THE MEDIATING POWER OF SPORT

RESEARCH IN THE SOCIOLOGY OF SPORT

Series Editor: Kevin Young

Recent Volumes:

Volume 1:	Theory, Sport and Society – Edited by Joseph Maguire and Kevin Young, 2001
Volume 2:	Sporting Bodies, Damaged Selves: Sociological Studies of Sports-Related Injury – Edited by Kevin Young, 2004
Volume 3:	The Global Olympics: Historical and Sociological Studies of the Modern Games – Edited by Kevin Young and Kevin B. Wamsley, 2005
Volume 4:	Tribal Play: Subcultural Journeys Through Sport – Edited by Michael Atkinson and Kevin Young, 2008
Volume 5:	Social and Cultural Diversity in a Sporting World – Edited by Chris Hallinan and Steven J. Jackson, 2008
Volume 6:	Qualitative Research on Sport and Physical Culture – Edited by Kevin Young and Michael Atkinson, 2012
Volume 7:	Native Games: Indigenous Peoples and Sports in the Post-Colonial World – Edited by Chris Hallinan and Barry Judd, 2013
Volume 8:	Sport, Social Development and Peace – Edited by Kevin Young and Chiaki Okada, 2014
Volume 9:	Sociology of Sport: A Global Subdiscipline in Review – Edited by Kevin Young, 2016
Volume 10:	Reflections on Sociology of Sport: Ten Questions, Ten Scholars, Ten Perspectives – Edited by Kevin Young, 2017
Volume 11:	Sport, Mental Illness, and Sociology – Edited by Michael Atkinson, 2018
Volume 12:	The Suffering Body in Sport: Shifting Thresholds of Pain, Risk and Injury – Edited by Kevin Young, 2019
Volume 13:	Sport and the Environment: Politics and Preferred Futures – Edited by Brian Wilson and Brad Millington, 2020
Volume 14:	Sport, Alcohol and Social Inquiry: A Global Cocktail – Edited by Sarah Gee, 2020
Volume 15:	Sport, Social Media and Digital Technology: Sociological Approaches – Edited by Jimmy Sanderson, 2022

Volume 16:	Doping in Sport and Fitness – Edited by April Henning and Jesper Andreasson, 2022
Volume 17:	Athletic Activism: Global Perspectives on Social Transformation – Edited by Jeffrey Montez de Oca and Stanley Thangaraj, 2023
Volume 18:	Gambling and Sports in a Global Age – Edited by Darragh McGee and Christopher Bunn, 2023
Volume 19:	Emergent Sociological Issues in Family and Sport – Edited by Steven M. Ortiz, 2023
Volume 20:	The Postcolonial Sporting Body: Contemporary Indian Investigations – Edited by Veena Mani and Mathangi Krishnamurthy, 2024

RESEARCH IN THE SOCIOLOGY OF SPORT   VOLUME 21

THE MEDIATING POWER OF SPORT: GLOBAL CHALLENGES AND SPORT CULTURE IN CHINA

EDITED BY

ENQING TIAN
East China Normal University, China

AND

NICHOLAS WISE
Arizona State University, USA

United Kingdom – North America – Japan
India – Malaysia – China

Emerald Publishing Limited
Emerald Publishing, Floor 5, Northspring, 21-23 Wellington Street, Leeds LS1 4DL

First edition 2024

Editorial matter and selection © 2024 Enqing Tian and Nicholas Wise.
Individual chapters © 2024 The authors.
Published under exclusive licence by Emerald Publishing Limited.

Reprints and permissions service
Contact: www.copyright.com

No part of this book may be reproduced, stored in a retrieval system, transmitted in any form or by any means electronic, mechanical, photocopying, recording or otherwise without either the prior written permission of the publisher or a licence permitting restricted copying issued in the UK by The Copyright Licensing Agency and in the USA by The Copyright Clearance Center. Any opinions expressed in the chapters are those of the authors. Whilst Emerald makes every effort to ensure the quality and accuracy of its content, Emerald makes no representation implied or otherwise, as to the chapters' suitability and application and disclaims any warranties, express or implied, to their use.

British Library Cataloguing in Publication Data
A catalogue record for this book is available from the British Library

ISBN: 978-1-83753-079-3 (Print)
ISBN: 978-1-83753-078-6 (Online)
ISBN: 978-1-83753-080-9 (Epub)

ISSN: 1476-2854 (Series)

Printed and bound by CPI Group (UK) Ltd, Croydon, CR0 4YY

INVESTOR IN PEOPLE

CONTENTS

About the Editors   ix

About the Contributors   xi

Introduction – The Mediating Power of Sport: Global Challenges and Sport Culture in China   1
Nicholas Wise and Enqing Tian

Chapter 1   Embodied Turn? Reviewing and Reflecting on the Study of Chinese Traditional Sports Culture   11
Zhen Zhang

Chapter 2   Chinese Sports Heroes and Nationalism at Mega-Sporting Events   29
Gen Li

Chapter 3   Debates on Football and Chinese National Identity   49
Kaixiao Jiang and Jinyu Liu

Chapter 4   Chinese Football Fandom: Growing With the Changing Chinese Society   73
Kaixiao Jiang and Liam O'Callaghan

Chapter 5   The Commercialisation of Chinese Professional Football: Transition and Evolution   99
Yang Ma

Chapter 6   Jack and the Visiting Giants: The Development of Chinese Baseball   111
Xiaoqian Richard Hu

Chapter 7   From an Expatriate-Only Sport to an Asian Games Sport: The Development of Cricket in China   129
Boyang He, Dominic Malcolm and Chunyang Xu

**Chapter 8   Esportisation: The Inclusion of Esports in the
Hangzhou Asian Games**   *143*
Jianping Hong and Jiandong Yi

**Chapter 9   Running Culture in China: Conceptualising Notions
of Power and Self**   *163*
Zhanbing Ren

**Chapter 10   Challenges in Reforms of Chinese Elite Sports:
Towards a New Development Mode**   *183*
Dehao Ma and Liu Ji

**Chapter 11   From 'Imported' to 'Local': Framing Foundations on
the Sociology of Sport in China**   *205*
Qiang Gao and Le Zhou

ABOUT THE EDITORS

Enqing Tian is an Associate Professor at the East China Normal University, China. His scholarly interests include the social issues of sociology of sport and geography of sport, with a particular emphasis on sense of place. His recent publications appear in *Leisure Sciences*, *International Review for the Sociology of Sport*, *Sport in Society* and *The International Journal of the History of Sport*.

Nicholas Wise is an Assistant Professor in the School of Community Resources and Development at Arizona State University in the United States. In 2012, he received his PhD at Kent State University in Ohio and has conducted research on sport around the world. His work focuses on geographical and sociological understandings of sport, contested identities, placemaking, destination competitiveness and major events. He has edited 10 books on topics related to sport, events and tourism development, and his work appears in *Leisure Sciences*, *International Review for the Sociology of Sport*, *Sport in Society*, *Event Management* and *Managing Sport and Leisure*. He is also a Senior Fellow of the Higher Education Academy (AdvanceHE).

ABOUT THE CONTRIBUTORS

Qiang Gao is a Professor at East China Normal University, China. His scholarly pursuits centre on the realms of the philosophy of sport, with a particular focus on the metaphysical and ontological dimensions within the field of Sport Philosophy. His notable contributions have been published in renowned academic journals such as the China Sport Science, Journal of Shanghai University of Sport, Journal of Beijing Sport University, Journal of Chengdu Sport University and Journal of Wuhan Sports University.

Boyang He is an Assistant Professor at the Xi'an Jiaotong University. His research interests include sociology of cricket, figurational sociology and decolonising research methodology. His recent publications appear in *Sport in Society* and *The International Journal of the History of Sport*.

Jianping Hong is an Associate Professor in the School of Journalism and Communication at Beijing Sport University. He has served as a Visiting Scholar at University of Otago (New Zealand). His research focuses on sociological analysis of sport and the media, and his current research interests include: Sport and Global Communication, Economics and Sociology of eSport.

Xiaoqian Richard Hu is an Associate Professor at the Tsinghua University. Dr Hu has invested most of his academic effort in Olympic studies and sport policy research. He is also well known in the Chinese sport science community for his dedication to the advancement of qualitative research in sport social science. His recent publications can be found in *European Sport Management Quarterly*, *Sport in Society* and *International Journal of the History of Sport*.

Liu Ji is a Professor at East China Normal University in China. His main research direction is physical education.

Kaixiao Jiang is a Lecturer in Sport Management at Liverpool Hope University, UK. His primary research interest is sports fandom, which is about the relationship between fans and their sports teams but also a means of observing people's lifestyles in various communities. He is particularly interested in Chinese football fandom and is dedicated to exploring how this topic reflects Chinese people's attitudes towards their national and local communities.

Gen Li is a Lecturer at the college of P.E. and sport, Beijing Normal University, China. His scholarly interests include sociology of sport and history of sport, particular emphasis on sport for development and sport history of modern China.

He participated in the preparation of the sociology of sport textbook in China. His recent publications appear in some Chinese academic journals.

Jinyu Liu is a Lecturer in Psychology at Manchester Metropolitan University, UK. Her research focuses on the influence of social determinants on healthy intentions and health-related lifestyle choices. She is particularly interested in how social identity influences people's response to societal norms in relation to adult dietary behaviour and physical activity status.

Dehao Ma is a Professor at East China Normal University, China. His main research direction is sports policy and governance. His recent publications appear in *China Sport Science*, *China Sport Technology* and *Journal of Physical Education*.

Yang Ma is an Associate Professor in sport governance at Wenzhou University, China. His research interests reside in sport governance in China in general and Chinese football governance in particular. He has recently published articles in *International Journal of Sport Policy and Politics*, *Managing Sport and Leisure* and *Sport in Society*.

Dominic Malcolm is a Professor of Sociology of Sport at Loughborough University. He has authored 5 monographs, edited 9 anthologies and written over 100 journal articles and book chapters. These publications cover a wide range of subjects within the sociology of sport, ranging from cricket, Eliasian sociology and the intersection of sport, medicine and health.

Liam O'Callaghan is an Associate Professor at the Liverpool Hope University, UK. As a researcher, he is interested in the social history of Ireland and the history of sport. He has been an invited conference speaker in the United States, Germany and Ireland, and his work has also been the basis of media interviews on RTE Radio, The Irish Times and The Wall Street Journal.

Zhanbing Ren is a Professor at the Shenzhen University, China. His scholarly interests include the social issues of running culture in China, exercise and health, with a particular emphasis on the relationship among physical activity and mental health, social relations and social connectedness.

Chunyang Xu is a Lecturer at Physical Education Department at Tongji University. He was a former national player for the Chinese men's cricket squad and an active coach of the team. His research interests are mainly in physical education and sports training. His most recent publications have been published in Sports Space and Modern Sports Science.

Jiandong Yi is a Professor in the School of Physical Education and Health at Wenzhou University. His expertise is in the study of the Olympics and Global Sport Governance. He has served as a Visiting Scholar at Victoria University (Australia) and Columbia University (USA). His recent publication appears in *The International Journal of the History of Sport*.

ABOUT THE CONTRIBUTORS

Zhen Zhang is an Associate Professor at the East China Normal University, China. His research focuses on sports philosophy, mainly studying the epistemological issues of embodied cognition in sports. His recently published papers are in the *Journal of Sports Science*, *Journal of Shanghai University of Sports* and *Thought and Culture*.

Le Zhou is currently a PhD student at East China Normal University, China. Her research interests lie in the fields of philosophy of sport and sport history. Her recent publications have been featured in the *Journal of Chengdu Sport University*.

INTRODUCTION – THE MEDIATING POWER OF SPORT: GLOBAL CHALLENGES AND SPORT CULTURE IN CHINA

Nicholas Wise[a] and Enqing Tian[b]

[a]*Arizona State University, USA*
[b]*East China Normal University, China*

ABSTRACT

This first chapter is the introduction to the book. The purpose of this book is to address and better understand why China tightly embraces modern sport in contemporary times. Some view this as an indicator of glocalisation and a result of Western industrial civilization putting pressure on China to showcase their strengths as a nation. Some important considerations to explore are China's mediated ability to play and compete with the west. Sport is also seen as a channel of observing global political and economic challenges, especially those in the current context of the COVID-19 pandemic and the intense tensions between communities, which certainly inspires further academic development. Given China's recently remarkable achievements in sport, it is high time to show the world more inside stories of sport development across the nation. The contributors of this collection bring foundational Chinese context to each chapter as they examine changing sport cultures at different scales.

Keywords: Sociology of sport; China; global sport; sport culture; modern sport; social transformation; nationalism; sports development

China is a rising power in the realm of global sports given their investment in sport and success in international competitions and recent hosting of large-scale events (see Chu, 2020; Dreyer, 2022; Wise, 2020). Sport is important no matter the context, may it be related to culture, economics or politics, as there are sociological and geographical implications that frame the importance of sport in society today (see Tian & Wise, 2020; Wise, 2015; Wise & Kohe, 2020). For decades, scholars have placed attention on sports sociology research in China to understand attitudes towards sport as China has long had ambitions to succeed in sport globally (Kong et al., 1990), may this be policy and promotion through hosting mega-events (Zheng et al., 2019) and establishing a new image (Chen, 2012) or investing in the development of different sports (e.g. He & Malcolm, 2021; Li & Liu, 2022; Li et al., 2020).

China has spread the playing field by focussing on different intentions locally and regionally based on encouraging physical activity of people of all abilities (Sun et al., 2019), healthy well-being (Xu et al., 2019), fandom patterns (Gong, 2020) and everyday leisure routines (Sui & Yang, 2023; Tian & Wise, 2022). Given the global importance of football (or soccer), much work aligns the growth and popularity of the sport with China's role in the globalisation of sport (see Bond et al., 2018; Newman et al., 2021; Tian, 2017).

Each of these, among others, that frame global and local dimensions of sport come into focus in subsequent chapters in this book. Much work focuses on spotlighting major- or mega-sporting events, but from a development standpoint, it is important that we consider local grassroots dimensions of sport in our research (see Wise, 2014) so that we can critically explore who is impacted by sport (Wise & Whittam, 2015). This is especially important that we continue to focus on local impacts as we see countries showcase themselves in the globalised world of hosting large-scale events (Hall & Wise, 2019; Li, 2021; Roche, 2017).

The purpose of this book is to address and better understand why China tightly embraces modern sport in contemporary times. Some view this as an indicator of glocalisation and a result of Western industrial civilization putting pressure on China to showcase their strengths as a nation (Lu & Fan, 2013). Some important considerations to explore are China's mediated ability to play and compete with the west. Sport is also seen as a channel of observing global political and economic challenges, especially those in the current context of the COVID-19 pandemic and the intense tensions between communities, which certainly inspires further academic development. Given China's recently remarkable achievements in sport (Zheng & Chen, 2016), it is high time to show the world more inside stories of sport development across the nation. The contributors of this collection bring foundational Chinese context to each chapter as they examine changing sport cultures at different scales.

Sociology of sport researchers have focused on a wide range of topical areas (Tian & Wise, 2020), and in recent years, more attention has focused on sociological aspects of sport across China. Cultural and political aspects of sport are integral to the study of sport and sociology, adding critical depth to how we think about the impact of sport on societal actions and measures (Manzenreiter, 2015; Wise & Harris, 2019). Other important aspects concern the increasing importance of soft power (Chen et al., 2012; Wise & Ludvigsen, 2023), technology (Wong & Meng-Lewis, 2023) and big data (Tian, 2020), as sport is at the centre of these discussions which impact us socially and emotionally. Emotional aspects of sport and events that people participate in showcase the power of sport to connect people (Gellweiler et al., 2019). Elements of heritage and development are also important directions when we think about sport and destination development as addressed in chapters in a recent collection by Wise and Jimura (2020).

This book outlines a number of sociological themes that sports scholars interact with. Topical areas chapters delve into focus on the challenge and reform of elite sports, nationalism and sport for development in China. Chapters focus on mega- and major-events and sports such as baseball, soccer and running, and along with the sociological and regional considerations, chapters provide important historical contexts of different sports as well. Mega-events especially are used by nations to leverage future impacts, create a new image or build a new visitor economy (Wise & Maguire, 2022). Chapters also introduce a range of social theories to address the different conceptual considerations sports scholars consider.

Some thinkers that sports scholars commonly engage with include theoretical foundations and inspirations from Elias, Bourdieu, Foucault and Cornell among others to address the issues of mediating power and sports culture (Tian & Wise, 2020). These conceptual directions are relevant when discussing sport in China as they help us think about sporting aspirations, fandom, branding, mega-events, competitiveness and gender in sports. Chapters throughout this volume offer critical insight into glocalised sporting cultures and political hegemony. In the final section, two contributors offer theoretical underpinning to reflect on current trends in line with traditional Chinese culture of sport and the sub-discipline in China with a philosophical version for researching sociology of sport in China going forward.

By analysing the relationships between sport and social transformation in China, the book will examine how and why the sport plays a key role in China's rise in the 20th and 21st centuries. The book will integrate a number of topical directions addressed above to discuss how and why China embraces modern sport. Important in this is how China embraces the Olympic Movement and also creates new forms of influence in the world through sports to showcase their presence in the international sports arena (see Wise, 2020).

Featuring major sports and events, original documents and interviews with a wide breadth of insiders, this book, for the first time, provides a sociological guide to understand the relationship between China's social structure and sport. Some previous scholars addressed sport but they are not grounded in sociological perspectives. For instance, Riordan and Jones (1999) edited a collection on sport and physical education in China. This collection provided readers with a history of physical education in China and directions for management. Fan and Lu (2015) examined key issues in sport in China longitudinally from 1949 to 2012.

From a disciplinary standpoint, this book offers sociological insights to what Fan and Lu (2015) address based on their overview of history, politics and society pertinent to sport in China. Chapters in this collection go further and offer contemporary analyses on the social issues in China sport with micro-, meso- and macro-scopic perspective but do address historical foundations as well that lend to modern practice. Chu (2020) highlights the inseparable nature between politics and sporting mega-events in China. Events are a global phenomenon (Wise & Harris, 2019), and Chu (2020) reviews 20 bidding cases to demystify domestic and international political reasons behind event bids as they pertain to building relationships, social structures and the development of a dominant sporting culture with international influence in China.

To offer a summative overview the book, this collection is organised into this introduction and 11 chapters. The introduction chapter here (this chapter you are reading) frames the importance of sociology of sport research in China today and offers here an overview of each chapter. Chapter 1 positions the tradition and development of sport in China in light of recent mega-events. Chapters 2 and 3 frame directions on nationalism, and then into particular examples of sport in China, where Chapter 4 relates to national identity and football. Chapter 5 continues with football, Chapter 6 into baseball, Chapter 7 on cricket, Chapter 8 offers directions on e-sports and Chapter 9 looks at running culture. Chapters 7 and 8 also provide insights into the Asian Games. Chapters 10 and 11 bring the collection together, with Chapter 10 offering scope on a new development mode and Chapter 11 offering new directions to bring together foundations and conclude this collection. We now provide some details on what each chapter contributes to this edited collection.

Chapter 1 on an *Embodied Turn? Reviewing and Reflecting on the Study of Chinese Traditional Sports Culture* by Zhen Zhang examines the study of traditional Chinese sports and identifies issues within research areas. This chapter introduces new interpretative perspectives and approaches within the framework of bodily sociology. The chapter addresses links between locally-informed sports practices and the formation of socialized individuals and considers three main themes: self-giving, the creation of bodily value and the construction of national identity through sports. The chapter advocates for further bodily sociological studies of Chinese sports culture, which could enhance the understanding of Chinese studies among Western scholars and contribute to a genuine embodied turn in this field of study.

In modern China, sports and nationalism always have close connection, and nationalism is the important reason for the promotion of Chinese sports. Chapter 2, titled *Chinese Sports Heroes and Nationalism at Mega-Sporting Events*, by Gen Li considers relationships between Chinese sports and nationalism in globalised China. They argue this focus has been under-researched by scholars, and more academically focused research can devise more influencing factors when studying relationships between sports and nationalism in China with regards to globalisation. This chapter focuses on the Beijing 2008 Olympic Games and considers stories of three Chinese sports heroes. In many respects, the three athletes focused in this chapter represent the national image of China. Under the influence of the mass media, market economy and sports professionalisation, nationalism still exists in Chinese sports and the concept of 'winning glory for the nation'. The relationship between Chinese nationalism and sports shows the important implications of rapid Chinese sports development.

Chapter 3, *Debates on Football and Chinese National Identity*, by Kaixiao Jiang and Jinyu Liu critically evaluates whether football can attain recognition as a national sport in China. This chapter addresses policy considerations, especially surrounding Article No. 11, released by the Chinese government in 2015, which aims to develop a new national strategy centralised on the sport of football. The focus here is to also foster consumption and enhance national soft power using football given the sports global popularity. With football the national sport of many countries around the world, the goal here is to encourage Chinese football fans to support the national football team. This chapter addresses literature comparisons with established Chinese national sports such as Chinese martial arts, badminton and table tennis. The chapter reveals that football currently falls short of meeting the general criteria of nation-wide popularity to be considered a national sport. It also proves that football fails to meet the criterion of politics, hindering its identification as a national sport in China. The chapter rebuts the assumption and advocates for the validity of comparing how fans assess their fandom for local and national football teams.

Chapter 4 continues with a focus on football. *Chinese Football Fandom: Growing with the Changing Chinese Society* by Kaixiao Jiang and Liam O'Callaghan explores how the development of football fandom for the Chinese national team and local football clubs is strongly associated with societal changes and builds on whilst offering different arguments from the previous chapter. Although the performances of Chinese football teams, especially the national team, have failed to impress the world, football remains the most popular because of millions of supporters with loyalty and passion. Most studies related to fans mainly focus on the economic and political implications of spectatorship along with the rise of China. Nevertheless, few articles are available to answer the fundamental questions, such as 'when did these supporters come out?' and 'what were the factors of the development of fandom?' This chapter considers archival records and published documents over the last decades to offer a comprehensive and historical analysis of the development of football fandom in the People's Republic of China. As such, this chapter does not intend to be the most authoritative one but is one of the rare sources to lay down the foundation for research on Chinese football fandom. Furthermore, this chapter also proves that studies on football fandom can be a useful window for observing Chinese society.

The Commercialisation of Chinese Professional Football: Transition and Evolution by Yang Ma is the focus of Chapter 5. This chapter articulates the transition to and evolution of the commercialisation of Chinese professional football, continuing this core theme of football through the middle chapters of the book. The author argues that there are different turning points that we need to direct our attention to, framed around two major findings. First, there exists a distinct 'Chinese way' of commercialising football. However, it does not indicate that Chinese football doggedly avoided the Western governance model. For the club governance, Chinese football authorities set about recommending privately operated enterprises, large and medium-sized state-owned enterprises. Second, the commercialisation transitions of professional football in China were triggered by exogenous policy shifts, rather than endogenous changes in market structures, resulting in higher horizontal financial fragility than is associated with the commercialisation model adopted in more developed Western markets.

Chapter 6 by Xiaoqian Richard Hu focuses on the development of Baseball in China, titled *Jack and the Visiting Giants: The Development of Chinese Baseball.*

Chinese baseball represents a singular case of investigation into how China responds to sport globalisation. Baseball is a relatively peripheral sport in China. Nonetheless, it is important to examine the development of Chinese baseball and its interplay with the global sport giants and international events such as the Olympic Games and the Major League Baseball. Given the influence of sport globalisation, we also identify the consistent dominance of Chinese sport authorities and the spectrum of local stakeholders' reaction towards globalisation. The chapter provides a critical discussion of the relationship between marginal position of Chinese baseball in the local sport system and the rationale of its response to sport globalisation.

Little work to date has focused on Cricket's development in China, and Boyang He, Dominic Malcolm and Chunyang Xu address this in Chapter 7. Their chapter titled *From An Expatriate-only Sport to An Asian Games Sport: the Development of Cricket in China* provides an exhaustive analysis on the development of cricket in China in order to advance existing theories of cricket's development and consider future implications for the international game. This chapter builds on work by He and Malcolm (2021) and He et al. (2023) which are foundations to the assessment of the development of cricket in China. The authors note that there are two key historical eras surrounding the sport: 1. Cricket as an 'expatriate-only' game and 2. Cricket as an 'Asian Games sport'. The first era, Cricket as an 'expatriate-only' game, is constructed according to three key phases: early development; post-war and the 'opening-up' era. The second era, Cricket as an 'Asian Games sport', is constructed according to five periods over the past few decades. These include the budding period (2003–2005), peak period (2006–2010), stable period (2011–2014), trough period (2015–2018) and revival period (2019–present). By providing this more comprehensive analysis of the development of cricket in China, it argues that cricket in contemporary China (mainland) exists within two distinct strands; that is, a grassroots game kept alive by a resourceful expatriate diasporic community, and a state-led game, largely underpinned by the Asian Games that embedded in the educational system.

Chapter 8 by Jianping Hong and Jiandong Yi focuses on a phenomenon that is gaining attention in China and around this world, this being esports. This chapter, *Esportisation: The Inclusion of Esports in the Hangzhou Asian Games* considers the inclusion of esports in a major event. The significance of this event marks that Asia once again takes a lead in the global esportisation, and this chapter investigates a series of events in the inclusion process of esports by looking into the history of making all this possible. This chapter is based on process-sociology and actor network theory to analyse the type characteristics of esports events during the Hangzhou Asian Games. The chapter examines how key stakeholders' interact and balance in the network composed of international sports organisations. The development is different from other sports given its base is emerging esports organisations and esports game companies instead of sporting governing bodies. The chapter also examines the functions of global game industrial economic geography, local cultural politics, esports geopolitics and Olympic values in esports sportization, aiming to reveal the implications of esports inclusion in the Asian Games on the debate of whether esports meets the criteria to be classified as a 'sport' and its enlightenment of digital strategy to the inclusion esports in the Olympics.

Chapter 9, *Running Culture in China: Conceptualising Notions of Power and Self*, by Zhanbing Ren considers the scale of running events in China which have increased dramatically. In China, running is not only a social phenomenon but also a historical and cultural phenomenon. It is noted that running in China is an organic part of human culture and takes on distinct sociological values. This chapter offers insight into the development of Chinese running culture and how this has emerged from ancient and modern Chinese running cultures. The chapter is conceptually based on Foucault's notions of disciplinary power theory, bio-power and the technologies of the self. This chapter discusses running culture in China for the first time under Foucault's theoretical framework and thus argues that running culture in China constructs the subjectivity of the Chinese runners under the joint action of the technologies of power and the technologies of the self. Findings acknowledge how Chinese Runners present and express themselves by showing a 'sense of presence'. Runners illustrate the implicit or explicit meaning and value of a particular way of life through running. It is also found that China's running policy under the technologies of power meets the needs of runners whereby power is not oppressive but productive.

Dehao Ma and Liu Ji focus on different elite sports in China in Chapter 10. *Challenges and Reforms of Chinese Elite Sports: Towards a New Development Mode* address the national government's expectation of transformation, administrative system reform, economic transition, social demand structure's upgrading and population change impacting sport across China. Against these considerations, in order to make this reform better adapted to China's reality and future development, the chapter suggests that Chinese traditional elite sports development mode should shift its driving forces of development from single to multiple and thus change its administrative system from government-oriented to society-oriented. The authors also speak to the importance of developing training concepts from instrumentalism to humanism. They argue that this will improve its construction of development from unbalanced to balanced and alter its effectiveness of development from extensive to intensive so to better achieve sustainable development.

The final chapter in this collection, Chapter 11, *From 'Imported' to 'Local': Framing Foundations on the Sociology of Sport in China*, by Qiang Gao and Le Zhou reflects on the development of sport sociology in China. They address sports sociology, and this notion as a transition from an 'imported' Western concept to a 'localised' Chinese discipline. In doing this, they also focus on the role of the Body in this process. This chapter offers some descriptive insight into the development of sport sociology in China to frame directions going forward. For instance, new characteristics of the study of sport have emerged in China; therefore, it is important to recognise some of the differences and similarities between Eastern and Western ideologies, especially regarding the concept of the 'Body' in research. In doing so, this chapter provides a unique perspective on the development of sport sociology in China, highlighting the role of the Body and the process of localization and this development of sports sociology in contemporary Chinese scholarship.

This book was inspired by the need to offer a collection useful for students, scholars and policymakers focussing on sport and sociological considerations in China. Over the past 40 years, sport programmes and courses at both the undergraduate and graduate level have been introduced in several universities across China, particularly in the areas of sport sociology, sport management and sport politics. However, the emergence of these programmes/courses has not seen a commensurate growth in research or publications to meet the needs of its students and teachers. This volume would make a significant contribution to filling this gap.

This book is the first English collation of chapters united in a single volume that offer both theoretical and empirical directions on sporting cultures and sports development in China. The contents and contributions offered in this book are organised for academic researchers, sport practitioners and as noted students who are expressing interest in the study of sport. The content will cater to readers in China to examine topical directions for different sports while also capturing attention of readers in various international settings to think about the sociology of sport from their own cultural context. This volume will provide various standpoints from sociology perspectives pertinent to how we understand sport policy, development and management. We now direct you attention to the following 11 chapters.

REFERENCES

Bond, A. J., Widdop, P., & Chadwick, S. (2018). Football's emerging market trade network: Ego network approach to world systems theory. *Managing Sport and Leisure*, *23*(1–2), 70–91.

Chen, N. (2012). Branding national images: The 2008 Beijing summer Olympics, 2010 Shanghai world expo, and 2010 Guangzhou Asian games. *Public Relations Review*, *38*(5), 731–745.

Chen, C. C., Colapinto, C., & Luo, Q. (2012). The 2008 Beijing Olympics opening ceremony: Visual insights into China's soft power. *Visual Studies*, *27*(2), 188–195.

Chu, M. P. (2020). *China's quest for sporting mega-events: The politics of international bids*. Routledge.

Dreyer, M. (2022). *Sporting superpower: An insider's view on China's quest to be the best*. Independently Published.

Fan, H., & Lu, Z. (2015). *The politicisation of sport in modern China: Communists and champions*. Routledge.

Gellweiler, S., Fletcher, T., & Wise, N. (2019). Exploring experiences and emotions sport event volunteers associate with 'role exit'. *International Review for the Sociology of Sport*, *54*(4), 495–511.

Gong, Y. (2020). Reading European football, critiquing China: Chinese urban middle class fans as reflexive audience. *Cultural Studies*, *34*(3), 442–465.

Hall, G., & Wise, N. (2019). Sport and social transformation in Brazil. *Bulletin of Latin American Research*, *38*(3), 265–266.

He, B., & Malcolm, D. (2021). The development of cricket in China. *Sport in Society*, *24*(8), 1372–1387.

He, B., Yang, J., & Malcolm, D. (2023). 'Cricket is perfectly suited to the Chinese people': The contemporary development of Chinese cricket. *International Journal of the History of Sport*, *40*(9), 830–850.

Kong, X. A., Niu, X., & Qiu, B. (1990). A summary of sport sociology research in the People's Republic China. *International Review for the Sociology of Sport*, *25*(2), 93–107.

Li, L. (2021). Contesting sustainability of mega-events in Chinese metropolises: A narrative and practise review. *Frontiers in Sustainable Cities*, *3*, 687315.

Li, P., & Liu, W. (2022). Research on the participation of Chinese sports cultural elite in ice and snow sports. *Frontiers in Public Health*, *9*, 1–8.

Li, H., Nite, C., Weiller-Abels, K., & Nauright, J. (2020). The development of women's professional ice hockey in China: Leveraging international competition to change institutionalized gender norms. *Sport in Society*, *23*(3), 523–538.

Lu, Z., & Fan, H. (2013). *Sport and nationalism in China*. Routledge.

Manzenreiter, W. (2015). Assessing the sociology of sport: On culture and political economy. *International Review for the Sociology of Sport*, *50*(4/5), 524–529.

Newman, J. I., Xue, H., Chen, R., Chen, Y., & Watanabe, N. M. (2021). Football and cultural citizenship in China: A study in three embodiments. *Sport in Society*, *24*(12), 2222–2245.

Riordan, J., & Jones, R. E. (Eds.). (1999). *Sport and physical education in China*. E & FN Spon.

Roche, M. (Ed.). (2017). Mega-events, globalisation and urban legacy: Events in China in the early twenty-first century. In *Mega-events and social change* (pp. 223–245). Manchester University Press.

Sui, W., & Yang, J. (2023). Running middle-class–marathon craze in transforming period of China. *Sport in Society*, *26*(5), 745–756.

Sun, S., Yan, R., Mao, A., Chao, L., & Jing, T. (2019). China and the development of sport for persons with a disability, 1978–2008: A review. *Sport in Society*, *14*(9), 1192–1210.

Tian, E. (2017). China's 'G-7 revolution' in soccer. *International Journal of the History of Sport*, *34*(17–18), 1915–1932.

Tian, E. (2020). A prospect for the geographical research of sport in the age of Big Data. *Sport in Society*, *23*(1), 159–169.

Tian, E., & Wise, N. (2020). An Atlantic divide? Mapping the knowledge domain of European and North American based sociology of sport, 2008–2018. *International Review for the Sociology of Sport*, *55*(8), 1029–1055.

Tian, E., & Wise, N. (2022). Dancing in public squares – Toward a socially synchronous sense of place. *Leisure Sciences, Latest Articles*. https://doi.org/10.1080/01490400.2022.2099490

Wise, N. (2014). Layers of the landscape: Representations and perceptions of an ordinary (shared) sports landscape in a Haitian and Dominican community. *Geographical Research*, *52*(2), 212–222.

Wise, N. (2015). Geographical approaches and the sociology of sport. In R. Giulianotti (Ed.), *Routledge handbook of the sociology of sport* (pp. 142–152). Routledge.

Wise, N. (2020). Eventful futures and triple bottom line impacts: BRICS, image regeneration and competitiveness. *Journal of Place Management and Development*, *13*(1), 89–100.

Wise, N., & Harris, J. (Eds.). (2019). *Event, places and societies*. Routledge.

Wise, N., & Jimura, T. (Eds.). (2020). *Tourism, cultural heritage and urban regeneration*. Springer.

Wise, N., & Kohe, G. Z. (2020). Sports geography: New approaches, perspectives and directions. *Sport in Society*, *23*(1), 1–10.

Wise, N., & Ludvigsen, J. A. L. (2023). New notions of soft power: Impact rhetoric in mega-event bid documents. *Local Economy*, *38*(4), 306–311.

Wise, N., & Maguire, K. (Eds.). (2022). *A research agenda for event impacts*. Edward Elgar.

Wise, N., & Whittam, G. (2015). Special edition: Regeneration, enterprise, sport and tourism. *Local Economy*, *30*(8), 867–870.

Wong, D., & Meng-Lewis, Y. (2023). Esports diplomacy – China's soft power building in the digital era. *Managing Sport and Leisure*, *28*(3), 247–269.

Xu, H., Meng, Y., & Li, J. (2019). Well-being of cycling tourists in Hainan, China. *Sport in Society*, *22*(8), 1449–1465.

Zheng, J., & Chen, S. (2016). Exploring China's success at the Olympic games: A competitive advantage approach. *European Sport Management Quarterly*, *16*(2), 148–171.

Zheng, J., Chen, S., Tan, T.-C., & Houlihan, B. (2019). *Sport policy in China*. Routledge.

CHAPTER 1

EMBODIED TURN? REVIEWING AND REFLECTING ON THE STUDY OF CHINESE TRADITIONAL SPORTS CULTURE

Zhen Zhang

East China Normal University, China

ABSTRACT

This chapter examines the 'embodied turn' in the study of traditional Chinese sports and identifies issues within this area of research. It introduces new interpretative perspectives and approaches within the framework of bodily sociology to elucidate the link between locally-informed sports practices and the formation of socialized individuals. The chapter categorises the current research into three main themes: self-giving, the creation of bodily value and the construction of national identity through sports. It then integrates these themes with the findings of embodied sociology. The chapter compiles and analyzes the existing literature on traditional Chinese sports culture from both Chinese and international scholars, offering insights into the status, rationale and challenges of bodily sociological research. By contextualising the concept of the embodied turn in traditional Chinese sports culture – through concepts such as self-givenness, self-techniques, the generation of value and the creation of collective memory – the chapter discusses the impact of bodily sociology on cultural research. The chapter advocates for further bodily sociological studies of Chinese sports culture, which could enhance the understanding of Chinese studies among Western scholars and contribute to a genuine embodied turn in this field of study. Providing one of the initial explorations of embodied studies in traditional Chinese sports, the chapter reveals a transition from broad cultural interpretations and symbolic, structuralist sociology to a phenomenological approach in sports cultural studies. It posits that the bodily sociology approach is beneficial for sports studies although current research has not yet fully realized the embodied turn.

Keywords: Traditional Chinese sport; embodied turn; body sociology; self-techniques; bodily skills and arts; inter-subjective

INTRODUCTION

The sociology of the body has emerged as a significant area within sociological inquiry, influencing research in China, particularly in the realm of traditional sports. Over the past decade, an 'embodied turn' has been observed in the sociological study of Chinese Traditional Sports Culture. Researchers have increasingly adopted bodily sociology perspectives, examining aspects such as the physicality of sporting skills, ritualistic practices in sports, the tactile relationship between mentor and apprentice and the corporeal identity of groups, ethnicities and the nation.

Traditional Chinese sports, including *wushu* (martial arts), archery, *cuju* (ancient football), *dragon boat racing* and *wrestling*, share a commonality: the intense interactivity between the athlete and their environment, as well as between athletes themselves. These sports encompass more than just physical prowess; they incorporate a physical ritual rooted in Chinese culture that transcends mere technique, embodying Chinese moral values.

This observation leads to two lines of inquiry. First, the embodied perspective of bodily sociology provides a lens to delve into the complex interplay between the subject's experience and social and technical phenomena in traditional Chinese sports. Second, the integration of Western body sociology theories and methods with Eastern philosophy enriches the interpretative power of bodily sociology in the context of China. This east–west synthesis offers English-speaking scholars a valuable framework for a deeper understanding of traditional Chinese sports.

The importance of an embodied sociological approach in the study of traditional Chinese sports lies not only in the choice of topics but also in the methodological approach. Given these considerations, this chapter is structured into five sections. The first section introduces key aspects of embodiment in traditional Chinese sports. The subsequent section demonstrates how these sports serve as a means to shape individuals, focussing on how the body interacts with itself and the environment to forge an ecological and organic self. The third section addresses the construction of inter-subjectivity within sports and movement culture. The fourth section examines how embodied sports shape the identities of groups, peoples and nations. Finally, the chapter concludes with a critical reflection on the challenges of the embodied turn, including the need for gender perspectives and a power analysis in the critique of traditional Chinese sports and their role in constructing ethnic and national identities, with particular attention to centralised body politics.

EMBODIED TECHNIQUES AND SKILLS IN CHINESE TRADITIONAL SPORTS CULTURE

Embodiment emerged from the extensive intersection of epistemological philosophy with disciplines like cognitive science, linguistics, sociology and anthropology. Its influence has earned it the title of 'second cognitive revolution'. The paradigm encompasses six key concepts: (1) structural coupling between subject and environment; (2) historical embodiment through accumulated structural coupling; (3) proprioceptive embodiment; (4) organismoid embodiment; (5) embodiment of autopoietic, living systems and (6) social embodiment (Ziemke, 2003). Gallagher summarises embodiment across 4E dimensions: *Embodied, Embedded, Extended, and Enacted* (Newen et al., 2018, p. 2) condensing human existence into profound contextual interactions between self, others and world across both physical and semantic reality. In the learning, mastery and development of any physical skill, individuals are deeply embedded within the everyday practices of Chinese life, which, through a protracted historical sedimentation, are imbued with the collective memory of the Chinese people, centred around ethical norms and a worldview in harmony with nature. Hence, the embodied subjects bearing traditional Chinese sports profoundly embody the '4E' as articulated by Gallagher and also represent an excellent manifestation of Ziemke's five categories of embodiment.

The first meaning of embodied subject underscores proprioception – the spatial reference point where the 'self' emerges through self-recognition. The Delphic maxim of 'know thyself' can become intuitive essence through embodiment. Embodiment is integral to bodily understanding in activities like training, performing, wrestling or fighting; the body is the prime starting point. Embodiment is an existential condition; the body generates subjectivity and grounds intersubjectivity experientially (Farrer & Whalen-Bridge, 2011, pp. 3–9). We understand ourselves and the world primarily by inward and outward self-perception. Sports deepens this understanding, rendering it more intuitive (Wise, 2015). When wholly absorbed in archery, I clearly sense my breathing rhythm, arm tension, stabilising core tension, the condensing space around and the target approaching me. Ancient philosopher Liezi used an extreme example:

> Can you still shoot accurately at the target when you are on a high mountain, walking on the edge of danger, with a bottomless chasm under your feet? A true expert in the art of archery can do so even when stepping on a dangerous rock, near an abyss, or even with his feet hanging two centimetres outside, with his expression unchanged and his body still maintaining the best archery condition.
>
> (Fang Yong, 2013, p. 333)

Perceiving the self in meta-praxis activities is the highest goal Chinese philosophers and sportsmen share. The philosopher Lie-zi adopts to the archery arts as an example because it is more intuitive and resonant. The philosophical basis behind this narrative body metaphor points to Merleau-Ponty's perceptual phenomenology of 'I am my body' rather than 'I have a body'. In the traditional Chinese sporting training perspective, the self and the body belong to the same subject, and the self needs to be constructed through some various of intentional metaphor of the body and related movement. For example, Chinese martial artists place great importance on the unrestricted control self-consciousness through deep breathing (diaphragmatic movements) by sinking the breath into a perceptual space in the abdomen called the 'Dantian' (inside navel's vacuum) – the body's centre of gravity in the centre of the abdomen (Cao & Zhao, 2014). In Chinese body metaphors, the *Dantian* is a symbol of bodily perception, an index to help practitioners visualise their strength in combat. The psychologist Jung noted in his 'Studies On Alchemical Conceptss' that the *Dantian* is 'the point of gyratory movement and a centre (*Die Kreisbewegung und der Mittelpunkt*)'. When all consciousness is focused, one's sense of object disappears into an embodied experience of 'the accomplishment' (*Die Vollendung*) (Jung et al., 1978, pp. 30, 52, 56).

The concept of the 'embodied subject' encompasses a second dimension, termed 'embeddedness', which manifests in traditional Chinese martial arts through three distinct levels of embedding: (1) within the movement or stance's intrinsic principles, whereby the body naturally and effortlessly expresses the essence of the technique; (2) in relation to the world, which entails the pursuit of a universally applicable form that is intrinsically integrated within the body; (3) concerning the other, which involves uncovering principles within all concealed movements or stances. This level of embedding engenders a profound comprehension of others' action patterns through one's own tangible and living presence (Cave, 2019, p. 8).

In disciplines such as Chinese wrestling, Wing Chun's 'sticky hands', and Taijiquan's 'pushing hands', participants are compelled to engage in a mutual 'sticking' and 'following' process. In these interactions, the offencive and defensive roles are intimately intertwined, employing techniques that include merging, borrowing, following and adhering to the principle of being 'last to move, first to arrive' (Wile, 1999, p. 19). These practices constitute a form of intersubjective bodily engagement in which the practitioner is deeply interconnected with the opponent's body. This profound attunement enables one to preempt the opponent's intention to apply force, thereby destabilising their base, leading to a loss of balance and disarray. Thus, the application of these living principles within the immediate 'living body' is crucial to mastering invincibility (Zhang et al., 2017).

The third dimension of meaning for the embodied subject pertains to the extension of corporeality within its historical and cultural milieu. Athletes do not exist in a vacuum, separate from their sense of self; rather, they are deeply intertwined with their identities, histories and cultures, with each continuously shaping the other. For instance, the physical expressions observed in the traditional game of *cuju* enable participants to experience a transition from the individual body to the collective body, and from there to the societal and global bodies, culminating in an understanding of both bodily and worldly spaces (Xiao, 2016).

The physical actions and body schemas developed through *cuju* kicking allow for the performance and expression of Chinese cultural forms – thus rendering them as visible and identifiable social realities through the celebratory and festive practices associated with the game. Farrer and Whalen-Bridge (2011, p. 48) contend that the practice of Chinese martial arts is both a projection and an extension of the body into culture and simultaneously constructs the subject as an embodiment of 'Asian identity and heroic practitioners'. Consequently, the technical styles of traditional Chinese sports not only reflect tendencies pertinent to specific historical periods but also find expression in sporting discourses. These discourses range from religious expressions, such as in Shaolin martial arts, to cultural ideologies, including the precedence of virtue and respect for teachers in martial training, as well as sporting expressions (e.g. 'stop where it should stop') and body postures (e.g. triangular stances, dragon and monkey forms).

Scholars concur that traditional Chinese practices should not be interpreted merely as a journey of embodied cognition from one art form to another or from one culture to another. Instead, they represent a process of individual immersion into the community, wherein the physical practice of sport shapes ideology, community identity, morality and the psychological patterns of the self. Bowman adds that the acquisition of embodied knowledge by martial artists occurs within a specific historical context and is completed in the 'place of the body-in-cultivation' (Bowman, 2011, p. 70). Allen (2013) concurs, noting that martial arts are, in fact, part of religious practice, particularly within Zen Buddhism and Daoism. These traditions inform the discourses of Chinese Shaolin martial arts and Wudang martial arts, imbuing Chinese martial arts with religious connotations. Consequently, the physicality of the practitioner is influenced by Buddhist or Daoist ideologies, which emphasise non-violence and effortless action, both in the technical systems and in the offencive and defensive strategies employed.

The fourth category of meaning within the framework of embodiment is enactive, which emerges from the phenomenological foundations of embodiment. This perspective regards the embodied subject as possessing the capacity for active generation. In the rich tapestry of traditional Chinese sports, a profound influence of Confucian ethics is evident, particularly in the emphasis on introspective self-examination. This is well articulated by Confucius: when the archer misses the centre of the target, he should reflect on oneself and seek for the cause of his failure in himself (Legge, 1960, p. 396). This principle underscores the importance of proactive self-scrutiny and the enactment of an integrated psychophysical subjectivity within the process of a gentleman's character cultivation. In traditional Chinese sports, such as archery, this ethos is not merely a mental exercise but a holistic practice that engages both mind and body in a dynamic and active generation of character (Zhang & Ju, 2020).

Here, the athlete is not a passive participant but an active agent, embodying a capacity for self-generation and self-improvement. This active generation is a crucial aspect of the embodied subject, where the cultivation of physical skills is inseparable from the development of moral virtues and the pursuit of personal excellence. The body subject, therefore, is not only engaged in the physical execution of sports but is also actively involved in the ethical and character-building dimensions of the practice, embodying the Confucian ideal of a harmonious unity between the inner self and outward actions. Otherwise, the Chinese have long revered the perpetual power of nature, within which humanity resides, and have thus developed diverse rituals for engaging with the natural world.

These rituals often involve physical activities and play that are deeply rooted in human instincts and the fundamental desire for enactive engagement. Scholars of traditional Chinese sports draw upon the concept of enactive embodiment, exploring the dynamic interplay that defines both human interaction and the formation of communal identity. The belief that appropriate physical activity can enhance life's vitality is informed by the Chinese notion of symbiosis between humans and nature (Chang & Yang, 2022). This belief underpins the 'embodied turn' research paradigm, which articulates a distinctly Chinese perspective on embodiment, marked by the interrelated dynamics of life, society and identity.

SELF-GIVENNESS: TRADITIONAL CHINESE SPORT AS A TECHNIQUE FOR SHAPING THE INDIVIDUAL

Contemporary pedagogical research underscores the unique contribution of physical self-techniques in sports to personality development and self-actualisation. This holds true across individual and team sports, which catalyze an ontological awareness – the fulfilment of one's life through 'first-personal givenness' as described in phenomenology. Tanaka (2011, p. 130) draws from the 'Nikāyas' to propose that the self's constitution – its perception and experiences – emerges within the 'I' that encompasses totality, essentially a flux within the stream of consciousness.

It is important to note that in Buddhist philosophy, the concept of the self resonates with the phenomenological notion of 'self-givenness', which pertains to the subject's perception and cognition of its own mode of existence. The subject ascertains its existence and meaning through the perception and experience of its body, psyche and environment. In this context, the subject is engaged in self-grasping or self-affirmation, a process which necessitates a perceptive engagement with a creative bodily activity that further facilitates the affirmation and apprehension of the self.

The efficacy of combat training, such as in Chinese martial arts, lies in the perpetual awareness and fine-tuning of the 'I' within the dynamic consciousness of offence and defence, integrating the 'momentary I' into a 'whole I' through movement introspection. Particularly, the discomfort of rigorous training and the striving to surpass personal limits are pivotal in the self's emergence. In collective expressions like *dragon boat racing* or *dragon and lion dances*, the synergy with others fosters a comprehensive 'inner body feeling' – a confluence of proprioception and identity. The coordinated rowing to the drum's beat *in dragon boat racing* and the precise spatial maneuvering in *dragon and lion dances* provoke an internal bodily awareness, an understanding of one's spatial orientation and a sense of belonging within a social context. These movements through space also reinforce how we thing about place and one's presence through participation (Tian & Wise, 2022).

Zahavi (2005) asserts that the self transcends mere subjectivity, embodying a reflexive first-person perspective within the experiential structure. Self-awareness is not simply an internal recognition but an active participant in experience, revealing consciousness's architecture. This form of self-awareness is not an insular, detached consciousness, nor is it confined to the brain; rather, it is a consciousness deeply engaged with the world. The self's emergence relies on an ontological sense of world immersion, continuously shaping a holistic perception of both the external environment and the self. Engaging with the world implies physical involvement, and sports training exemplifies such active participation. Skill acquisition in sports is based on several demands: (1) the practitioner's full commitment to self-selection, as technical improvement hinges on this dedication; (2) the endurance of arduous training, which fosters profound self-perception by necessitating a resilient self and (3) the development of advanced technical abilities, which enhances self-esteem. Consequently, the deliberate choice to embrace and adapt to the rigours of training cultivates self-esteem, self-confidence, self-discipline and a profound sense of self.

In the context of traditional Chinese sports, the concepts of self-givenness and self-technology represent two distinct yet interconnected processes of self-perception and self-cultivation. Self-givenness can be understood as a more passive process, where the individual comes to recognise and accept their inherent abilities and limitations through the natural unfolding of physical activities. It is a process of self-discovery that emerges from the embodied experience of participating in sports, allowing for an intuitive understanding of one's own body and capabilities (Farrer & Whalen-Bridge, 2011). On the other hand, self-technology refers to the active practices of self-cultivation that are deeply embedded in traditional Chinese sports (Kauz, 2014). This involves the deliberate learning and mastering of specialised skills and techniques aimed at enhancing one's physical and mental faculties (Mainland, 2018). It is a proactive approach to self-improvement that requires discipline, dedication and a systematic method of training. In sports such as martial arts, archery and Tai Chi, practitioners engage in rigorous routines to refine their movements, increase their strength and agility and cultivate a focused and resilient mindset (Allen, 2015).

In can be argued that for effective self-cultivation in traditional Chinese sports, stringent prerequisites often apply. These may include a commitment to regular practice, adherence to ethical and philosophical principles and guidance from experienced masters. The cultivation of both body and mind is seen as essential, with an emphasis on the harmonious development of physical prowess and moral integrity. The practitioner must not only learn the external forms but also internalise the deeper values and meanings behind the movements, embodying the principles of balance, harmony and self-awareness that are central to the philosophy of traditional Chinese sports. This dual engagement with self-givenness and self-technology fosters a holistic development of the individual, where the cultivation of the self is both a personal journey and a disciplined practice (Schrenk, 2014, pp. 103–104).

In traditional Chinese sports, equal emphasis is placed on 'skills' and 'arts', with the latter representing a pursuit of metapraxis – a concept signifying actions that reflect upon themselves and aim at self-transcendence. Kauz contends that Chinese physical arts are dedicated to the construction of personal meaning, directing individuals towards self-perfection or realization, and he encapsulates this as 'education for character training' (Kauz, 2014, p. 274), highlighting the transformative knowledge inherent in Chinese martial arts. The practitioner is not simply engaging in active participation; rather, they are shaping their subjectivity through interactions with the physical arts. This subjectivity is not predetermined but emergent and evolving. Throughout the progressive journey of sports training, the individual encounters profound psychological and physical satisfaction, which serves to integrate fragmented life experiences, often a byproduct of modern existence, and fosters the continuous, holistic formation of the unconscious body in self-reflection.

The art of physical sports suggests an ongoing process of creation, resonating with the notion of subjectivity as an open-ended form. French philosophers, including Foucault, Lefebvre and Sartre, favoured the term 'œuvre' to describe this perpetual creative endeavour. The richness and diversity of traditional Chinese sports enable the 'art' within these practices to be fully appreciated in multiple dimensions: (1) as an aesthetic experience, (2) as an emotional expression, (3) as spontaneous action beyond practical utility, (4) as a medium with potential symbolic meanings, (5) as a form that is complex yet coherent and (6) as an original character of the practitioner.

Traditional Chinese sports, through their performative physical expressions, are instrumental in fostering interoception and proprioception, which are pivotal to understanding the self from both philosophical and sociological perspectives. Schrenk (2014) posits that the depth and vitality of 'art' within these sports enhance the body's sensory engagement with movement, suggesting that the more nuanced and dynamic the art, the more profound the encounter.

Such encounters can be facilitated by the rich tapestry of 'arts', which in turn can enable a more varied and creative subjectivity to emerge. However, the physicality of sports arts is distinct from other artistic disciplines due to the rigorous and often grueling nature of their training, which – as previously discussed – demands perseverance through tedium and pain as integral to athletic development.

Drawing on Nietzschean philosophy, Monahan argues that the martial artist's journey involves an ongoing process of overcoming internal conflicts and fears, contributing to the continuous transcendence and sublimation of the self (Monahan, 2007). In martial arts, this transcendence is directed inward, with the ultimate aim being self-competition, a means to realize the full potential of the human body. The practitioner's intense emotions serve as a relentless driving force, rooted in the sensory experiences of the physical self. Martial arts, it can be claimed, are unparalleled in their capacity to evoke profound emotional responses. Mainland (2018, p. iv) encapsulates this interplay of subjectivity within martial arts with the evocative phrase 'embodying the way of iron and silk', vividly conveying the philosophical essence of martial arts as a discipline that shapes the self.

The construction of the self, transcendence and introspection are not solely mental activities of an individual subject; rather, they are grounded in inter-subjective practical activities, particularly in traditional Chinese society. The ethics of mastery, religious ethics and clan ethics, deeply embedded within bodily perception, are integral to learning and training activities, forming a part of daily spiritual practice. These elements are vital to the constitution of the heroic figure, a key source of Chinese values. The 'I' in this context is an inter-subjective entity, a social construct, which holds even greater significance in the realm of traditional Chinese sports.

THE PRODUCTION OF WORTH: CHINESE TRADITIONAL SPORTS AS SELF-TECHNIQUES FOR SHAPING INTERSUBJECTIVITY

Schutz (1967) articulates the concept of 'intersubjectivity' as the shared understanding among individuals across various contexts, positing it as essential for all immediate human experiences within the lifeworld. This shared subjectivity enables individuals to comprehend others and themselves during face-to-face encounters, interpersonal interactions and dialogue (Schutz, 1967, p. 190). Subjective self-awareness and the notion of free will are, in fact, continuously shaped and informed by the interpretation of specific perspectives. Within the framework of embodied sociology, the conception of any idea is understood as emerging incrementally from daily life, making the practice of sport a process of engaging with others, as well as with historical and cultural contexts.

In Chinese archery, the five categories of skill emphasise not only technical prowess (such as hitting the target consecutively three times, shooting through the target or hitting the target with an arrow placed upon it) but also the importance of behaviour that aligns with Confucian etiquette among fellow archers. Earning respect within the community and a sense of value is contingent upon the physical manifestation of various 'skills-etiquette' (Yang, 2022). Jennings contends that the postures and motor skills in Chinese martial arts foster a 'skills-emotion' connection with 'others' (including masters, teammates and rivals), within a dynamic context of force adaptation. He notes that Chinese martial arts serve as 'socio-linguistic' resources (Jennings, 2010, p. 289), imbued with distinct genre and culture.

This cultural richness has led to a proliferation of stylistic variations that evolved from a technically homogeneous form of combat, resulting in diverse body positions and training methodologies in China. Masters from various schools have devised their routines and movements not primarily for combat efficacy but to signify cultural identity, offering self-contained explanations for these practices. Consequently, Chinese martial arts schools have transcended mere categorisation by fighting skills and now represent distinct local fighting styles. Researchers such as Dai and Lu (2021) have identified that the offencive and defensive manoeuvres in Chinese martial arts have given rise to a plethora of value narratives. For instance, *Wing Chun*'s *Chi-Sa*, which translates to a tense arm or hand, actually denotes a two-person sparring technique aimed at enhancing a practitioner's sensitivity and reaction time. However, the intent is not to cause harm or incapacitate others, especially within the relationships of master, disciple and fellow practitioners.

In contrast to Western sports, where competition and rivalry predominate, traditional Chinese sports represent an embodied approach to constructing social and ethical relations, thereby shaping value subjectivity. From the perspective of embodied sociology, these sports underscore an ecological ethos, pursuing a holistic social role where competition techniques transcend mere abstract fighting methods to become a form of 'performance art' steeped in religious ethics. Young posits that the 'morality' and 'etiquette' found in Japanese and Korean martial arts originate from the ethical framework of Chinese martial arts, with martial arts practice serving as a fundamentally 'social' form of self-cultivation (Young, 2014, pp. 212–213). Here, the self is perceived not as an isolated entity but as inherently situated within a nexus of social relations, rendering the martial artist's subjectivity as intersubjective, rooted in relational empiricism and daily experience. This constitutes a meta-praxis of 'ethical life', bearing the weight of Confucian values, with 'Dao' (Ways) at its core.

'Dao' in this context transcends a metaphysical philosophical concept; it emerges from embodied experiences of daily life, thus constituting a 'meta-praxis'. The synthesis of physical sensation with the spirit of sport during exercise exemplifies this profound alignment. Jennings et al. (2010) employ the term 'Secular Religion' to describe *Wing Chun*, suggesting that its practice encompasses a 'Dao' derived from quotidian religious practices and holds sacred significance for practitioners. In Chinese secular religions, deities are not the focal point of worship; instead, there exists a 'historical complex' where specific historical figures (ancestors) are revered through rituals, with the Sifu (master) symbolising this transmission. The Sifu epitomises not only an individual but also embodies a revered personality and sacred values integral to the genealogy of movement techniques. Kauz (2014, p. 277) observes a shared ethos between Chinese martial arts and the Stoic philosophy of ancient Rome, where the arts are pursued to foster a spirit of aiding the vulnerable and nurturing the genteel, with education aimed at character development and filial piety as the bedrock of social norms.

Traditional Chinese sports are not mere physical exercises; they are deeply rooted in the philosophical tenets of Confucianism, Buddhism, and Daoism, thereby fostering a secular spirituality that is holistic in nature. Brown (2016, p. 317) from Cardiff University posits that Taijiquan exemplifies this integration, drawing upon Daoist principles, Confucian morality and ethics, as well as cosmological views, to translate these abstract cultural elements into tangible physical practices. This translation enables the physical embodiment of Chinese culture as a faith, blending religious and holistic spiritualities seamlessly. In a separate study, Brown (2013) also contends that Chinese martial arts serve as a conduit for incorporating diverse spiritual and religious elements into the practitioner's body through disciplined movement. Over time, athletes incorporate a behavioural habitus into the transmission of sport techniques and rituals, thereby renewing them and embedding their bodies within the historical and cultural milieu.

Amidst the 'embodied turn' in sociological inquiry, scholars examining traditional Chinese sports have recognized the necessity of manifesting philosophical and religious concepts through physical skills. These skills, once embodied, become inter-subjective symbols of value. Consequently, in sociological research on the value of traditional Chinese sports, the body should be foregrounded as a critical component of the interactive subject and a direct expression of value identity. Some academics argue that the marginalisation of the body – due to modernisation, industrialisation, urbanisation, and informatization – constitutes the primary reason for the decline of traditional Chinese sports (Loh & Loong, 2016; Zhang & Guo, 2022). Individuals detached from the embodied experiences of their cultural heritage are unable to construct tangible, meaningful values, leading to an existential void. Echoing Bourdieu's 'The Logic of Practice', values are inherently part of an authentic inter-subjective bodily experience, and sports offer a profound means to cultivate this genuine, contextualised perception.

THE CREATION OF COLLECTIVE MEMORY: TRADITIONAL CHINESE SPORT AS EMBODIED SKILLS OF A NATIONAL NARRATIVE

Drawing from the French philosopher Jean-François Lyotard, considerations addressed in this section are meant to distinguish between two forms of knowledge: narrative and scientific. Lyotard (1984, p. 18) posits that knowledge transcends mere object-specific generalizations or denotative statements, encompassing practical competencies such as 'knowing how', 'knowing how to live' and 'knowing how to listen' (savoir-faire, savoir-vivre and savoir-écouter). In the realm of traditional Chinese sports, a substantial portion of knowledge is narrative in nature. This narrative knowledge is inextricably linked to bodily skills, whether in physical combat or performance, and the embodiment within narratives extends the body as an element of collective culture. Guo's (2020) research on the *Song Jiang Jhen*, a martial arts tradition shared by *Fujian* and *Taiwan*, reveals that the individual and collective memories of its practitioners shape their national identities. The heroic narratives embedded in these physical performances foster a shared cultural and ancestral connection among individuals on both sides of the Taiwan Strait.

Similarly, Wan Jianzhong (2016) explores traditional sports in western China, suggesting that through bodily collisions and interactions, participants reinforce their ethnic self-perceptions and identities, with physical identity being paramount. Moreover, the maintenance and reinforcement of sports as a universal practice are essential for the sustenance of physical identity. Xu Xinjian (2013) refers to this phenomenon as the 'social expression of the ethnic body', highlighting the narrative skills' extension into the social realm.

Traditional Chinese sports serve as a fertile medium for crafting heroic narratives and collective memory. Disciplines such as *archery*, *martial arts*, *cuju* and *dragon boat* racing not only embody cultural significance but also sculpt the value-laden image of the Chinese hero through the corporeal practice of these sports. Bowman draws upon philosopher Judith Butler's conceptualisation of the heroic persona as a form of 'fantasy reality', which plays a dynamic role in connecting social norms (values) with the living subject as a spiritual reality, thereby forging self-identity. This connection is not merely a process of spiritual self-formation but an ethical permeation and cultural construction of 'being-in-the-flesh'.

Contrary to past beliefs that individuals had minimal impact on culture, being merely products of their environment, contemporary insights reveal that sports, amplified by the rise of visual media, enable individual bodily techniques to exert substantial cultural influence. Bowman highlights how Bruce Lee's 'heroic subjectivity' (Bowman, 2011, p. 69) emerges from diverse cultural interactions and integrations, rooted in the technical prowess of his kung fu. Lee's embodiment of martial arts allows for the materialisation of aspirational values, fostering a connection with the visceral experiences of diverse groups, nationalities and countries. Lee's films have catalysed this effect, positioning him as a structural icon that bridges Eastern and Western cultures, revolutionises perceptions of Chinese martial arts and reshapes the Western portrayal of Asian masculinity, facilitating a deep historical interweaving of two heroic traditions.

Drawing from the Chinese philosophical principle of 'intergradations of body and state', which extends from self-cultivation to family governance and state management, some scholars infer the individual's value as an 'individual of the nation-state', positing that the essence of traditional national sports culture resides in bodily skills (Zhou et al., 2021; Sun & Ye, 2022). Thus, traditional Chinese sports inherently embody a 'power authenticity', suggesting that the historical tradition of the sport is subject to continuous reinvention. The cultural narrative of the sport resembles 'historiography' (Bowman, 2016). For instance, Taijiquan is not an ancient martial art fixed in time; rather, it represents the perpetuation of collective ideology from its inception to the 19th century. Judkins and Nielson (2015, p. 3) further argue that the contemporary image of *Wing Chun* is deeply entwined with the 'quasi-biographical' narratives of Hong Kong cinema, where cinematic portrayals of Bruce Lee and his master Yip Man have crafted a storied representation of *Wing Chun*.

The exploration of bodily narratives and metaphors has significantly advanced the sociology of the body, fostering a nuanced understanding of the interplay between individual bodily skills and a collective sense of body identity. A pivotal shift in the study of traditional Chinese sports has been the emphasis on the 'extended' category, which is intricately connected to China's unique political climate and historical legacy. The foundations of Chinese national identity are steeped in the ancestor veneration of antiquity, prompting a national imagination that leans heavily on the collective memory and heritage encapsulated in rituals.

The ancients attributed political significance to natural phenomena, as epitomised by the traditional notion of 'the harmony between heaven and humanity'.

This concept positions the celestial realm as the wellspring of moral and ethical codes – transcendent yet non-volitional. This insight enriches the 'extended' category with an 'enactive' dimension. Consequently, numerous Chinese scholars have leveraged an embodied framework to investigate traditional sports' contribution to national and ethnic identity. Conversely, Western scholars like Bowman, observing from an external vantage point, contend that Taijiquan, rather than being an authentically ancient practice, is a product of political narratives crafted since the 19th century.

AN EMBODIED TURN?

Within the context of embodied philosophy's substantial influence and the assimilation of embodied cognition into various humanities disciplines, the study of traditional Chinese sports culture has undergone an 'embodied turn'. This shift has redirected focus from broad cultural interpretations, communicative explorations, pedagogical analyses and anthropological descriptions towards a profound examination of the social epistemological underpinnings of the human body relationship. It includes delving into proprioception, tangible social interactions, identity awareness and national identity within sporting contexts. This transition represents a paradigmatic evolution from symbolic interpretation to a corporeal focus and from structuralist to phenomenological sociology in cultural studies (Chang & Yang, 2022; Chen et al., 2022; Ma & Gao, 2023; Zhang & Guo, 2022; Zhang et al., 2014).

However, within these conceptual directions and arguments, a key question remains: has the field truly embraced the 'embodied turn'? Presently, several critical gaps persist, including (1) a glaring deficiency in the analysis of personal skill details in sports, with research often remaining too abstract; (2) a notable absence of gender sociological perspectives, with research frequently adopting a gender-neutral stance; (3) a predilection for collective memory and national consciousness, which risks misinterpretation as generalised collectivism or nationalism and (4) a limited and superficial engagement with the enactive aspect.

The current research paradigm in traditional Chinese sports is predominantly oriented towards overarching narratives, lacking a nuanced exploration of practical sensibilities. While there is a recognized focus on the embodied nature of sporting skills and mind-body integration, the existing studies tend to be overly abstract and macroscopic, failing to investigate the specific skill details that shape the practitioner's experience. For instance, the rhythm and technique employed by drummers during *dragon boat* training sessions instill a sense of proprioception in paddlers, synchronizing their collective strength, yet such intricacies remain underexplored. Moreover, there is a deficiency in dynamic historical analysis concerning the evolution and innovation of sports skills. Despite *cuju*'s long-standing popularity from the pre-Qin era through the Ming and Qing dynasties, concrete studies on the development of its techniques are scarce. Furthermore, body sociology, as a Western research paradigm, has not been fully mastered or deeply applied by local Chinese scholars. Consequently, the study of traditional Chinese sports has not genuinely realized an 'embodied turn', given that the sociology of physical skills has yet to be thoroughly and authentically analysed and interpreted.

Second, the topic of embodied gender has been notably underexplored in the study of traditional Chinese sports. Researchers have predominantly adopted a gender-neutral perspective, which feminists argue is a subtle manifestation of patriarchy. The origins of Chinese sports in an ancient agrarian society, coupled with traditional gender norms, meant that activities requiring physical strength, combativeness or exposure often excluded women. Even when women participated, their contributions were frequently marginalised in historical narratives. This historical exclusion partly explains the absence of women from the annals of Chinese sports. Furthermore, contemporary scholars demonstrate a lack of gender sociological awareness, failing to adequately investigate the sociological aspects of sports practiced by women, such as *female cuju, wrestling, pitch-pot games* and *skating*.

There is also a dearth of research into the embodied experiences of female athletes in these sports. Conversely, certain traditional Chinese sports, like *Taijiquan, Ba Duan Jin* (Eight-Section Brocade Qigong) and *Wu Qin Xi* (Five-Animal Frolics), are imbued with feminist undertones through their Taoist philosophies and connections to eco-feminist thought. However, local Chinese researchers have not sufficiently engaged with the sociology of the female body. This oversight presents a significant challenge: within Western scholarship, the study of women's experiences is fundamental to the sociology of the body, and its absence complicates the recognition of an 'embodied turn' among Western scholars committed to political correctness.

Third, a paradigmatic conflict emerges within the research on collective memory in traditional Chinese sports. Current scholarship primarily focuses on the unifying value produced when ethnic minorities or various ethnic groups partake in traditional sports collectively, examining the implications for establishing a communal identity and a national collective memory (Dai, 2011; Guo, 2020; Ma & Gao, 2023; Zhang, 2019). However, this research paradigm faces significant challenges, including

- The prevailing research paradigm emphasises grand narratives, diverging from the foundational tenets of the sociology of the body, which prioritises micro-level, tangible and quotidian life studies.
- From the viewpoint of numerous Western scholars, China's unique multi-ethnic nation-state structure often appears enigmatic and is consequently conflated with collectivism or even nationalism. As a result, research on traditional Chinese sports that underscores national unity risks being misinterpreted through the lens of nationalist ideology.
- The competitive sports of ethnic minorities, such as Mongolian wrestling, which stem from interpersonal physical contests, inherently possess an

exclusivity that seems at odds with the collective memory associated with forging a broader Chinese national community. In essence, the fundamental logic behind the 'embodied turn' becomes contentious and susceptible to misinterpretation within this research context.

Fourth, the exploration of enaction remains superficial. While the essence of enaction resonates with the Chinese philosophical notion of the 'co-existence of heaven and human', an extensive literature review indicates a gap: researchers in the field of traditional Chinese sports have not thoroughly investigated and analysed the concept of embodiment, at times even overlooking it. The absence of this critical concept of embodiment in research undermines any claim of a successful 'embodied turn'.

In summary, scholars in the field of traditional Chinese sports have recognized the significance of the embodied paradigm within the sociology of the body, incorporating it into a range of studies and generating numerous findings. However, a detailed and in-depth analysis of these contributions reveals several issues within the so-called 'embodied turn' that demand scholarly attention.

CONCLUSIONS

This chapter has critically examined the scholarship on embodiment within traditional Chinese sports. As humanities and social science research increasingly embraces an embodied perspective, scholars of traditional Chinese sporting culture have also recognized and begun to integrate this approach. By adopting an embodied framework – a stance that fosters a heightened awareness of corporeality – researchers have been able to delve into the cognitive experiences of athletes and participants in traditional Chinese sports. This focus on embodiment not only enriches the research but also provides insights into the significance of traditional Chinese sports in the construction of human subjectivity and the formation of ethnic identity.

FIVE KEY READINGS

Allen, B. (2015). *Striking beauty: A philosophical look at the Asian martial arts.* **Columbia University Press.**

The first book to focus on the intersection of Western philosophy and the Asian martial arts, Striking Beauty comparatively studies the historical and philosophical traditions of martial arts practice and their ethical value in the modern world. Expanding Western philosophy's global outlook, the book forces a theoretical reckoning with the concerns of Chinese philosophy and the aesthetic and technical dimensions of martial arts practice. Striking Beauty explains the relationship between Asian martial arts and the Chinese philosophical traditions of Confucianism, Buddhism and Daoism, in addition to Sunzi's Art of War. It connects martial arts practice to the Western concepts of mind-body dualism and materialism, sports aesthetics and the ethics of violence. The work ameliorates Western philosophy's hostility towards the body, emphasising the pleasure of watching and engaging in martial arts, along with their beauty and the ethical problem of their violence.

Dai, G. (2011). *Bodily culture of Chinese martial arts.* **People's Sports Publishing House.**

This book elaborates on Chinese martial arts as a cultural embodiment of physical behaviour, with its own cultural generative laws, and as an embodiment of Chinese culture. Compared with the cultural characteristics of Western sports, the cultural implications exhibited and implied by Chinese martial arts are more about the concept of unity between man and nature, the spirit of moral integrity and a polite sense of competition. These concepts, spirits and consciousness contain the cultural genes of the Chinese nation and are the crystallization of the wisdom of the Chinese nation.

Farrer, D. S., & Whalen-Bridge, J. (Eds.). (2011). *Martial arts as embodied knowledge: Asian traditions in a transnational world.* **Suny Press.**

This book provides a wide-ranging scholarly consideration of the traditional Asian martial arts. Most of the contributors to the volume are practitioners of the martial arts, and all are keenly aware that these traditions now exist in a transnational context. The book's cutting-edge research includes ethnography and approaches from film, literature, performance and theatre studies.

Judkins, B. N., & Nielson, J. (2015). *The creation of Wing Chun: A social history of the Southern Chinese martial arts.* **SUNY Press.**

This book explores the social history of southern Chinese martial arts and their contemporary importance to local identity and narratives of resistance. Hong Kong's Bruce Lee ushered the Chinese martial arts onto an international stage in the 1970s. Lee's teacher, Ip Man, master of Wing Chun Kung Fu, has recently emerged as a highly visible symbol of southern Chinese identity and pride. Benjamin N. Judkins and Jon Nielson examine the emergence of Wing Chun to reveal how this body of social practices developed and why individuals continue to turn to the martial arts as they navigate the challenges of a rapidly evolving environment. After surveying the development of hand combat traditions in Guangdong Province from roughly the start of the 19th century until 1949, the authors turn to Wing Chun, noting its development, the changing social attitudes towards this practice over time and its ultimate emergence as a global art form.

Sun, Q., Lijuan, M., & Li, C. (2023). *Illustrated book of traditional Chinese sport.* **World Scientific Pub Co Inc.**

Employing archaeology, anthropology, sociology and iconography, this book employs a multidisciplinary approach to delve into Chinese sports. A distinguishing feature is its documentation of Chinese sports history and culture, drawing from diverse sources like mythology relics, rock paintings and ancient literature. Through both visuals and text, it maps out the inception, growth, transformation and spread of ancient Chinese sports across different epochs.

REFERENCES

Allen, B. (2013). Games of sport, works of art, and the striking beauty of Asian martial arts. *Journal of the Philosophy of Sport, 40*(2), 241–254.
Allen, B. (2015). *Striking beauty: A philosophical look at the Asian martial arts*. Columbia University Press.
Bowman, P. (2011). In D. S. Farrer & J. Whalen-Bridge (Eds.), *The fantasy corps of martial arts, or, the "communication" of Bruce Lee*. SUNY Press.
Brown, D. (2013). Seeking spirituality through physicality in schools: Learning from "eastern movement forms". *International Journal of Children's Spirituality, 18*(1), 30–45.
Brown, D. (2016). Taoism through Tai Chi Chuan: Physical culture as religious or holistic spirituality? In M. Souza, J. Bone, & J. Watson (Eds.), *Spiritual across disciplines research and practice*. Springer.
Bowman, P. (2016). *The Intimate Schoolmaster and the Ignorant Sifu: Poststructuralism, Bruce Lee, and the Ignorance of Everyday Radical Pedagogy* (p. 131). Knowledge, Spirit, Law.
Cao, H., & Zhao, G. (2014). Embody-perception exercise and acquisition of martial art skills. *Journal of Shandong Institute of Physical Education and Sports, 30*(02), 59–62.
Cave, P. (2019). *The Tai Chi space: How to move in Tai Chi and Qi Gong*. Aeon Books Ltd.
Chang, Z., & Yang, L. (2022). Body turn: The embodied cognition of Taijiquan on the Confucian view of heaven and human. *Journal of Physical Education, 6*, 25–30.
Chen, B., Yuzhu, J., & Wang, G. (2022). Embodied practice and internal logic of Chinese Wushu Somaesthetics. *Journal of Tianjin University of Sport, 37*(1), 119–124.
Dai, G. (2011). *Bodily culture of Chinese martial arts*. People's Sports Publishing House.
Dai, G., & Lu, A. (2021). Wushu: A culture of adversaries. *Journal of the Philosophy of Sport, 46*(3), 321–338.
Fang, Y. (2013). *Zi Zang – Daoist Division – Lie Zi Volume* (Vol. 3). National Library Press.
Farrer, D. S., & Whalen-Bridge, J. (Eds.). (2011). *Martial arts as embodied knowledge: Asian traditions in a transnational world*. Suny Press.
Guo, X. (2020). Memory, identity and community: A study on body performance and discourse narration of national traditional sports in Wushu perform culture of Songjiang array on both sides of the Taiwan strait. *China Sports Science, 40*(07), 79–87.
Jennings, B. G. (2010). *Fighters, thinkers and shared cultivation: Experiencing transformation through the long-term practice of traditionalist Chinese martial arts*. University of Exeter.
Jennings, G., Brown, D., & Sparkes, A. C. (2010). "It can be a religion if you want": Wing Chun Kung Fu as a secular religion. *Ethnography, 11*(4), 533–557.
Judkins, B. N., & Nielson, J. (2015). *The creation of Wing Chun: A social history of the Southern Chinese martial arts*. SUNY Press.
Jung, C. G., Jung-Merker, L., & Rüf, E. (1978). *Studien Über Alchemistische Vorstellungen*. Walter-Verlag.
Kauz, H. (2014). The martial spirit. In J. Donohue (Ed.), *The overlook martial arts reader* (Vol. 2). Woodstock New York.
Legge, J. (1960). *The Chinese classics: Confucian analects, the great learning, and the doctrine of the mean*. Hong Kong University Press.
Loh, H., & Loong, L. (2016). *The body and senses in martial culture*. Palgrave Macmillan.
Lyotard, J. F. (1984). *The postmodern condition: A report on knowledge*. University of Minnesota Press.
Ma, C., & Gao, L. (2023). Embodied ethics of Wushu: Theoretical selection and practical requirements to promote Chinese Wushu ethics in school physical education. *Journal of Sports Research, 37*(3), 87–94.
Mainland, M. (2018). *Kung Fu is inside the body: A phenomenological inquiry into cultivating martial art practices*. University of Waterloo.
Monahan, M. (2007). The practice of self-overcoming: Nietzschean reflections on the martial arts. *Journal of the Philosophy of Sport, 34*(1), 39–51.
Newen, A., De Bruin, L., & Gallagher, S. (Eds.). (2018). *The Oxford handbook of 4E cognition*. Oxford University Press.

Schrenk, M. (2014). Is proprioceptive are possible? In G. Priest & D. Young (Eds.), *Philosophy and the martial arts*. Routledge.

Schutz, A. (1967). *The phenomenology of the social world* (1st ed.). Northwestern University Press.

Sun, W., & Ye, S. (2022). Body: The foothold of the return of national traditional sports culture. *Journal of Nanjing Sports Institute*, (02), 75–80.

Tanaka, K. (2011). In D. S. Farrer & J. Whalen-Bridge (Eds.), *Self-awareness and the self*. Suny Press.

Tian, E., & Wise, N. (2022). Dancing in public squares – Toward a socially synchronous sense of place. *Leisure Sciences, Latest Articles.* https://doi.org/10.1080/01490400.2022.2099490

Wan, J. (2016). Body experience and body significance of western traditional ethnic sports. *Northwestern Journal of Ethnology*, (03), 153–158+177.

Wile, D. (1999). *Tai Chi's ancestors: The making of an internal martial art*. Sweet Ch'i Press.

Wise, N. (2015). Geographical approaches and the sociology of sport. In R. Giulianotti (Ed.), *Routledge handbook of the sociology of sport* (pp. 142–152). Routledge.

Xiao, J. (2016). The generic property of Chinese traditional Cuju: Kick sports games and analysis of their characteristics as a body culture. *Journal of Chengdu Sport University*, *42*(4), 51–55.

Xu, X. (2013). Social expression of ethnic body: Researching the national minority traditional sports meeting from the view of anthropology. *Journal of Chongqing University of Arts and Sciences (Social Sciences Edition)*, *32*(1), 61–63.

Yang, T. (2022). On the "physical literacy" of Chinese traditional archery. *Journal of Sports Research*, (01), 81–90.

Young, D. (2014). Bowing to your enemies. In G. Priest & D. Young (Eds.), *Philosophy and the martial arts*. Routledge.

Zahavi, D. (2005). *Subjectivity and selfhood*. MIT Press.

Zhang, J., Tian, S., & Xi, F. (2014). Body, cultural form and Chinese traditional sports culture. *Journal of Sports Adult Education*, *30*(1), 59–62.

Zhang, Z. (2019). *Memory imagination identity: The body historical genealogy of Chinese Wsushu*. People's Sports Publishing House.

Zhang, Y., & Guo, L. (2022). The embodiment path of school physical education for forging a sense of community for the Chinese nation through traditional national sports. *Journal of Ethnology*, *13*(05), 100–107+141.

Zhang, Z., & Ju, F. (2020). Philosophical implication of ancient Chinese physical literacy. *China Sport Science*, *40*(9), 89–97.

Zhang, J., Zhou, H., & Tan, T. (2017). Embodied cognition and philosophical research of Wushu teaching: Body, situation and cognition. *Journal of Wuhan Institute of Physical Education*, *51*(1), 67–71.

Zhou, L., Zhang, W., & Wang, W. (2021). Research on present situation and development countermeasures of MOOCs of traditional national physical education-based on the theory of physical cognition. *Journal of Dalian Minzu University*, *23*(03), 281–285.

Ziemke, T. (2003). What's that thing called embodiment? *Proceedings of the Annual Meeting of the Cognitive Science Society*, *25*, 1305–1310.

CHAPTER 2

CHINESE SPORTS HEROES AND NATIONALISM AT MEGA-SPORTING EVENTS

Gen Li

Beijing Normal University, China

ABSTRACT

In modern China, sports and nationalism always have close connection, and nationalism is the important reason for the promotion of Chinese sports. However, the relationship between Chinese sports and nationalism in globalised China could be much more examined by academics, as well as its influencing factors. This chapter selects the Beijing 2008 Olympic Games as the context and representative three Chinese sports heroes in the period of globalisation to study. The findings show that in some extent, Beijing 2008 Olympic Games and three Chinese sports heroes represent the national image of China in the globalised world, also bearing the burden of washing away historical humiliation and pursuing national glory. Furthermore, it is manifested that China have a complex nationalism in the process of hosting the 2008 Olympic Games. Under the influence of mass media, market economy and sports professionalisation, nationalism still exists in Chinese sports, but people gradually start to reflect on the 'Juguo Tizhi', the traditional Chinese sports system and the concept of 'winning glory for the nation'. The relationship between Chinese nationalism and sports shows the important implications of rapid Chinese sports development.

Keywords: Chinese sports; nationalism; Beijing 2008 Olympic Games; sports hero; celebrity; sports development

INTRODUCTION

After the 1980s, China started a new journey of reform. This journey involved opening up and rapid market economic reform. New policy was implemented, and this allowed Chinese people to go overseas more often. This also resulted in enhanced relationships between China and foreign countries, making them much closer. China also became truly globalised, and almost every aspect developed significantly, especially around manufacturing and trade, and this also included sports and an expanded events portfolio (Wise, 2020). During this period, Chinese nationalism gradually began to show new characteristics, and the development of national power made Chinese nationalism much stronger. At that times, Chinese nationalism shows different proposition, such as defending the dignity and status of the Chinese nation, pursuing the maximisation of the interests of the Chinese nation, supporting the political system established by The People's Republic of China and supporting the promotion of the values represented by the Chinese nation in the international community (Shen, 2007).

The development of Chinese nationalism has been influenced by different areas and factors. The sports area is a good example, as it is closely related to Chinese nationalism, which is also an important reason for the promotion of Chinese sports (Brownell, 1995; Lu & Fan, 2019). However, the relationship between Chinese sports and nationalism in a globalised China could be more deeply discussed by academics. All events create impacts, and nationalism is a form of social impact in relation to place (Wise & Harris, 2019; Wise & Maguire, 2022). Especially in the context of the Beijing 2008 Olympic Games, the issue of nationalism as reflected in the stories of some representative Chinese sports heroes has revealed meaningful implications. This chapter focuses on the following questions: What are the characteristics of sport and nationalism that shows in the Beijing 2008 Olympic Games? How do the stories of Chinese sports heroes show the relationship between Chinese sports and nationalism in the context of Beijing 2008 Olympic Games? This paper will select some representative cases for study, including Beijing 2008 Olympic Games as a mega event and three Chinese sports heroes.

BEIJING 2008 OLYMPIC GAMES: A STORY SYMBOLISING *NATIONAL REVIVAL?*

The study of national in sport is an important research direction (Bairner, 2001; Tian & Wise, 2020). The Chinese in the early 20th century asked the 'Three Olympic Questions', the last of which was when China would be able to host an Olympic Games. This dream began to be realized in China in the 1990s, when in December 1991, the Chinese Olympic Committee submitted an application to the International Olympic Committee (IOC) announcing China's government bid for the 2000 Summer Olympics. The bid was supported by China's leader at that time, Deng Xiaoping, who said to the leader of the Chinese Sports Committee during an inspection of the Asian Games facilities, 'Have you made up your mind about bidding to host the Olympics? Why are you afraid to do this?' (Xiong & Zhong, 2010, p. 253) In the final vote in 1993, Beijing lost by only two votes to Sydney, Australia. The bid was very competitive at that time; the finally defeat caused great disappointment in China. According to the New York Times, some Peking university students planned to march to the United States (US) Embassy after the failed Olympic bid was stopped by police (Tyler, 1993; Wang, 2014, p. 224).

After the failure of the previous bid, the Chinese government decided in 1998 that Beijing would again bid to host the 2008 Summer Olympic Games. In 2000, the IOC announced that Beijing had officially qualified to bid for the Summer Olympics. On 13 July 2001, the IOC held a meeting in Moscow to vote for the host city of the 2008 Olympic Games. After two rounds of voting, Beijing won the right to host the 2008 Summer Olympics (Zhu, 2015). As the news back to China, it instantly ignited immense nationalism within China. The People's Daily, the Chinese official newspaper, reported the information about the Olympic bid on its front page, with a particular extra page. In the report, this newspaper described the scene in Beijing as follows:

> In the living scene, people hold the national flag and wave them, throwing flowers and banners into the sky again and again [...] joyful singing and dancing until midnight. The lights are brilliant, the people are flowing, the colourful flags and the songs are flying from Tiananmen Square to the Asian Games Village, from Wangfujing and Xidan to Peking University and Tsinghua University. This historic night will be remembered in the hearts of Chinese people. This night belongs to Beijing, and this night belongs to China. (Zhu, 2015)

CCTV, the Chinese official television station, spent a great deal of time and resources to cover the entire process and celebration of the bid (Varrall, 2020). Before the live broadcast of the Olympic bid, all planned programs were adjusted or removed to accommodate the full coverage of the bid, and CCTV spent 14 hours of programming around the bid, using a total of four channels for the broadcast. After the news of the successful bid, CCTV reporters quickly sent news of the celebrations in China and even arranged 13 correspondent stations worldwide to quickly send back reports of the celebrations of Chinese people around the world. CCTV's attention to this Olympic bid reached a very high level in terms of the timing and scale of coverage.

In terms of content, CCTV's coverage focused on landmarks of national significance in Beijing. The first look was at the Chinese Century Monument, a symbol of the history of Chinese civilization, where Jiang Zemin and other national leaders participated in the celebrations and where CCTV captured the grand scenes of the leaders celebrating with the people. Afterwards, the CCTV's coverage moved to Chang'an Street, Tiananmen Square and Zhongnanhai, the centre of Beijing and Chinese government. By the side of Chang'an Street, cheering crowds entered the camera, and the success of the Olympic bid was expressed in the form of a national celebration (Peng, 2005). Through the Chinese media's coverage and reproduction of the Olympic bid, the themes of 'Chinese nation' are highlighted, and these concept as an 'imagined community' becomes more real and vital, becoming the basis of identity that inspires Chinese nationalism.

In the view of the Chinese government, the success of the Olympic bid should be given the great significance of washing away historical shame and pursing national rejuvenation. In a commentary by Xinhua News Agency, which is another official media, it was stated that

> In the past, it was nearly impossible to break the record of zero Olympic gold medals; today, China has achieved the top three in the Olympic games. In the past, the government did not know what the Olympic Games were; now, Beijing has succeeded in its second bid to host them. The Olympic Games have witnessed the rapid rise of the Chinese nation from the "Sick Man of East Asia" to the giant of the East and the fantastic transformation of China from poverty to standing on the world stage. (Wang, 2001)

Another report also mentioned that Chinese people had waited too long for the success of the Olympic bid, and hosting the 2008 Olympics is an important opportunity for China in the new century. 'We should strive to make great success in the 2008 Beijing Olympics games because it will greatly stimulate the nationalism and patriotism across the country and promote the development of China's reform, opening up, and socialist modernisation (Zhu, 2015)'. It should be said that the imminent arrival of the Olympic Games became a nationalist feast that many people in China were looking forward to. The media's nearly 24-hour broad coverage of the successful Olympic bid also reflects a construct of 'banal nationalism'.

During the Olympic period following the successful bid (known as Olympiad in ancient Greece), China's government and people are working hard to create an excellent national image in order to welcome the Olympics and friends around the world. The Beijing government accelerated the construction of city facilities, and the Olympic stadium and new buildings symbolising modernity were built. On the cultural side, the government carries out a spiritual-building campaign to welcome the Olympics. The 11th of each month was designated as a special 'education day' to appeal citizens to build a good image for the Olympics. Government have provided cab drivers with opportunities and helps to learn basic English (Lovell, 2008). Beijing TV station producing programs on the etiquette of watching the games and linking it to the image of the Chinese nation. Some social organisations also publish initiatives in the media, calling on people to 'drive less for the Olympics' to meet the environmental requirements of the Olympics (Fu, 2014, p. 60). And as mentioned above, the Chinese government has further increased its investment in elite sports to achieve a breakthrough in performance at home.

The nationalism of the Chinese public was even more obvious in the torch relay of the Beijing Olympics. The Beijing Olympic torch relay began in March 2008 with the theme 'Journey of Harmony', echoing the country's policy of 'peaceful rise'. The torch relay began in Greece and covered 20 cities on five continents (IOC, 2007). Protests by opponents erupted in many cities, including San Francisco, Paris, London, Seoul and Istanbul, where the torch was passed. These opponents, who mainly included groups from anti-Chinese government, tried to obstruct and disrupt the torch relay, and clashes broke out with local Chinese students who supported China. The most violent conflict erupted in Paris when several protesters tried to seize the torch from disabled athlete Jin Jing, causing the torch to be extinguished several times and Jin Jing to be injured. The torch relay in Paris also showed unfavourable security. Hence, a massive protest demonstration against France and a boycott of the French enterprise Carrefour appeared in China (BBC Chinese, 2008).

The protest was initially mobilised on the Internet, with actions spreading across several cities in China where Carrefour is present. Due to the seriousness of the situation, the Chinese government shifted from an initial laissez-faire attitude to a pacified approach, with Xinhua News Agency and People's Daily publishing commentary articles titled 'Nationalism passion should be put on a rational way' and 'Turning Nationalism sentiment into national aspirations' and expressing appreciation for Carrefour's business practices in China, which eventually led to the finish of the protests (Ni & Zhao, 2008). Jin Jing, who was injured due to her efforts to protect the torch, was appreciated by the Chinese government and the public that she was selected as one of the top 10 'Touching China' by CCTV in 2008. 'Touching China' is a programme of CCTV. It is held once a year and selects most impressive and touching Chinese people and teams through a variety of ways. This TV programme is very influential in Chinese society. The disruption of the Olympic torch relay was also included in the subsequent best-selling book 'Why China is Unhappy', which embodied nationalism and was seen as solid evidence of Western opposition to China (Guo, 2009). Before the torch relay, the Chinese public also initiated a boycott of some Western media because of their different opinions on political issues such as Tibet independent. This series of events brought Chinese nationalism to a high level even before the 2008 Olympics.

On 8 August 2008, the Beijing Olympics opening ceremony was finally held at the Bird's Nest, the Chinese national stadium (People's Daily Online, 2008). This opening ceremony, directed by the famous Chinese director Zhang Yimou, took massive resources and was an extremely grand spectacle. Zhang Yimou highlighted Chinese elements in his performance, including Chinese calligraphy, painting, writing, opera, ancient music and other symbols representing traditional Chinese culture, to present China's long and prosperous civilization to the world. In the entrance moment, the symbol of nationalism was highlighted. A nine-year-old girl, Lin MiaoKe sang 'Sing the Motherland' in a slow rhythm, and 56 children dressed in traditional Chinese costumes of 56 ethnics walked into the stadium together, holding the flag of the People's Republic of China.

The 56 children undoubtedly represent 'the Chinese nation', a concept of representation that also constructs the official Chinese historical narrative. The concept of 'the Chinese nation' first emerged in the early 20th century. Under the promotion of the government and academic world, this concept gradually became a central part of the grand narrative and ethnic policy. According to the IOC's subsequent statistics, the opening ceremony of the 2008 Beijing Olympics was watched by a staggering eight billion Chinese audience (People's Daily Online, 2008). The opening ceremony, full of national symbols and recreating the Chinese nation tradition, touched many Chinese people. Through this nationalistic spectacle, the Beijing Olympics opening ceremony was given multiple meanings as a national festival and ritual (Wu & Yun, 2008). In this moment of national celebration, the concept of Chinese nation was reaffirmed and further contributed to the shaping of the 'imagined community' of China.

After the opening ceremony, the Beijing Olympic Games started. The Chinese team played really well at home, and the Chinese Olympic Glory strategy in sports and significant investment in athletics paid off. In the Beijing Olympics, the Chinese team won 48 gold medals and broke 10 world records, setting the best result since China's participation in the Olympics Games (Xinhua News Agency, 2008). More importantly, the Chinese team taking first place at the gold medal table. This achievement is a great success for Chinese sports. Chinese government President Hu Jintao, at the closing ceremony of the Beijing Olympics, highly praised the achievements of the Chinese team and highly combined their excellent performance with 'the motherland': 'Our athletes remembered the trust of the motherland and the Chinese people ranked first at the gold medal table of the Beijing Olympics and Paralympic Games, and They have achieved both sports achievements and spiritual legacy, brighten the Olympics, win glory for the motherland, and make a wonderful gift to the motherland and the people (Xinhua News Agency, 2008)'. For the success of the Beijing Olympics, he even called as a collective victory of the Chinese nation.

The Chinese people, with perseverance and hard work, have fulfiled the century-long expectation of the Chinese nation, fulfiled the wish of the Chinese at home and overseas, won high praise from the international community and made a great contribution to the history of the modern Olympic movement. The Chinese people have been pursuing and struggling for a whole century to realize the Olympic dreams, a 100-year expectation of the Chinese nation, and have made persistent and tenacious efforts for several generations. The successful realization of the 100-year Olympic dream is another historic triumph to achieve the great rejuvenation of the Chinese nation. (Xinhua News Agency, 2008).

Hu Jintao's speech reflects the 'national rejuvenation' significance of hosting the Olympics for China and the 'Chinese nation'. The success of the Olympic Games is a symbol of modern China, proving that it has an important place in the world and is no longer the last empire of the poor and weak. The magnificent show of the Beijing Olympics was also enough to rally the nationalism of Chinese. This was exemplified by tons of bestseller books about nationalism that came out after the Beijing Olympics (e.g. China Is Unhappy, The Mandate of Heaven Is a Great Nation, etc.). Liu Peng, Director of the State General Administration of Sports, also published an article entitled 'From "Sick Man of East Asia" to Great Sports Power' after the Beijing Olympics, emphasising that the Beijing Olympics showed the amazing results of China's sports development, which was the dream of the 'Chinese nation' for a 100 years.

The first place at the gold medal table had the symbolic value of washing away the shame of 'East Asia's sick man' (Liu, 2009). Through the performance of elite sports, the physical and national strength of the 'Chinese nation' has indeed reached a level that cannot be underestimated. For a century, Chinese sports and nationalism have been closely intertwined, and the metaphorical relationship of using sports to prove 'national power' reached a peak at the Beijing Olympics.

Some scholars have pointed out that one of the significant characteristics of Chinese nationalism since modern times is the sense of self-respect and inferiority. The former sense stems from the prosperity of China's ancient civilization, which makes Chinese people want to recreate this glory in the present. The latter stems from China's humiliating history of bullying by other countries in the modern era, which makes Chinese people particularly eager to prove their status in the world (Lovell, 2008). China's hosting of the Olympic Games and its efforts to develop elite sports are all manifestations of this complex nationalism. Interestingly, the motto of the Beijing Olympics games is 'One World, One Dream'. In terms of the connotation of the Beijing 2008 Olympic games, this 'One Dream' is more like the dream of the great rejuvenation of the Chinese nation. From this perspective, maybe the nation's dream in the Beijing Olympics may be more prominent than Olympism, which is the pursuit of global unity. China's rejuvenation is the most profound impression of this Olympics has left on the world (and on China itself).

SPORTS HERO'S AND NATIONAL IMAGE: LIU XIANG, YAO MING AND LI NA

In the globalised new era, athletes are increasingly viewed as celebrities (e.g. Andrews & Jackson, 2001; Wise & Harris, 2010). With the progress made in elite sports, China has seen more world-champion athletes emerge. With the development of mass media and the market economy in China during this period, the breadth and depth of sports communication have increased dramatically, and the popularity of champion athletes has been enhanced (Keeler & Nauright, 2005). In the context of the Beijing 2008 Olympic Games, three athletes were closely connected to nationalism issues: Liu Xiang, Yao Ming and Li Na. The complex aspects of nationalism combined with sports were reflected in each of them, and it was enough to cause a lot of thoughts and debate. In the context of China's gradual globalisation, their influence is not only limited to the country but also represents the image of China in the world.

Liu Xiang: From National Hero to Controversial Figure

China's 110m hurdler Liu Xiang, who won the 2004 Athens Olympics, quickly became one of China's most prominent athletes. On 28 August 2004, Liu Xiang won the men's 110m hurdles match at the Athens Olympics with a world record time of 12.91 seconds, shocking Chinese when the news came out (China Daily, 2004). The official Xinhua News Agency issued a congratulatory report with the theme 'Liu Xiang wins a gold medal and raises the spirit of the country', The official newspaper, People's Daily, published several reports celebrating Liu Xiang's victory. The titles of the reports, such as 'The strong motherland is powerful motivation, China's flying man amazes the world!' And 'Asia has me, China has me!' And 'Foreign news agencies praise Liu Xiang with enthusiasm, Chinese take the world stage', all reflecting obvious nationalism sentiments

(Ge, 2013, p. 25). In the propaganda approach of the reports, the narrative of building national heroes coexisted with the grand narrative of breaking the 'sick man of East Asia' sign. Two of the reports included such content as follows:

> More than 70 years ago, when the Chinese first appeared in the Olympic Games, the only competitor, Liu Changchun, was also standing in the 100-metre starting line. But he was eliminated in the preliminary contest, and the newspapers posted a cartoon saying that Liu Changchun was a one-person race. At that time, the humiliating image of the "Sick Man of East Asia" was carried on the Chinese nation. Twenty years ago, ... the world watched in amazement as Xu Haifeng's crisp gunshot shot down the first-ever Chinese Olympic gold medal and told the world that the image of the "Sick Man of East Asia" had been thrown. Liu Xiang won the Olympics championship shows that as long as Chinese people work together as one, they can create miracle after miracle. (Chen Zhao, 2004)

> Who said the Chinese are the "sick man of East Asia" on the track? The "Chinese flyer" has banned those who look down on the Chinese. Liu Xiang's speed today shows that the Chinese can create legends not only in the economic field but also in any other field with "Chinese speed". (Yang, 2008)

The report evokes the humiliating history of the Chinese nation in modern times. The combination of Liu Xiang's and Xu Haifeng's images symbolised washing the shame of the 'Sick Man of East Asia' and rebuilding the nation's glory. At that time, various media, including newspapers, television and magazines, vigorously reported Liu Xiang's victory with themes such as 'the flying man' and 'China's pride', and the public also actively discussed Liu Xiang on the Internet, which quickly portrayed Liu Xiang as an athlete representing Chinese hero image (Fu, 2014, pp. 78–106; Ge, 2013, pp. 22–33). On an online survey conducted by Sina.com on 31 August 2004, the topic was 'Which Chinese sports star do you think can be called a national hero?' Liu Xiang received 35% of the votes, surpassing Yao Ming, who received 15% of the votes and was ranked first. Liu Xiang won the 'Touching China' Person of the Year in 2004, and the image of him receiving the award wearing the national flag was repeatedly shown on television screens to the Chinese public (Ge, 2013, p. 31). It can be said that Liu Xiang has become a hero in Chinese sports through nationalistic media propaganda.

While the public had higher hopes for Liu Xiang, he withdrew from the 2008 Beijing Olympics and the 2012 Athens Olympics due to injury, failing to win any medals. The result gradually changed Liu Xiang's image from national hero. Liu Xiang failed to finish normally due to injury, the media was divided into two factions. One faction take a tolerant attitude, believing that Liu Xiang's standing on the field was a victory; the other faction began to question why Liu Xiang insisted on playing if he was injured and whether there were more interests behind (Fu, 2014, pp. 97–106). Many people also changed their supportive attitude towards Liu Xiang. They thought he was performing, questioning the truth of the matches. It is not an exaggeration to say that Liu Xiang has changed from what people once saw as a national hero to a controversial athlete (Ge, 2013, pp. 45–57).

The controversy about Liu Xiang's withdrawal has undoubtedly triggered debates in the media and public. Its controversies reflect the Chinese people's complex feelings about the sports system and nationalism. Liu Xiang is an athlete trained by traditional Chinese sports system, the 'Juguo Tizhi', whose goal is to train world champions to win glory for the nation (no author, referenced as: The International Journal of the History of Sport, 2012). Liu Xiang went on the field knowing he was injured and failed to finish the match tragically. Because of his significant influence, the State General Administration of Sports and his team have made him the focus of their work. Whether he continues to appear on the field with injured is something he cannot decide only by himself. He has been under the huge pressure because of the word 'Motherland'.

When Liu Xiang's mother was interviewed, she said, 'Now Liu Xiang is the son of the country, and could only give him back to me after the Olympics. If one day Liu Xiang is no longer a champion, I hope everyone could forgive him (Zhu & Zhang, 2012)'. And his coach Sun Haiping revealed that an officer from the State General Administration of Sports had told Liu Xiang that if he could not win the gold medal at the Beijing Olympics, all his past achievements would have no meaning (Wang, 2015). The nationalism shown by the Chinese public in the sports was not only reflected in Liu Xiang's win in Athens but also in the questioning that he suffered after his defeat. Some Chinese people are not tolerant of the former 'flying man' and 'pride of China'. Athletes in the 'Juguo Tizhi' system have been firmly tied to national glory in the historical evolution of the China. The controversy about Liu Xiang's career as an athlete shows the model of Chinese people's understanding of sports in the grand narrative of 'winning glory for the nation'.

Yao Ming: Little Giant in the Globalised World

Another athlete who had a huge impact during this period was Yao Ming, who played in the American National Basketball Association for the Houston Rockets from 2002 to 2011 (Keeler & Nauright, 2005). Yao was born in 1980 in Shanghai, China, his parents were both basketball player. At 2.26 metres tall and with fantastic shooting and centre skills rarely seen anywhere else in the world, he was known as the 'Mobile Great Wall' of Chinese basketball. In 2002, Yao was draughted by the Houston Rockets as the first pick and started his National Basketball Association (NBA) career. After a short adaptation period, Yao quickly gradually became a great player, being selected to the All-Star team several times. At the national team level, Yao has also become a leader of the Chinese team, leading the Chinese men's basketball team to the last eight of the 2008 Beijing Olympics and almost beating the dominant team Spain (Keeler & Nauright, 2005). After Yao retired in 2011 due to injury, he was recognised as China's most successful men's basketball player of all time. After retiring, Yao entered the business world, buying the management rights of his former team, the Shanghai Sharks and became active in China's basketball activities, later becoming president of the Chinese Basketball Association and still has great influence in Chinese sports area.

Yao's rise has two implications for China's sports and national image. First, Yao's remarkable success in his career symbolises that the Chinese no longer have only a 'sick man' physical image. It inspires the Chinese public to imagine and be passionate about the new national image identity. His success also marked the changed of the Chinese body image. Yao Ming is a basketball centre who stands at 2 metres 26, which makes him a very tall person even in the professional basketball world. The Chinese media has also intentionally highlighted Yao's height by calling him the 'Little Giant', His success in the intensely masculine NBA has reversed the stereotype of the Chinese body image as thin and weak (Cao, 2007). One scholar of the sociology of sport has pointed out that sport is inherently conservative and contributes to the official nationalism. And the sport has specific characteristics that allow it to serve as a tool for national unity (Maguire, 2002, p. 153). Yao Ming's image in China shows this point of view. The rapid development of Chinese sports media has served as a platform for propagating this nationalism. The official newspaper Jiefang Daily has described it as follows.

> Yao Ming is the pride of more than one billion Chinese and more than ten million people in Shanghai. Yao Ming's spirit and image are the "face" of the new globalised era of Chinese. Yao has opened the views of Americans with his excellent ball skills and easy-going, humourous personality. Yao Ming is no longer an ordinary person. Because of this, Yao Ming says, I recognise that this is a national responsibility, and I must take on this responsibility. (Xue, 2003)

In the reports, Yao Ming's image is closely linked with the image of the country and Chinese people, and he represents the 'face' of China in the world. For Chinese people at home and overseas, every brilliant performance of the black-eyed, yellow-skinned Yao Ming in the NBA is enough to construct an imagined community and enhance their identity with 'the Chinese nation'. This imagined community is built on the dissemination of various Chinese media (Fu & Li, 2007).

Second, Yao Ming's success in the NBA, both in performance and commercial aspects, means that China is beginning to enter the market economy of global sports. When Yao's commercial value is fully exploited by the global capitalist market, not only does he become an international sports star but also a metaphor for China's imminent presence in the world. In Time Magazine's 2004 'World's 100 Most Influential People', Yao Ming was selected as the only NBA athlete (TIME, 2004). Transnational corporations like Nike, Reebok, Toyota and Visa have all run their businesses around Yao and the Houston Rockets that he plays for.

The NBA has extensively expanded its blueprint in the Chinese market with Yao's success (Cao, 2007). Yao Ming's personality is friendly, humble and humourous. He became a great ambassador for cultural exchange between China and the US, allowing the American public to increase their understanding of China. Yao was selected to the Naismith Basketball Hall of Fame in 2015 for his outstanding performance on the court and worldwide influence (Neuharth-Keusch, 2016). Along with the development of China's economy and modernisation, Yao has provided a bridge for China's integration into the global marketplace. His 'huge' and 'successful' images demonstrate that Chinese people are not only physically new but also beginning to play a more critical role in the globalised market area.

As an athlete trained by 'Juguo Tizhi', the traditional Chinese sports system run by government, Yao Ming has maintained his loyalty to playing for his country even after entering the NBA, a developed commercial league. Compared to Wang Zhizhi, another Chinese men's basketball player who refused the national team call-up for his NBA career and eventually fell out with the Chinese Basketball Association, Yao Ming has put playing for his country first, even at the cost of possible injury. A journalist once asked Yao if he would choose to give up the national team in the future because of NBA games, and Yao's answer was direct: 'I don't think the word "choose" should be used for the national team' (Jiefang Daily, 2004). Yao's dedication to his country has enabled him to maintain his image well and secure his commercial value in China. Throughout Yao's career, he had almost no negative news. Whether in his service to his country, private life or other issues, Yao has maintained a good image. This has also made him a favourite sports star among advertisers, the public and he has been able to navigate within various areas.

Li Na: Breaking Through Out of a Traditional System

Li Na, the Chinese female tennis player, has had quite a rebellious experience, which makes people rethink profoundly on sports and Chinese nationalism. Born in 1982, Li Na was sent to a sports school by her father at age five to practice badminton (New York Times Chinese, 2013). Because her shoulders were too broad and her wrists were not flexible enough, she was advised to abandon badminton and practice tennis, which was not very popular in China at that time. Li Na's training as a teenager was entirely under the traditional sports system, which was very hard and strict, so she did not enjoy tennis at that time. With her hard training, her tennis level improved rapidly, and she was already ranked number one in China by age 20. However, she chose to retire at this time, due to her poor physical and mental condition and coaches overtrained her (New York Times Chinese, 2013). Li Na returns to her hometown of Hubei and went to college with her boyfriend, Jiang Shan.

More than a year after this retirement, the new director of the Chinese Tennis Management Centre, former volleyball star Sun Jinfang, came to visit Li Na and let her make a comeback. Sun suggested that Li Na could gradually adopt a 'flying solo' model. The government would no longer control her training and game plans but Li Na herself. Instead of paying 65% of the prize money she receives to the government, she would only have to pay about 8–12%, but she would also be responsible for her training and competition expenses (Li, 2012, pp. 102–107). Li Na eventually decided to come back to tennis, and this 'flying solo' model was formally launched at 2008, after that her game performances promoted rapidly (New York Times Chinese, 2013).

In 2010, Li Na reached the Australian Open semi-finals and get into the top 10 in the world (CCTV, 2010). A year later, she beat top seeds to reach the final, and on 4 June 2011, Li Na won the French Open final with a historic victory over her opponent. As a result of this breakthrough Grand Slam victory, top brands signed endorsement deals with Li Na and the Women's Tennis Association (WTA) even expanded its plans to add events in Asia. After hard training, Li Na eventually reached her peak by winning the Australian Open in 2014 and coming second in the world rankings. In the second half of 2014, Li Na finally chose to retire due to injury. Her achievement undoubtedly made history for Chinese tennis and caused a huge impact both at China and overseas.

Li Na's career has brought many thoughts on the relationship between Chinese sports and nationalism, which can be summarised into two main points. First, Li Na's 'flying solo' model was a breakthrough attempt of the 'Juguo Tizhi', and its success has further led discussions on the 'Juguo Tizhi' and the nationalism in Chinese sports (The International Journal of the History of Sport, 2012). After 2008, the Chinese Tennis Management Centre announced that three other tennis players could choose the 'flying solo' model and become real professional players (Pu et al., 2019). Before that, except for a few sports such as football and basketball, which have undergone professional reforms, most Chinese athletes had lived their entire careers under the 'Juguo Tizhi' of Chinese sports. Athletes under the 'Juguo Tizhi' enter sports teams from junior high school or earlier and are then selected to advance to adult-level, provincial and national teams. Athletes who grow up in this system are responsible for all their training, competition, even life by the government. While the national system protects athletes, they also lose much freedom in choosing their career path. Their ultimate goal is to 'win glory for the nation' and achieve good results in international competitions. Behind this goal, many personal thoughts and pursuits have to give way.

Tennis is a highly professional sport worldwide, and it was only sport in 2008 that China finally allowed its players to 'flying solo' and enter real professional life. After Li Na's breakthrough, there was a discussion on whether China should liberalise the professionalisation of the sport and cease the 'Juguo Tizhi' (Quan, 2011). Interestingly, Cai Zhenhua, who was then the director of the State General Administration of Sports, argued that the model of 'flying solo' was not good enough for the growth of athletes and the goal of 'winning glory for the nation' (Li, 2009). Under the 'Juguo Tizhi', it's all about winning the gold medal, and there have been incidents of 'match fixing' that violate sportsmanship in China. After this incident with the Chinese badminton team, the head coach Li Yongbo said, 'I don't agree with match fixing, people get hurt in every bad match, and I can't bear it, but in China, our ultimate goal is the national interest' (Sina Sports, 2008). This comment was critical and real. The other side of the Chinese sports 'Juguo Tizhi' is that the state power dominates almost every Chinese athlete, reflecting strong collectivism and nationalism. The breakthrough of the 'flying solo' system in tennis symbolises the meaning of rise of individualism and the market economy.

Second, Li Na sometimes makes remarks that are not in line with the main theme of 'winning glory for the nation', which is rare among Chinese athletes and has provoked media and public debates on the relationship between sports and nationalism. It should be noted that Li Na's 'solo flight' was really implemented after 2008 (Pu et al., 2019). Before the Beijing 2008 Olympic Games, the main theme of 'winning glory for the nation' was still difficult to be challenged. After Li Na suffered a heartbreaking loss in the 2013 French Open, the official Chinese media Xinhua news agency asked her to explain the disappointing result to Chinese fans. She immediately fought back: 'It was just a loss. I just lost one match. Do I need to apologize Chinese audience (Wang & Shang, 2013)?' This comment provoked much criticism from Chinese public. People's Daily criticise Li Na for 'behaving like a child' and suggested she should return to the usual way of Chinese athletes 'winning glory for the nation' (Zhong, 2013). However, perhaps because of her experience of 'flying solo', Li Na has always considered playing for herself rather than for her country. She is a new anomaly among Chinese athletes. When Li Na was asked in 2011 what motivated her to participate in the Grand Slams, she smiled and said, 'The prize money' (Li, 2012, p. 262). After winning her second Grand Slam at the Australian Open, Li Na also did not thank her country and system for training her but expressed her gratitude to her personal team, family and sponsors (Pu et al., 2019). This act caused controversy in China again. Li Na had expressed her opinion on this issue.

After the Grand Slam in France, some media described it as 'China's victory'. Don't exaggerate. I am just an athlete. I can't represent a country. I can only represent myself and do what I want to do. Those great duties that others put on me are just those people who wish to express their ideas, which actually have nothing to do with me.

I represent no one, and I don't want to represent anyone. I just want to represent myself. (Li, 2012, p. 283)

This expression of Li Na's individualistic attitude has contributed to a reflection by the media and the public on the concept of 'winning glory for the nation'. Some influential domestic media commented that Li Na and Yao Ming, two of China's most successful athletes, had never won an Olympic gold medal. This success in professional sports is the best commentary on the 'Juguo Tizhi'. Li Na's success has expanded the influence of tennis in China, and Li Na doesn't have to thank the country (Southern Metropolis Daily, 2011; Tencent Sports, 2011). Li Na's attitude of 'playing for herself but not for the country' also caused heated debates on the internet. The online media Tencent Sports published a survey titled 'How do you rate Li Na's speech?' in which 67% of netizens thought Li Na's speech was 'decent and no problem', while only 12% thought she 'should thank the country' (BBC Chinese, 2012; Tencent Sports, 2014). This result would probably not have occurred in China 10 years ago. We can understand the professionalisation of sports, the market economy and the impact of globalisation really changed the Chinese people's ideas.

In the globalisation era, the cases of three Chinese sports heroes show that the institutional reform of Chinese sports at a crossroads, and people's notion that Chinese sports must 'win for the nation' is beginning to change. In the context of the 'Juguo Tizhi' and the globalised sports market, Liu Xiang is trapped in the system, Yao Ming is comfortable in both circumstances, and Li Na has managed to escape. These three sports heroes with international-level influence show the image of China and Chinese nationalism. Alan Bairner (2001) points out that nationalism in sports gradually becomes a force of resistance to globalisation. Despite the increasing integration of markets and cultures in global sports, nationalism in sports has not died out in the context of globalisation and has even expanded to some extent. In the case of China, after Chinese sports encountered the globalised market, the original concept of 'winning glory for the nation' was impacted. Although the nationalism sentiment in sports still exists, people have started to reflect on the shortcomings of the original concept and the institution associated with it. It can be argued that the Chinese nationalism in sport to rebel against globalisation is not so obvious. The images of Liu Xiang, Yao Ming and Li Na were given national significance meaning to wash the shame of 'the sick man of East Asia' and recreate the nation's glory. This echoed the background of China's gradual increase in national power and was one of the reasons for the persistence of nationalism in China after the 1990s. Their success satisfied the national self-esteem that the Chinese people needed as the country grew stronger.

CONCLUSION

Hosting the Beijing 2008 Olympics is a very important event for China and a milestone in the development of Chinese sports. At the beginning of the 20th century, a Chinese newspaper asked famous China's 'Three Olympic Questions': (1) When will China send athletes to the Olympic Games? (2) When will China win Olympic gold medals? (3) When will China host the Olympic Games (Zhang, 2014)? The first two goals have long been reached, and after the heartbroken failure of the Olympic bid in 2000, the third goal were finally achieved in 2008. The hosting of Beijing 2008 Olympics had multiple significance. First, during this period, China was already on the path of reform and opening up and was gradually enhanced globalisation process. By hosting the Olympic Games, China presented a progressive and open image to the world. The success of the Beijing Olympics has also enabled the international community to know more about China and realize that China will have more influence in the future world. Second, in terms of sports achievements, Chinese athletes' performance in the Beijing 2008 Olympics also reached an all-time best, winning the first place in the Olympic gold medal list. This achievement proved the success of the Chinese government's Olympic Glory strategy that began in the 1990s. Chinese athletes' great performance has important symbolic significance and is conducive to building a good national image for China. At that time, all these factors helped Chinese nationalism to reach another peak.

In the context of the success of the Beijing 2008 Olympics, the stories of the three Chinese sports heroes have impressive meanings on the issue of nationalism. As an athlete, Liu Xiang has been trained under the traditional Chinese sports system, the 'Juguo Tizhi' throughout his whole career. His historic win at the 2004 Athens Olympics urges a climax of Chinese nationalism. However, his inability to finish the 2008 and 2012 Olympics due to injuries shocked and disappointed the Chinese public. Some Chinese people even attacked Liu Xiang on the Internet, showing another side of Chinese nationalism.

Yao Ming is a Chinese athlete with international influence. He was also trained under the 'Juguo Tizhi' and eventually entered the NBA league and became a top basketball player. His achievements and good image in the international sports world have made him the pride and idol of many Chinese people. Yao's excellent performance in basketball has also aroused the nationalism sentiment of many Chinese people. In the new era, Yao has achieved success in both sports and business area, while he has maintained his loyalty to his country. He became a representative figure and symbol in the globalisation of Chinese sports.

Li Na is another famous athlete in China. After breaking away from the 'Juguo Tizhi', Li Na has achieved a successful career by winning several Women Tennis Grand Slam. She used a new independent training model, known in Chinese parlance as 'flying solo', is an emerging model of sports training in China. This new model has led discussions in the Chinese media and the public on the issue of sports and nationalism. Li Na has also expressed her views on some of the idea of Chinese sports, such as the most important goal of sports is to winning glory for the nation. She believes that she plays tennis more for herself rather than for the nation. Some of her point of view, reflecting an individualism attitude, have sparked further discussion and reflection on the relationship between sport and the nation in China. All the three athletes participated in the 2008 Beijing Olympics. Their stories reveal different aspects of the relationship between Chinese sport and nationalism. In this context, Chinese athletes represent more than just themselves; pursing national glory is always a main theme in their careers.

FIVE KEY READINGS

Jarvie, G., Hwang, D.-J., & Brennan, M. (2008). *Sport, revolution and the Beijing Olympics.* **Berg.**

Sport, Revolution and the Beijing Olympics is a cultural history of sport in China that challenges many such ingrained Western assumptions. The authors unpick the relationship of sport to imperialism and revolution and examine its significance in China at governmental and everyday levels. In the process they successfully debunk harmful myths, such as the prevalence of drugs in Chinese sport among women athletes, and present a balanced view that is a much-needed corrective to popular understanding.

Hu, X. R., Liang, J., & Bairner, A. (2021). A rebel and a giant: change and continuity in the discursive construction of Chinese sport heroes. *Sport in Society***, 24(12), 2199–2221.**

The essay examines the changes and continuities in the construction of Chinese national sport hero(in)es after the Beijing 2008 Olympics and investigates this development in the context of the reform of Chinese elite sport.

Through employing Critical Discourse Analysis to interrogate the Chinese sport hero discourse from government-run media concerning two of the most renowned Chinese national sport hero(in)es, the paper identifies the maintenance, albeit with subtle changes, of the traditional nationalist account concerning the athletic and political qualities of Chinese national sport hero(in)es. Concurrently, there are also new features, which are argued to be the consequence of a shift in the political climate in Chinese sport, in the post-2008 construction of national sport hero. The paper concludes with a discussion, from a Foucauldian perspective, of the relationship between the discourse, knowledge and the power of/over discourse in the construction of Chinese elite athletes as national hero(in)es throughout the period.

Bairner, A. (2001). *Sport, nationalism, and globalisation: European and North American perspectives.* **State University of New York Press.**

Sport and nationalism are arguably two of the most emotional issues in the modern world. Both inspire intense devotion and frequently lead to violence. In this book, Alan Bairner discusses the relationship between sport and national identities in Europe and North America – specifically Ireland, Scotland, Sweden, theUS and Canada – within the context of a broader theoretical debate about the impact of globalisation in the modern era. Through a unique comparative perspective, the author sheds new light on the ways sport impacts the construction and reproduction of national identities. Ultimately, the work considers the role of sport in allowing nations and nationalists to resist, or at least come to terms with, powerful globalising pressures.

Bairner, A. (2015). Assessing the sociology of sport: On national identity and nationalism. *International Review for the Sociology of Sport,* **50(4–5), 375–379.**

Alan Bairner, one of the most influential scholars to study the socio-cultural relationship between sport and nation, reflects on the dynamics of national identity and nationalism in sport. Because the sociology of sport has too often taken for granted concepts such as nation, nation-state, nationality, national identity and nationalism, an ongoing need has been to engage debates about those concepts in mainstream nationalism studies. Because the most powerful form of national performance today may be seen in sport, understanding tensions between not only the national and global but also between the nation-state and the historic nation and between nationality and national identity remain key challenges. Complex dynamics of competing identities may be seen in exemplar studies of sport in Spain relative to Catalonia and the 'united' (or not) qualities of the United Kingdom relative to Ireland, Scotland, Wales and, indeed, England. In the future, it is posed that the study of sport and nation must move beyond reliance on media analysis and received notions of 'imagined community' and seek more access to and understanding of elite performers and organizational actors.

Zhouxiang, L., & Hong, F. (2019). China's sports heroes: Nationalism, patriotism, and gold medal. *The International Journal of the History of Sport,* **36(7–8), 748–763.**

Sport has been of great importance to the construction of Chinese national consciousness during the past century. This article examines how China's sport celebrities have played their part in nation building and identity construction. It points out that Chinese athletes' participation in international sporting events in the first half of the 20th century demonstrated China's motivation to stay engaged with the world and therefore led to their being regarded as national heroes. From the 1950s, China's status and relative strength among nations became measured by the country's success at international sporting events. The nation's appetite for gold medals resulted in the rapid development of elite sport but has placed a heavy burden on star athletes.

REFERENCES

Andrews, D. L., & Jackson, S. J. (2001). *Sport stars: The cultural politics of sporting celebrity*. Routledge.

Bairner, A. (2001). *Sport, nationalism, and globalization: European and North American perspectives*. State University of New York Press.

BBC Chinese. (2008, April 20). *Chinese people's protest against France continues to spread. BBC Chinese*. http://news.bbc.co.uk/chinese/simp/hi/newsid_7350000/newsid_7357000/7357098.stm. Accessed on June 14, 2024.

BBC Chinese. (2012, March 13). Li Na plays not for her country cause debate. http://www.bbc.com/zhongwen/simp/chinese_news/2012/03/120313_lina.shtml. Accessed on December 19, 2023.

Brownell, S. (1995, August 1). *Training the body for China: Sports in the moral order of the people's republic* (1st ed.). University of Chicago Press.

Cao, J. (2007). The media discourse production of sports stars: Yao Ming, masculinity and national image. *Journalism College*, *2007*(4), 143–152.

CCTV. (2010, February 2). Chinese Li Na makes history to enter WTA top 10. *CCTV*. https://english.cctv.com/20100202/101161.shtml. Accessed on February 19, 2024.

Chen, Z. (2004, August 29). The Chinese finally fly. *People's Daily*, A7.

China Daily. (2004, August 28). Brave Liu Xiang did it! Chinese fans jubilant. *China Daily*. https://www.chinadaily.com.cn/english/doc/2004-08/28/content_369582.htm. Accessed on February 19, 2024.

Fu, X. (2014). *The construction of nationalist discourse in sports media communication since the 1990s*. Huazhong University of Science and Technology Press.

Fu, X. J., & Li, B. C. (2007). The construction of national idols in the context of globalization: Yao Ming as a model. *Journalism*, *2007*(3), 40–41.

Ge, J. (2013). *Liu Xiang's media presence in the Olympic Games: A nationalism perspective*. Unpublished master's thesis, Anhui University, Hefei.

Guo, R. (2009). *Why China is not happy*. Five Continents Communication Press.

IOC. (2007, April 25). BEIJING 2008: BOCOG announces Olympic torch relay route. https://olympics.com/ioc/news/beijing-2008-bocog-announces-olympic-torch-relay-route. Accessed on February 19, 2024.

Jiefang Daily. (2004, October 7). Yao Ming, Liu Wei on the center. Jiefang Daily. https://sports.sina.com.cn/s/2004-10-17/1057391369s.shtml. Accessed on June 14, 2024.

Keeler, B., & Nauright, J. (2005). Team Yao: Yao Ming, the NBA, sporting goods and selling sport to China. *American Journal of Chinese Studies*, *12*(2), 203–218.

Li, J. (2009). Zheng Jie enters the final four to return to the top 20 of the worlds to respond Cai Zhenhua's doubts about solo flight. http://sports.sina.com.cn/t/2009-10-28/05284666967.shtml. Accessed on December 19, 2023.

Li, N. (2012). *Alone on the court*. CITIC Press Group.

Liu, P. (2009). From the "sick man of East Asia" to a sports power: 60 Years of sports in new China. *QIUSHI*, *2009*(16).

Lovell, J. (2008). Prologue: Beijing 2008 – The mixed messages of contemporary Chinese nationalism. *International Journal of the History of Sport*, *25*(7), 758–778.

Lu, Z., & Fan, H. (2019). China's sports heroes: Nationalism, patriotism, and gold medal. *International Journal of the History of Sport*, *36*(7–8), 748–763.

Maguire, J. A. (2002). *Sport worlds: A sociological perspective*. Human Kinetics.

Nanfang Metropolis Daily. (2011, January 30). Nandu: Li Na thanks sponsors first. The best irony of the national system. *Southern Metropolis Daily*. http://sports.qq.com/a/20110130/000487.htm. Accessed on December 19, 2023.

Neuharth-Keusch, A. J. (2016, September 9). Yao Ming enters Hall of Fame as global ambassador of basketball. *USA Today*. https://www.usatoday.com/story/sports/nba/2016/09/09/yao-ming-hall-of-fame-china-global-ambassador/90093276/. Accessed on February 19, 2024.

New York Times Chinese website. (2013). Li Na: Chinese tennis rebel. *The New York Times Chinese website*. https://cn.nytimes.com/sports/20130902/c02lina/. Accessed on December 19, 2023.

Ni, G., & Zhao, E. (2008, July 20). Turning patriotic fever into the will to serve the country. *People's Daily*. http://politics.people.com.cn/BIG5/1026/7140471.html. Accessed on March 2, 2017.

Peng, H. T. (2005). The national world imagination: A media study of the 2008 Olympic bid. *Twenty-first Century*, *2005*(1).

People's Daily. (2008, August 1). Beijing Olympics opening ceremony receives amazing appraisal. *People's Daily Online*. http://2008.people.com.cn/GB/128225/128445/7644820.html. Accessed on March 15, 2017.

Pu, G., Newman, J. I., & Giardina, M. D. (2019). Flying solo: Globalization, neoliberal individualism, and the contested celebrity of Li Na. *Communication & Sport*, *7*(1), 23–45.

Quan, H. (2011). How long could the "Juguo Tizhi" of competitive sports hold on. *Journal of Physical Education (in Chinese)*, (03), 20–25.

Shen, S. (2007). *Redefining nationalism in modern China: Sino-American relations and the emergence of Chinese public opinion in the 21st century*. Palgrave Macmillan.

Sina Sports. (2008). Dismissal of world champion to Ye Zhao Ying match fixing, Li Yongbo: Do not want to disguise. http://sports.sina.com.cn/o/2007-11-11/17543286194.shtml. Accessed on March 18, 2017.

Tencent Sports. (2011). Sports Teahouse: The country should thank Li Na. http://sports.qq.com/zt2011/thankslina/. Accessed on December 19, 2024.

Tencent Sports. (2014, January 27). Media: Li Na didn't say thank you to her country for winning the championship. *Tencent Sports*. http://sports.qq.com/a/20140127/003986.htm. accessed December 19, 2023.

The International Journal of the History of Sport. (2012). From Barcelona to Athens (1992–2004): 'Juguo Tizhi' and China's quest for global power and Olympic glory. *International Journal of the History of Sport*, *29*(1), 113–131.

Tian, E., & Wise, N. (2020). An Atlantic divide? Mapping the knowledge domain of European and North American based sociology of sport, 2008–2018. *International Review for the Sociology of Sport*, *55*(8), 1029–1055.

TIME. (2004, April 26). The 2004 TIME 100. *TIME*. https://content.time.com/time/specials/packages/article/0,28804,1970858_1970910_1972002,00.html. Accessed on February 19, 2024.

Tyler, P. (1993, September 24). OLYMPICS; there's no joy in Beijing as Sydney gets Olympics. *New York Times*. https://www.nytimes.com/1993/09/24/sports/olympics-there-s-no-joy-in-beijing-as-sydney-gets-olympics.html. Accessed on June 14, 2024.

Varrall, M. (2020, January 10). Behind the news: Inside China global television network. Lowy Institute. Accessed on February 19, 2024.

Wang, J. (2001, July 15). *Xinhua news agency: A century of great changes in China from the perspective of the Olympics*. Xinhua News Agency. http://sports.sina.com.cn/o/15161463.shtml. Accessed on December 19, 2023.

Wang, H. L. (2014). Understanding contemporary Chinese nationalism: Institutions, affective structures, and cognitive frameworks. *Cultural Studies*, *2014*(19), 189–250.

Wang, S. Z. (2015). Olympic champion Liu Xiang retires. *The New York Times Chinese edition*. https://cn.nytimes.com/china/20150408/c08liuxiang/. Accessed on December 19, 2023.

Wang, Z. J. & Shang, X. (2013, May 31). Li Na: Don't want to blame the weather for the defeat. Should I take a knee down to the fans? http://sports.titan24.com/tennis/2013-05-31/348032.html Accessed on May 3, 2017.

Wise, N. (2020). Eventful futures and triple bottom line impacts: BRICS, image regeneration and competitiveness. *Journal of Place Management and Development, 13*(1), 89–100.

Wise, N., & Harris, J. (2010). Reading Carlos Tevez: Football, geography, and contested identities in manchester. *International Journal of Sport Communication, 3*(3), 322–335.

Wise, N., & , Harris, J. (Eds.). (2019). *Event, places and societies*. Routledge.

Wise, N., & Maguire, K. (Eds.). (2022). *A research agenda for event impacts*. Edward Elgar.

Wu, J., & Yun, G. (2008). Cultural criticism of the opening ceremony of the Beijing Olympic Games. *Twenty-first Century, 2008*(12), 106–114.

Xinhua News Agency. (2008). *Hu Jintao's speech at the Beijing Olympic Games closing Ceremony*. http://news.xinhuanet.com/newscenter/2008-09/29/content_10133226.htm

Xiong, X. Z., & Zhong, B. S. (2010). *60 Years of sports in new China*. Beijing Sports University Press.

Xue, M. Y. (2003, January 2). *Yao Ming in the new year*. Jiefang Daily. https://sports.sina.com.cn/r/2003-01-02/0924373800.shtml. Accessed on June 14, 2024.

Yang, M. (2008). *China's speed amazes the world. Titan sports*. https://2004.sina.com.cn/comm/at/2004-08-28/0359104641.html. Accessed on June 14, 2024.

Zhang, B. (2014). Tianjin: The birthplace of the three Olympic questions. https://news.nankai.edu.cn/mtnk/system/2014/08/26/000198734.shtml. Accessed on December 19, 2023.

Zhong, W. (2013, July 1). Sports view: Stars should have a bottom line. http://sports.people.com.cn/n/2013/0701/c22172-22024684.html. Accessed on December 19, 2023.

Zhu, H. X. (2015, August 1). People's daily's three Olympic bids: Complex and emotional feelings across 22 years. http://politics.people.com.cn/n/2015/0801/c1001-27395997.html

Zhu, Y., & Zhang, J. (2012). Liu Xiang's mother: He is the son of the country. Please forgive him if he is not good. http://2012.sina.com.cn/cn/at/2012-08-08/070148613.shtml. Accessed on December 19, 2023.

CHAPTER 3

DEBATES ON FOOTBALL AND CHINESE NATIONAL IDENTITY

Kaixiao Jiang[a] and Jinyu Liu[b]

[a]Liverpool Hope University, UK
[b]Manchester Metropolitan University, UK

ABSTRACT

This chapter critically evaluates whether football can attain recognition as a national sport in China. Article No. 11, released by the Chinese government in 2015, aimed to develop a new national strategy centralised on the sport of football to foster consumption and enhance national soft power. Consequently, this also means encouraging Chinese football fans to support the national football team. Comparing the significance of local football clubs and the national football team to Chinese football fans is deemed meaningless and unable to generate useful information to comprehend Chinese people's attitudes towards local and national communities. Through literature comparisons with established Chinese national sports such as Chinese martial arts, badminton and table tennis, the discussion reveals that football currently falls short of meeting the general criteria of invention and popularity to be considered a Chinese national sport. In the specific Chinese context, it also proves that football fails to meet the criterion of politics, hindering its identification as a national sport. Consequently, the chapter rebuts the assumption and advocates for the validity of comparing how fans assess their fandom for local and national football teams.

Keywords: National sports; sport and national identity; football; Chinese society; Chinese national football team

INTRODUCTION

Identify is one of the most popular areas studied in the sociology of sport literature (Tian & Wise, 2020). In most areas of the world, people's national attachment is enhanced during watching their national teams' games (Bairner, 2001) and hosting large-scale events (Wise & Harris, 2019). Sugden and Tomlinson (1998, p. 304) suggests that 'sport in general and football in particular have proven to be significant theatres for the expression of national identity', indicating that football is a more influential tool than other sports to stimulate people's sense of belonging to their nations from international spheres. This idea also appears to be recognised by the Chinese government as sport, and hosting major events is part of encouraging people to play sport locally and showcase China's international sporting prowess (Wise, 2020).

In 2015, the State Council of the People's Republic of China (PRC) published Article No. 11 – The Notice on the Overall Plan of Chinese Football Reform and Development (2015). A subsequent governmental instruction to Article No. 46 – *Opinion on Accelerating the Development of the Sport Industry and Promoting Sports Consumption* (State Council of the PRC, 2014) – aims to centralise football as a national strategy to develop Chinese sports consumption. Moreover, this government paper also identifies the government's target of becoming a sporting power, displayed after the successful organisation of the 2008 Olympics. Many see sport in China as a channel for promoting national soft power (Connell, 2018; Junio & Rodrigues, 2017; Tan & Bairner, 2018). Consequently, all Chinese social organisations have been involved in developing Chinese football since then. In other words, football may be developed as a new Chinese national sport – a symbol of the nation that triggers people to celebrate their national identity deeply (Bairner, 2009).

Among Chinese society, traditional Chinese sports, such as martial arts, and sports where China performs well internationally (and often wins gold medals), including table tennis and badminton, are recognised as national sports. These sports stimulate the Chinese people to celebrate their national identity (Liu & Fan, 2017; Lu & Fan, 2014). If football can occupy the same position as these established national sports, Chinese football fans may also place greater importance on supporting the national football team. The assumption's validity implies that comparing the significance of local football clubs and the national football team to Chinese fans is no longer meaningful (Jiang & Bairner, 2024). Furthermore, it suggests that studies aiming to explore Chinese people's attitudes towards their local and national communities through Chinese football fandom are considered valueless even though the sport is identified as a means of reflecting society (Jarvie, 2017).

Football seems to be among the top three popular sports among the Chinese people, capturing the strong interest of 40% of the Chinese population (Nielsen, 2022). However, the Chinese men's national football team has not achieved any remarkable records in major events (Chinese Football Institution, n.d.) since it was officially recognised by the Fédération Internationale de Football Association (FIFA) in 1974. Moreover, the team's failure to qualify for the 2018 and

2022 FIFA World Cup Finals indicates that the article published in 2015 remains unsuccessful in realising the governmental football dream.

In comparison to their male colleagues, the record of the Chinese women's football team seems to support the earlier assumption. Despite the relatively late emergence of the Iron Roses in the 1980s, the Chinese women's national football team has claimed victory nine times in the Asian Football Confederation (AFC) Women's Asian Cups and has been a consistent participant in the FIFA Women's World Cups (FWWC) since 1991 (Hong & Mangan, 2004; Venkat, 2022). Notably, China hosted two FWWCs in 1991 and 2007 (Williams, 2007), further solidifying the team's role in achieving the Chinese government's objectives. However, the lower rates of spectatorship, sponsorship and broadcasting for Chinese women's domestic games compared to men's imply that women's football still holds less influence in China (Cao & Geng, 2010; Zhou, 2020).

For instance, Shuang Wang, a key player who scored five goals in the 2022 AFC Women's Asian Cup, leading the Chinese women's national football team to victory, suggests that most Chinese football fans show limited interest in women's domestic games compared to men's. Female players only capture the attention of these fans when participating in major international events (Li, 2022). In essence, football in the Chinese context remains within the dominant realm of men, despite the women's team showing much promise. Therefore, the current national sport status of football in China is still primarily assessed and evaluated based on the performance of the men's national team. Despite the team's relatively weak performance, Chinese football fans continue to moderate their support for the national team. Understanding how they assess the importance of national and local teams provides a valuable window into observing the attitudes of the Chinese people towards their society.

This chapter addresses this assumption and questions whether football in China is a national sport that reflects the country's national identity. It first seeks answers to how sport contributes to enhancing people's national identities by reviewing the literature on the relationship between sport and national identity in international competitions and national sports. Next, based on a discussion on how perceived Chinese national sports stimulate Chinese national belongingness, the second section sets a series of debates to examine the optimal ways in which football can be recognised as a national sport by Chinese people and enhance their national identity.

SPORT AND NATIONAL IDENTITY

National identity is the cornerstone of studies examining the relationship between sport and national identity. This key concept relies on social identity and nationalism studies (Bairner, 2001). As one of an individual's social identities, national identity also guides an individual to believe who they are based on 'the totality of a person's individuality plus the idiosyncratic things that make that person unique' (Junge, 2014, p. 17). Because no one lives alone in human society, an individual's recognition of themselves results from self-evaluation of their relationships with other people in their lives, especially those in their unique spatial and temporal circumstances (Olson, 2003; Tajfel, 1978; Turner, 1985). National identity, therefore, is a result of an individual's constant interaction with their nation used to help people identify themselves within this community. While developing this social identity in a nation, individuals also forge a secure social bond– a sense of belonging – with the social community, as this is essential for individuals to survive in the history of human evolution (Baumeister & Leary, 1995; Fiske, 2018). Consequently, people's national identity is 'the foundation of their solidarity' as a nation (Barnard, 2003, p. 181). This idea raises the studies of sport and national identity, focussing on how sports appear to be useful to develop and enhance people's national identity (Cronin & Mayall, 1998).

Studies of nationalism, then, provide insights into how people develop their national identity. A nation is a political community, and nationalism is an ideology and movement that encourages people to develop and empower their communities into a nation (Gellner, 1983). Moreover, this political community, defined as the supreme entity, can be rooted in various forms of society, including ethnic/geographic affiliations and a shared constitution. The civic awareness developed by universal education that allows people to master this political community equally is the fundamental factor in nation-building (Anderson, 1991; Hobsbawm, 1992). While acknowledging their membership in the nation, people also contribute to the legitimacy of their national identity (Smith, 1995). As national identity stands as the pivotal factor in a nation's solidarity, the study of sport and national identity also seeks to examine how sports influence nationalism and shape the relationship between people and their nation (Allison, 2000; Bairner, 2001).

Within this study, international sports competitions have been examined as a clear 'vehicle' to enhance people's national identities and establish a distinct boundary for individuals to identify 'their nation' as opposed to 'others' (MacClancy, 1996, p. 2). Rituals in these competitions, such as honouring flags and singing anthems in the Olympic Games and the FIFA World Cups, are the most typical examples that underline the distinctions between nations in the stadiums (Bairner, 2009; Birrell, 1981). Meanwhile, the use of languages and the shared ideas produced by different national contexts remind people that they are from diverse communities with clear boundaries (Hargreaves, 1992). Inevitably, these elements enable people to acknowledge their national affinities with their national sports delegations, emphasising the support for national teams as the channel to celebrate their developed national identities.

The study of sport and national identity further delves into national sports and their impact on national identity. Sport is a way to connect people through shared associations (Wise, 2015) or through supporting national teams (Harris, 2008), Both facilitate people's connection and recognition of those sports or teams that give presence to a national symbolic status (Birrell, 1981). Consequently, athletes are also defined as heroes striving for national pride, and sports become opportunities to empower nations by promoting patriotism and a shared sense of identity (Allison, 2000).

In other words, people's national belongingness can be triggered during games played by their national teams. In addition, such emotional attachment can be exaggerated further via witnessing national teams' victories, particularly in the games against rivals related to tensions beyond the sports world (Bairner, 2001). For example, Chinese people thought highly of their victories during the football games against Japan in the Far East Championship Games (FECG) because they recognised those as the tool to moderate the humiliation caused by Chinese failure in the First Sino-Japanese War (1894–1895) and the agreement of the 21 Demands that offered Japan authority to control China (Fan, 2007; Lu & Fan, 2014). Therefore, supporting national teams is an automatic choice for people who have the desire to empower their nations.

National sports can be simply identified as those invented by specific nations (Bairner, 2001, 2009). Communities devise sports based on their living circumstances and lifestyles, allowing these sports to directly reflect the features of those communities (see Wise, 2015). For instance, buzkashi, being a horse-riding competition, not only mirrors the equestrian history but also the lifestyle of the Afghan people, particularly their admiration for superb horsemanship and stereotyped masculine values such as courage, strength, and dominance (Azoy, 2011). In other words, observing or participating in these national sports helps individuals establish a connection to the culture and lifestyles developed by their nations, thereby reinforcing people's sense of belonging to their nations (Duffy, 1997). Hence, a national sport can be viewed as evidence that nation and nationalism 'have no rivals' in the global era and 'remain indispensable elements of an interdependent world and a mass-communications culture' (Smith, 1995, pp. 159–160). It significantly influences people's behaviours and ideas when applied in international competitions, especially when compatriots of a nation are satisfied with a national team's success (Bairner, 2001). Such success would reinforce national pride and promote 'the idea of a national sport' according to Bairner (2001, p. 19).

However, most people worldwide prefer to play and watch sports invented elsewhere. Football, in particular, which originated in England, is claimed as a national sport by many other nations. In this context, Bairner (2009) recognises that most nations encounter an obstacle concerning the criterion of invention.

There are two main reasons for football being recognised as the national sport of nations outside of England. First, football spread from England in a relatively early era, resulting in people in other nations having a long-term interaction with this sport (Archetti, 1996; Elias & Dunning, 1986; Maguire, 1999). Second, it is acknowledged as a favourite sport. Morris (2016), from the perspective of human beings' primitive lifestyles, suggests that playing football can evoke people's intensity as predators, contributing to this sport becoming a favourite. By contrast, Duke and Crolley (1996, p. 1) regard its straightforward and low-cost participation as the primary factor leading football to be the 'world's number one game' with the largest number of participants and spectators in the stadium or in front of the television. Regardless of which factor makes football a favourite among nations, Bairner (2009) suggests the concept of 'popularity' as a crucial criterion to define national sports in most nations where we see mass levels of support through spectatorship.

DEBATE 1: CAN FOOTBALL MEET THE CRITERIA OF INVENTION AND POPULARITY IN CHINA

The previous section has indicated that supporting national sports teams is an automatic choice for people to celebrate their national identity. It also highlights the role of the national sport in stimulating people's sense of nationhood. Following that, the previous section explores the criteria of invention and popularity for people to acknowledge their national sports. To assess whether football can evoke Chinese people's national belongingness as effectively as other established Chinese national sports, the following sections reference Chinese martial arts and badminton (Liu & Fan, 2017; Lu & Fan, 2014).

Invention and Cultural Affinity

Cuju was recognised by FIFA as one of the early forms of football games in 2004 (Connor, 2015; FIFA.com, 2004), evidencing that football could be a Chinese-invented sport or, at the very least, has a close connection. This Chinese form of the football game was first played in the Warring States Period (403 BC–221 BC) for military training, encompassing the discipline, organisation and tactics of soldiers (Stride & Vandenberg, 2019; Timm, 2015; Yang, 2014). Similar to Shields and Bredemeier's1996 suggestion that militarism results in the origins of sports, most Chinese traditional sports were also invented for military purposes. Among these sports, it is undeniable that Chinese martial arts or wushu is the most famous one, sharing the same origin as cuju (Lu & Fan, 2014).

The development of Chinese martial arts has a rich and lengthy history. Chinese legendary stories document this fighting skill as the legacy of the Yellow Emperor (黄帝), the ancestor of the Han people and a legendary military leader born in 2711 BC (Allan, 1984). According to this legend, the Yellow Emperor introduced the earliest martial arts to his tribe for effective hunting and defence in tribal battles. Although this story has not been examined by archaeology and anthropology, present evidence suggests that the Shang dynasty (1600 BC–1046 BC) could be the earliest time when Chinese people practised fighting skills. Similar to the legendary story, evidence shows that the skills of attack and defence were initially used for animal hunting (Jia, 2001; Li, 2009; Ma, 2007). They were gradually developed as a crucial component of military training, with the tools for hunting also serving as weapons for killing. In contrast to its historical context, Chinese martial arts are currently primarily organised as a sport for exhibition and combat competitions (Lu & Fan, 2014). Despite its diminished role in modern military training, the extensive and continuous history of wushu renders it an indispensable element of Chinese culture. Therefore, observing and engaging in Chinese martial arts can evoke a sense of belonging among the Chinese people to their nation.

In contrast, football cannot fulfil the same role in triggering people's national attachment as Chinese martial arts. Chinese people do not have the same continuous tradition with football as they do with wushu. According to Goldblatt (2007), there was a nationwide ban on cuju during the Qianlong period (1644) in the Qing dynasty. The rulers of the Qing dynasty were the Manchu people who assumed control of China from the Han people, and they sought to eliminate any potentially subversive elements through crowd gathering. As a Han-invented form of a team sport, cuju was inevitably forbidden by the regime. Nevertheless, it was unlikely for the Qing dynasty to impose a nationwide ban on wushu, as it was also utilised for the dynasty's military training. Moreover, being a form of individual sport/exercise, wushu could be preserved and passed down through generations (Lu & Fan, 2014; Stride & Vandenberg, 2019). Since few people can still engage in the traditional way of playing cuju, the claim that modern football has an authentic connection to cuju should be moderated. In other words, modern football cannot occupy the same historical affinity position as Chinese martial arts. Developing the connection between football and cuju may only be a strategy to promote and maintain the popularity of football in the Chinese context, especially when the national team has not yet achieved outstanding records during the rise of the Chinese football dream.

The cultural significance in Chinese society is another factor that prevents football from being identified as the same national sport as Chinese martial arts. Before its decline in the Qing dynasty, cuju was as popular as modern football in many countries, as it entertained the public (Yang, 2014). In the Song dynasty (960–1279), professional cuju clubs emerged to train cuju players and represent communities in the Han area. In addition, since the Han dynasty (202 BC–220 BC), playing cuju as a ceremony in particular festivals was a tradition (Cui, 1991; Goldblatt, 2007; Yang, 2014). Hence, cuju was a favoured sport and a form of entertainment for the Chinese populace throughout history.

Similar to cuju, the Chinese people have also imbued martial arts with cultural meaning, transforming them from mere fighting skills to cultural symbols for festivals and ceremonies. A notable example is juedi (角抵, one of the earliest Chinese wrestling skills). Juedi is identified as a legacy of Chi You (蚩尤), the god of war in the legendary story, so people involved in military training in ancient China esteemed this fighting skill (Allan, 1984; Reid & Croucher, 1983). However, during the age between the Qin and the Han Dynasties (221 BC–220 BC), juedi was transformed into a ceremony of worshipping gods to invoke courage and strength for people, especially soldiers preparing for war (Acevedo & Cheung, 2010). Performers transitioned from soldiers to priests, adorning masks with horns to underscore their connection to mythical beasts or Chi You, often depicted with horns on their heads. Such a ceremony persisted until the end of the Qing dynasty (Tong, 2005). However, the key difference between Chinese martial arts and cuju in terms of cultural value is that these fighting skills also integrate with Chinese philosophies, especially Confucianism.

Its name, wushu, serves as proof of this engagement, emphasising the notion of stopping fighting to advocate the core Confucian idea of benevolence (Lu & Fan, 2014). The term wushu refers to the skill of wu (武), and wu is a Chinese word originated from a combination of characters in the Shang dynasty (1600 BC–1046 BC), incorporating zhi (止), the pictogram of feet and ge (戈), the most common weapon (Wu, 2023). Thus, this word embodies the nature of fighting skills, utilising both weapons and feet for attack and defence. Yet, after aligning with the concept of benevolence in the Zhou dynasty (770 BC–256 BC), the skill of wu evolved to represent a combination of compassion, kindness, empathy and genuine concern for the well-being of others. Eventually, zhi, as a component of the skill of wu, evolved beyond its original reference to feet and embodied its most common meaning – stopping – a sense that still applies today. Wushu has also adapted to this new concept, learning to fight to stop the fight, emphasising the diminishing value of battles and wars between people. Moreover, Confucianists highlighted the connection between wushu and an individual's quality. Archery was used to test this development because an outstanding archer needed to undergo long-term rigorous physical and mental exercise (Ames & Rosemont Jr, 1999; Jiang, 1993). In the Confucianists' *Book of Rites* (礼记), the archery competition was a gentlemanly contest with strict requirements of etiquette and cautious attitudes towards rivals. Since Confucianism became the dominant ideology of Chinese society in the Han dynasty, wushu has become an irreplaceable symbol in the Chinese context.

Furthermore, the Chinese people not only seek to showcase societal values through their participation in martial arts but also perceive the physical movements of fighting skills as a means to comprehend the laws of the universe (Li & Zhao, 2017; Lu & Fan, 2014). Followers of Taoism believe that the motion of wushu exercises can aid in understanding the Tao (the nature of the universe) to attain a state of immortality (Bai, 2010). According to *Wang Zong-yue's Theories of Tai Chi* (王宗岳太极拳论) (Li, 2016; Wang, 1991), practising Tai Chi involves combining physical and mental training. The movements incorporate the Yin-Yang philosophy and the worldview of five elements (metal, wood, water, fire and earth) to encourage practitioners to sense the power and truth of the universe (Bai, 2010). While becoming immortals may be a fantastical notion, Taoists have recognised the benefits of wushu exercises in promoting human physical well-being, as exemplified by the Five Mimic-animal Exercise (五禽戏), invented by Hua Tuo (Lu & Fan, 2014). By emulating the movements of five different animals (tigers, deer, bears, apes and cranes), the series of exercises was designed to help individuals enhance their physical health. Although different schools invented various types of wushu to practice their philosophies, the practice of Chinese martial arts has become a cultural symbol denoting a strong Chinese identity (Lu & Fan, 2014; Ma, 2007).

Cuju is a Chinese-invented sport and a cultural symbol, akin to Chinese martial arts. However, the significance of wushu in reflecting Chinese philosophies creates a substantial gap between these two sports in terms of social significance for the Chinese people, especially if cuju is primarily used as a form of entertainment (Cui, 1991; Yang, 2014). Moreover, due to this lack of a direct lineage, cuju may only be classified as one of the unconnected football-like sports played in ancient China (Goldblatt, 2007). In other words, present-day Chinese individuals face a challenge in connecting the relationship between cuju and football, making it difficult to recognise modern football as Chinese property, hindering the extraction of historical affinity and stimulation of national identity.

Popularity and Nationalism

While the national football team has not yet achieved outstanding success, China stands as a formidable sporting power globally, particularly evident in the medal standings of the Summer Olympics (Giulianotti, 2015). However, most modern sports played by Chinese athletes in contemporary world sports mega-events, including football, were not originally invented in the nation. Instead, Chinese people have actively participated and engaged in modern sports since the late 19th century (Morris, 2004). Over the long-term interaction with modern sports, some of these sports played in international competitions meet the criteria of popularity, with high rates of participation and spectatorship, so they are also recognised as Chinese national sports (Bairner, 2009). Badminton, as a Chinese gold medal event, serves as a typical example. Thus, this section identifies badminton as a reference to examine whether football can also develop an affinity with the Chinese national identity and become a symbol of China.

In terms of historical affinity, Chinese people's interactions with football and badminton share the same root. After China failed in the Opium Wars in the late 19th century, treaties signed by the Qing dynasty allowed Western Christian missionaries, including members of the Young Men's Christian Association (YMCA), access to inland China for religious preaching (Duara, 1996). Through the process of Christianisation, these missionaries established churches and Western schools throughout China and introduced Western lifestyles and values to the Chinese people. The YMCA's promotion of its identified masculine culture among Chinese people ultimately contributed to the inception of modern physical education and sporting games, including football and badminton (Garrett, 1970; Morris, 2004; Riordan & Jones, 1999). Moreover, as Shanghai was the first place to welcome the initial wave of YMCA groups in 1885, football and badminton were originally introduced in this place (Fan, 2007; Rizak, 1989). The shared duration of interaction with Chinese people may suggest that football could hold the same position as badminton in becoming a Chinese national sport.

Such an assumption may also be validated regarding the same duration of the national representative status for both sports teams. Furthermore, the Chinese national football team even predates the badminton team. After the YMCA established Western schools to promote physical education and modern sports in China, they also organised the first international sports event in Eastern Asia, the FECG, in 1913 (Fan, 2007). Football has been one of the compulsory events since the inception of FECG. Players from schools in Tianjin and Shanghai, where football was relatively popular at that time, formed the first Chinese national football team through an ad-hoc arrangement and participated in the inaugural FECG (Shen et al., 1995). By contrast, China did not have a badminton national team until the 1920s when the Wanguo (万国, thousands of countries) International Badminton Games (WIBG), a regular international badminton event, was established in Shanghai. The national badminton team mainly consisted of the Shanghai Feisuo (飞梭, the flying shuttle) Badminton Club, and most players were returning overseas Chinese students at St. John's University (Lian, 2018). Before that, badminton was a recreational activity for the upper class. Moreover, badminton was not included as an event in FECG, which was more influential than WIBG as it inspired the development of today's Asian Games (Fan, 2007). Although the Chinese national football team did not win the championship in the first FECG, China held the title from the second one until 1934, when China withdrew from the FECG against Japanese support for Manchukuo's independence (Fan, 2007). In this respect, football was much more popular than badminton at that time, which may strengthen football's qualification to be a Chinese national sport.

In terms of spectatorship rates, badminton and football both attract large numbers of audiences in China (Nielsen, 2016). However, a report from the General Administration of Sport of China (2015) suggests that the football participation rate among Chinese people is much lower than that of badminton, indicating that the participation rate is the primary obstacle to football meeting the criterion of popularity to achieve Chinese national sport status. Based on the discussion above, such a difference should have emerged after 1934, when China concluded its FECG participation (Fan, 2007). Moreover, the Sino-Japanese War and the subsequent Civil War (1937–1949) did not provide Chinese people with a peaceful environment and the opportunity to participate in influential international competitions for both sports (Rizak, 1989). In other words, the development of football after the establishment of the PRC in 1949 is the main factor in the decline of its participation rate, preventing it from sharing the same position as badminton.

The decline did not occur until the two national sports teams restored their federation-acknowledged international competitions between the 1970s and the 1980s. After the Second World War, China was also influenced by the Cold War, amidst potential conflicts between the Soviet Union and the US. In anticipation of a potential world war, China emphasised the importance of sports in enhancing the physical fitness of its people to provide more qualified soldiers (Zhao, 1998). Consequently, physical education and sports competitions were quickly reinstated, and the government also developed its elite sports system for football and badminton, respectively. Following the first National Football Championship in 1951, the elite football player system and the Chinese Football Association (CFA) were established (Dong & Mangan, 2001; Jin & Zhang, 2014). Similarly, badminton was reinstated as one of the events in the first National Four-Ball Games (首届全国四项球类大赛, featuring basketball, volleyball, tennis and badminton) in 1953. Badminton in Chinese is 羽毛球, a ball with feathers, so it is also acknowledged as a ball game among Chinese. Subsequently, the Chinese Badminton Association was organised in 1958 (Luo & Cheng, 2002). Due to the earlier establishment of domestic football games and relevant governing body compared to badminton, football retained its status as the more popular and influential sport in the early years of the PRC.

Until the improvement of Sino-American relations in the 1970s and its subsequent effects, such as the recognition of the PRC's member status in the United

Nations (UN) and the International Olympic Committee (IOC), both national sports teams were able to restore their games acknowledged by the Badminton World Federation (BWF) and FIFA (Jiang & Bairner, 2019; Luo & Cheng, 2002). However, since 1974, the Chinese national football team has not achieved any outstanding records in competitions acknowledged by FIFA and the IOC (the Chinese Football Institution, n.d.). Its most notable appearance was in the 2002 FIFA World Cup finals, where, unfortunately, no goals were completed during the tournament (Jiang & Bairner, 2019). By contrast, after the Chinese Badminton Association was admitted by the BWF in 1981, the national badminton team achieved remarkable success. They won the World Men's Team Championship in 1982, participating for the first time in the Thomas Cup. Following this, China secured the Women's Team Championship in the 1984 Uber Cup. Between 1986 and 1987, the team clinched both the World Men's Team Championship and the Women's Team Championship. Additionally, they swept all five individual contests at the fifth World Badminton Championships, making history as the first country to win all badminton championships contested in a season (Wang, 2014). Hence, the primary difference between badminton and football lies in the respective records of the two national sports teams in these mega-events.

According to Bairner (2001), people's sense of belonging to their nation can be stimulated by viewing the success of their national sports teams. In turn, people will pay more attention to those sporting successful national teams. Moreover, such an effect can be exaggerated if those teams win games against particular rivals, especially the tensions caused by the world beyond sports. When comparing the performance records of China's national football and badminton teams in international competitions, the Chinese people have more opportunities to celebrate their national identity through the success of the national badminton team. In contrast, the football team is often seen as having fewer promising prospects, resulting in fewer participants than the badminton one.

Furthermore, Chinese nationalism also plays a crucial role in influencing the impact of these teams' records on participant rates in international competitions. The beginning of Chinese nationalism also resulted from Western colonialism and imperialism in the 19th century (Chang, 2004). Qichao Liang was the first to bring the concept of nation and nationalism into China. He proposed the notion of the Chinese nation as the union of all Chinese ethnic groups, which is the foundation for today's PRC constitution to define the nation. Thus, Liang's nationalism is the dominant theory of Chinese nationalism. Influenced by Yan Fu's translated version of Thomas Henry Huxley's *Evolution and Ethics*, Liang attached social Darwinism to his nationalism to empower China (Chang, 1971). It is important to note that Yan Fu was a famous translator and introduced many Western ideas to China in the late 19th century. As a result, challenges from outside China are considered a natural selection in the evolution of all Chinese people (Liang, 2016). In turn, people become sensitive to challenges from out of China. The national football team's records have not met the requirement of Chinese nationalism against the challenge from out of China, so it is unlikely for people to pose a strong interest in participating in football. In other words, although football attracts many Chinese people's attention, it cannot be recognised as a Chinese sport to remind people's national identity.

DEBATE 2: CAN FOOTBALL MEET THE CRITERION OF POLITICS

According to Fan (2007, p. xx), the Chinese people have a perfect understanding of 'the relationship between sport and politics'. Such a comment initially referred to the Chinese people's attitude towards Japan in the FECG. As the Chinese people's first international sports competition, this tournament was also organised during the period between the first and the second Sino-Japanese War (1894–1945). Hence, this sporting event was also acknowledged as a platform to realise Chinese people's political expectations towards the tensions between these two nations. For example, the Second FECG took place in Shanghai in 1915, occurring six days after Yuan Shi-kai's government signed the 21 Demands, granting Japan power to control China (Young, 1977). Therefore, Chinese athletes expected to win back the reputation that they had lost on the battlefields and at the diplomatic table through the victories during this FECG, and spectators also celebrated those athletes' victories as a symbol against Japanese imperialism (Fan, 2007). In this respect, Chinese people have recognised that sports serve as a channel to express their political sentiments since they encountered international competitions. In addition, sports that genuinely align with their political aspirations are more likely to be popular among them (Fan & Xiong, 2002).

Indeed, table tennis is a typical Chinese national sport that evolved within a political context. Similar to badminton and football, the Chinese people's involvement in table tennis can also be traced back to the influence of the YMCAs in the early 20th century (Li & Xiao, 2012). However, Ping Pong Diplomacy, which facilitated the establishment of diplomatic relations between the US and the PRC in the early 1970s, significantly influenced the development trajectory of this sport and helped it become the most popular sport in China during the 1980s and 1990s, even earning the status of a national sport (Griffin, 2014; Han & Tan, 2005). In this respect, comparing the developments of table tennis and football can shed light on whether the Chinese political context will allow football to attain a similar status as table tennis as a national sport, as the State Council of China also intends to leverage its political influence to elevate the football industry and designate football as a national sport via the governmental article released in 2015 (Junio & Rodrigues, 2017; Peng et al., 2019; Tan et al., 2016).

Political Demand

The popularity of table tennis and football is related to politics in the Chinese context. Ping Pong Diplomacy, which eventually resulted in table tennis' position as a Chinese national sport, started with the friendship between Zedong Zhuang and Glenn Cowan and the friendly match between the table tennis teams of the

US and the PRC in the early 1970s (Griffin, 2014; Hong & Sun, 2000). Behind the story, such a successful diplomatic event is, in fact, associated with how the PRC and the US sought approaches to resolve their national and political crises (MacMillan, 2008). China, at that moment, coped with the pressure caused by the deteriorating relationship with the Soviet Union in the late 1960s (Lüthi, 2010; Zagoria, 2015), while the US also needed to seek a new partnership in Asia to reduce the power of the Soviet Union, particularly due to its failure in the Vietnam War (LaFeber, 1985). As a result, the table tennis games between China and the US contributed to the PRC's recognition by the UN, which subsequently contributed to China's representative status of the Chinese Olympic Committee (COC) in the IOC (Fan & Xiong, 2002; Griffin, 2014; Hong & Sun, 2000; MacMillan, 2008). Thus, the Chinese people have a special emotional attachment to table tennis, and this sporting participation, driven by the desire to ease the relationship between the PRC and the USA, led to table tennis becoming a popular sport in the Chinese context.

The development of football's popularity is also associated with Chinese politics. The beginning of the Chinese people's interest in football after the establishment of the PRC was associated with their viewing experience of the 1978 FIFA World Cup Finals (Jiang & Bairner, 2019). According to Chen and Hu (2008), that broadcast was required by Deng Xiaoping, who became a powerful leader of the PRC at that time and had a strong interest in football. However, this story was not a simple reflection of Deng's political power in China. Instead, Deng's requirement may be related to his promoted political campaigns of the opening-up policy and a socialist market economy (Ding, 2009; Qi, 2022). In order to develop China as a socialist and communist country, the Chinese Communist Party (CCP) initiated a series of socialist revolutions in the Chinese economy, industry and agriculture to eliminate any components of capitalism and Western society, such as the private and market economy. However, the subsequent political campaigns, especially the Great Proletarian Cultural Revolution that caused nationwide social disorder between 1966 and 1976, resulted in China's relatively underdeveloped status in industries and technologies compared with Western countries (Lu, 2004). Hence, the opening-up policy and socialist market economy conducted by Deng in the 1970s aimed to use Western capital to create a competitive environment for developing China. The 1978 World Cup broadcasting can also be interpreted as a sign of Deng's Socialist reformation (Qi, 2022). Because it was rare for a Chinese family to own a television and enjoy television entertainment at that time, that unforeseen broadcast allowed Chinese people to develop a special fondness for football (Jiang & Bairner, 2019).

Competitive Capability

After successfully hosting the 2008 Beijing Olympic Games, China announced its new target of becoming a powerful sporting country to develop its soft power and showcase the Chinese social system as commendable (Giulianotti, 2015). Considering that FIFA-acknowledged football games, especially the World

Cups, share a similar social influence to the Olympics in attracting spectators around the world, Chinese President Xi Jinping believed that entitling the football world championship could reliably establish China as an influential nation (Li & Fan, 2017; Tan et al., 2016). Consequently, the Chinese football dream emerged, and all Chinese social organisations are actively involved in implementing the national strategy of developing football (Tan & Bairner, 2018; Tan et al., 2016). In other words, football has now attained the same political foundation as table tennis, being acknowledged as a Chinese national sport.

Yet, the relatively weak competitive capability of the Chinese national football team presents obstacles to football meeting political demands and being recognised as a new national sport in China. The primary role of sports in serving politics is to develop national soft power and reputation, with the precondition being that national sports teams achieve outstanding records (Grix & Lee, 2013; Houlihan, 2000). This crucial function has been assigned to football by Article No. 11 (State Council of the PRC, 2015). However, the sole appearance of the Chinese national football team in the FIFA World Cup Finals, especially its absence in the 2018 and 2022 World Cups, implies that the team's competitive capability is insufficient to help football meet the required political targets (Chinese Football Institution, n.d.). Following the release of the governmental article in 2015, the national football team faced a series of issues, including Marcello Lippi's resignation as the manager of the Chinese national football team, limitations on naturalised players' playing time and corruption allegations against Li Tie, Lippi's successor (Church, 2019; Han et al., 2023; Smith, 2023; White, 2020). These challenges further underscore the daunting task facing the realisation of the Chinese football dream.

One specific Chinese football dream is to qualify for the FIFA World Cup Finals. The CFA appointed Marcello Lippi as the manager of the Chinese national football team in 2016 (Associated Press, 2016). However, following the team's inability to qualify for the 2018 World Cup Finals and facing challenges for the Qatar event, Lippi resigned as the team's manager. Subsequently, Li Tie was appointed as his successor. During the subsequent qualification matches for the 2022 FIFA World Cup Finals, concerns arose among fans regarding Li's managerial abilities, particularly about the restricted time for naturalised players who were recruited with substantial financial investment. He exposed various issues in the national team's management, including the failure of the naturalisation project.

By contrast, football could be identified as a Chinese national sport if the national football team can achieve the same success as table tennis. Following Ping Pong Diplomacy, the popularity of table tennis was significantly boosted, eventually leading this sport to become a gold medal event (Han & Tan, 2005; Li & Xiao, 2012). Since the 1988 Olympics, table tennis has been acknowledged as a Chinese medal event. China has won a total of 60 Olympic medals in table tennis, including 32 golds (Burke, 2023). In addition, China has achieved a dominant record in the Table Tennis World Championships with 151 golds since joining the tournaments in 1956 (Olympics.com, 2022). Such remarkable achievements have led to the International Table Tennis Federation implementing measures to limit their dominance, such as the system of waiting periods for Chinese players who change nationalities and wish to represent their new countries in the Olympics, to protect the development of table tennis in other nations (Oonk & Oonk, 2023). Although the main political demand for table tennis was to help China develop its diplomatic relations with other nations, the Chinese table tennis team's records in international competitions inevitably strengthened this sport's status as a national symbol and contributed to the delivery of Chinese soft power (Li et al., 2021).

Thus, although Article No.11 initially promoted football, especially with the support of schools that increased the number of children and young adult football participants when it was released (Tan & Bairner, 2018; Tan et al., 2016), it may only heighten Chinese people's attention to football at present. Without witnessing how the national team meets the political targets to deliver Chinese soft power, Chinese citizens cannot claim this sport as a powerful channel to reflect their social system positively (Houlihan, 2000). Hence, football's new Chinese national sport status remains unacknowledged yet.

CONCLUSION

In order to assess whether football can be recognised as a national sport after the release of Article No. 11 by the State Council of China, this chapter has conducted literature comparisons between football and other established Chinese national sports such as Chinese martial arts, badminton and table tennis. The discussions demonstrate that football, at present, cannot be identified as a national sport in China as it fails to meet the criteria of invention, popularity, and politics respectively. Consequently, further studies to understand Chinese people's attitudes towards their local and national communities by comparing the importance of local football clubs and the national football team to Chinese football fans are still warranted (Jiang & Bairner, 2024).

Among sports that stimulate nationalism, national sports play a more influential role in helping people recall their national affinity. In general, two criteria, invention and popularity, are applied to define a national sport (Bairner, 2001, 2009). Invention refers to a sport that originated in a particular nation. As sports are influenced by people's living circumstances and culture, engaging in and watching these sports can evoke their memories of interactions with nations, thereby invoking national affinity. A sport meeting this criterion can be recognised as a national sport in that nation. The Chinese people's involvement in football was influenced by the YMCA's introduction to Western lifestyles and values (Fan, 2007). Although FIFA recognises the connection between modern football and cuju, invented in ancient China (Connor, 2015; FIFA, 2004), the Qing dynasty's ban on playing cuju severed its connection with most Chinese people (Goldblatt, 2007).

It is unlikely to identify modern football as a Chinese-invented sport. Additionally, cuju, as a form used for public entertainment, does not help football attain the same position as Chinese martial arts, which embody Chinese social values (Cui, 1991; Lu & Fan, 2014; Yang, 2014). Hence, football cannot meet the criterion of invention, and its connection to cuju may be utilised to expand its popularity in the Chinese context.

A sport can also be designated as a national sport by a specific nation if it boasts high participation and spectatorship rates within the nation and has a national representative team in international competitions. This criterion is popularity, commonly employed to recognise sports invented in other nations as national ones (Bairner, 2009). Using badminton as an example to examine whether football meets the criterion of popularity, the chapter establishes that football is a popular sport with high spectatorship in the Chinese context. However, football's status as a Chinese national sport remains elusive due to its low participation rate. This is a consequence of the relatively low competitive capacity of the Chinese national football team in international competitions, failing to align with Chinese nationalism's goals of empowering China and demonstrating its ability to handle external challenges on the field (Chang, 1971; Liang, 2016). Consequently, Chinese people do not perceive football as a promising sport in which to participate. Football has yet to fulfil the two general criteria required to be recognised as a Chinese national sport.

In the Chinese context, politics plays a pivotal role in developing a sport as Chinese property (Fan, 2007; Fan & Xiong, 2002). This criterion provides a straightforward method to define football as a Chinese sport, analogous to how Ping Pong Diplomacy influenced table tennis's status in the Chinese context. After the Chinese government centralised football as a new tool to enhance the country's soft power, this sport shared the same political foundation as table tennis and garnered support from various social organisations. However, the primary obstacle hindering football from being recognised as the national sport lies in the weak competitive capacity of the national football team. This incapacity prevents football from serving as an effective tool for developing national soft power and reputation (Grix & Lee, 2013; Houlihan, 2000). Consequently, Chinese citizens are unlikely to assert that the records of their national football team positively reflect their social system. Without meeting the designated political demands, football's status as a Chinese national sport remains deniable.

Furthermore, the likelihood of the national football team becoming a world championship team in the short term is low. Therefore, studies exploring Chinese people's attitudes towards their local and national communities by comparing the importance of local football clubs and the national football team to Chinese football fans remain pertinent. However, a specific concern that should be addressed in future research is the decline of the Chinese national football team's affinity with the nation. This decline may imply that football can no longer have a positive impact on people's national belongingness in the international sphere. In most nation-states, including China, the composition of the national football delegation requires careful consideration to assess its ability to represent all ethnic groups in the nation (Cronin & Mayall, 1998; Devos & Banaji, 2005; Von Mises, 2006). A high dominance of a particular ethnic group in the national delegation can raise questions about the football team's representative status, and racial stereotypes within the team may lead to dislike from certain ethnic groups

(Lapchick, 2000). Ethnic stereotypes arise from historical accumulation in a context dominated by a particular group whose culture has been mainstream and influential in shaping national values (Devos & Banaji, 2005). Therefore, not all ethnic groups are equally represented in any national sports team, with the domination of one ethnic group being a common phenomenon, creating obstacles for some ethnic groups to identify with the national team's games (Tamir et al., 2016). Consequently, selecting which Chinese local football club fans serve as the sample to assess the importance of local football clubs and the national football team to Chinese football fans should involve a rigorous and cautious discussion.

Moreover, under the influence of globalisation, some national football teams have lost their national identities due to an increasing number of sporting migrants (Bairner, 2001; MacClancy, 1996; Mangan, 1996). Financial demands, multicultural experiences and opportunities to test/challenge themselves are the main factors contributing to the growing trend of sporting migration between different continents and hemispheres (Stead & Maguire, 2000). The Chinese national football team, at present, also recruits naturalised players to achieve its sporting targets, even though the naturalisation project was damaged during the process of qualifying for the 2022 Qatar World Cup (Han, 2023; Sullivan et al., 2023). Since it is becoming common to see more Chinese players from other nations, the Chinese people's recognition of their national team's representative status may decline. Alongside this phenomenon, how future research interprets the connection between athletic identity and Chinese national identity in national teams is key to validating the research in comparing the importance of local football clubs and the national football team to Chinese football fans (Sullivan et al., 2022).

FIVE KEY READINGS

Bairner, A. (2001). *Sport, nationalism, and globalization: European and North American perspectives.* **New York: State University of New York Press.**

In this book, Alan Bairner offers a perspective on the study of sport and nationalism by underlining the links between the recent evolution of sporting nationalism and globalisation processes. Sport and nationalism are arguably two of the most emotional issues in the modern world, and both inspire intense devotion and frequently lead to violence. The relationship between sport and national identities in Europe and North America, specifically Ireland, Scotland, Sweden, the US and Canada, are compared to show how sport impacts the construction and reproduction of national identities. Ultimately, the work considers the role of sport in allowing nations and nationalists to resist, or at least come to terms with, powerful globalising pressures.

Bairner, A. (2009). National sports and national landscapes: In defence of primordialism. *National Identities,* **11(3), 223–239.**

Through this article, Alan Bairner explores the relationship between landscape, sport and the formation and reproduction of national identities. Central to this discussion is the concept of national sports, with evidence being taken from various genres of sports-related literature and from a variety of nations. Just as the landscape provides the context in which national sports are played and watched, it is the playing and watching of these sports which, in turn, give the landscape added meaning. As a consequence of this, the nation, sport and landscape come to be recognised as interconnected texts which, taken as a whole, offer significant insights into the primordial formation of national identities.

Morris, A. D. (2004). *Marrow of the nation: A history of sport and physical culture in Republican China.* **Berkeley: University of California Press.**

Andrew Morris shows how sporting culture and ideology played a crucial role in the making of the modern nation-state in the Republic of China. In addition, this book provides the dramatic story of how Olympic-style competitions and ball games, as well as militarised forms of training associated with the West and Japan, were adapted to become an integral part of the modern Chinese experience. Hence, it offers a much-needed contribution towards understanding the origins of China's long quest to host the Olympic Games.

Lu, Z., & Fan, H. (2014). *Sport and nationalism in China.* **Routledge.**

This book examines the relationships between sport, nationalism and nation-building in China. Exploring the last 150 years of Chinese history, authors offer unparalleled depth and breadth of coverage and provide a clear grasp of Chinese sports nationalism from both macro and micro perspectives. The book also scans the whole spectrum of both modern and contemporary Chinese nationalism and interprets the most important issues on the course of China's nation-building, explaining why sport is so tightly bound up with nationalism and patriotism, and how sport became an essential part of nationalists', politicians' and educationalists' strategy to revive the Chinese nation.

Fan, H. (2007). Prologue: The origin of the Asian games: Power and politics. In H. Fan (Ed.), *Sport, nationalism and orientalism: The Asian games* **(pp. xii–xxiv). Routledge.**

In this chapter, Hong Fan introduces the origin and the development of the Asian Games, especially the influence of the YMCA. Meanwhile, this article also aims to explore the political confrontation between China and Japan at the Far Eastern Championship Games from 1913 to 1934. Eventually, this article highlights that the Chinese people have a comprehensive idea of the relationship between sports and politics, and it also provides evidence of how these people use sports to empower their nation.

REFERENCES

Acevedo, W., & Cheung, M. (2010). A historical overview of mixed martial arts in China. *Journal of Asian Martial Arts, 19*(3), 30–45.

Allan, S. (1984). The myth of the Xia dynasty. *Journal of the Royal Asiatic Society, 116*(2), 242–256. https://doi.org/10.1017/S0035869X00163580

Allison, L. (2000). Sport and nationalism. In J. Coakley & E. Dunning (Eds.), *Handbook of sports studies* (pp. 344–355). Sage.
Ames, R. T., & Rosemont, H. Jr. (1999). *The analects of Confucius: A philosophical translation*. Ballantine Books.
Anderson, B. (1991). *Imagined communities*. Verso.
Archetti, E. P. (1996). The moralities of Argentinian football. In S. Howell (Ed.), *The ethnography of moralities* (pp. 98–123). Taylor & Francis.
Associated Press. (2016). China appoint Marcello Lippi as manager of national team. https://www.theguardian.com/football/2016/oct/22/china-appoint-marcello-lippi-manager-national-football-team. Accessed on 19 February 2024.
Azoy, G. W. (2011). *Buzkashi: Game and power in Afghanistan* (3rd ed.). Waveland Press.
Bai, T. (2010). 论太极拳文化与道家哲学的关系 [Discussion on the relationship between Tai Chi and Taoism]. *Science and Wealth, 12*, 143–144.
Bairner, A. (2001). *Sport, nationalism, and globalization: European and North American perspectives*. State University of New York Press.
Bairner, A. (2009). National sports and national landscapes: In defence of primordialism. *National Identities, 11*(3), 223–239. https://doi.org/10.1080/14608940903081101
Barnard, F. M. (2003). *Herder on nationality, humanity, and history*. McGill-Queen's Press.
Baumeister, R. F., & Leary, M. R. (1995). The need to belong: Desire for interpersonal attachments as a fundamental human motivation. *Psychological Bulletin, 117*(3), 497–529. https://doi.org/10.1037/0033-2909.117.3.497
Birrell, S. (1981). Sport as ritual: Interpretations from Durkheim to Goffman. *Social Forces, 60*(2), 354–376. https://doi.org/10.1093/sf/60.2.354
Burke, P. (2023, May 20). *China reveals selection criteria in bid to continue table tennis domination at Paris 2024*. Inside the Games. https://www.insidethegames.biz/articles/1137131/china-paris-2024-table-tennis
Cao, W., & Geng, J. (2010). 对我国女足运动发展若干问题的反思 [Reflections on development of women's football]. *Journal of Hebei Institute of Physical Education, 24*(3), 54–57. https://doi.org/10.3969/j.issn.1008-3596.2010.03.015
Chang, H. (1971). *Liang Chi-chao and intellectual transition in China, 1890–1907* (Vol. 64). Harvard University Press.
Chang, H. (2004). 时代的探索 [Exploring the age]. Linking Publishing.
Chen, Z., & Hu, Y. (2008). 复刻回忆：世界杯与中国球迷的三十年 [World Cup memories since 1978]. *NetEase News*. http://news.163.com/special/00014DRO/worldcup78.html. Accessed on January 5, 2021.
Chinese Football Institution. (n.d.). *CFA 足球大数据* [Chinese Football Association Big Data]. http://wiki.cfadata.com/index.php?title=%E9%A6%96%E9%A1%B5. Accessed on December 5, 2023.
Church, M. (2019, November 14). Lippi quits as China coach after Syria defeat. *Reuters*. https://www.reuters.com/article/uk-soccer-worldcup-china-idUKKBN1XO2HS/
Connell, J. (2018). Globalisation, soft power, and the rise of football in China. *Geographical Research, 56*(1), 5–15. https://doi.org/10.1111/1745-5871.12249
Connor, N. (2015, December 23). China opens a shrine to mark its love affair with disgraced former FIFA president Sepp Blatter. *The Telegraph*. https://www.telegraph.co.uk/sport/football/sepp-blatter/12065899/China-opens-a-shrine-to-mark-its-love-affair-with-disgraced-former-Fifa-president-Sepp-Blatter.html
Cronin, M., & Mayall, D. (Eds.). (1998), *Sporting nationalisms: Identity, ethnicity, immigration and assimilation*. Frank Cass.
Cui, L. (1991). 中国古代蹴鞠的起源与发展 [The origin and development of Cuju]. *Cultural Relics of Central China, 2*, 59–66. CNKI:SUN:ZYWW.0.1991-02-010.
Devos, T., & Banaji, M. R. (2005). American = white? *Journal of Personality and Social Psychology, 88*(3), 447–466. https://doi.org/10.1037/0022-3514.88.3.447
Ding, X. (2009). The socialist market economy: China and the world. *Science & Society, 73*(2), 235–241. https://doi.org/10.1521/siso.2009.73.2.235

Dong, J., & Mangan, J. A. (2001). Football in the new China: Political statement, entrepreneurial enticement and patriotic passion. *Soccer and Society*, *2*(3), 79–100. https://doi.org/10.1080/714004853

Duara, P. (1996). *Rescuing history from the nation: Questioning narratives of modern China*. University of Chicago Press.

Duffy, P. J. (1997). Writing Ireland: Literature and art in the representation of Irish place. In B. Graham (Ed.), *In search of Ireland: A cultural geography* (pp. 64–86). Routledge.

Duke, V., & Crolley, L. (1996). *Football, nationality and the state*. Longman.

Elias, N., & Dunning, E. (1986). *Quest for excitement: Sport and leisure in the civilising process*. Blackwell.

Fan, H. (2007). Prologue: The origin of the Asian Games: Power and politics. In H. Fan (Ed.), *Sport, nationalism and orientalism: The Asian games* (pp. xii–xxiv). Routledge.

Fan, H., & Xiong, X. (2002). Communist China: Sport, politics and diplomacy. *International Journal of the History of Sport*, *19*(2–3), 319–342. https://doi.org/10.1080/714001751

FIFA.com. (2004, October 19). The cradle of football. *Fédération Internationale de Football Association*. https://www.fifa.com/news/the-cradle-football-94490

Fiske, S. T. (2018). *Social beings: Core motives in social psychology* (4th ed.). Wiley.

Garrett, S. S. (1970). *Social reformers in urban China: The Chinese YMCA, 1895–1926* (Vol. 56). Harvard University Press.

Gellner, E. (1983). *Nations and nationalism*. Cornell University Press.

General Administration of Sport of China. (2015). 2014 年全民健身活动状况调查公报 [Survey on public sports and physical activities participation in 2014]. http://www.sport.gov.cn/n16/n1077/n1422/7300210.html

Giulianotti, R. (2015). The Beijing 2008 Olympics: Examining the interrelations of China, globalization, and soft power. *European Review*, *23*(2), 286–296. https://doi.org/10.1017/S1062798714000684

Goldblatt, D. (2007). *The ball is round: A global history of football*. Penguin.

Griffin, N. (2014). *Ping-pong diplomacy: The secret history behind the game that changed the world*. Simon & Schuster.

Grix, J., & Lee, D. (2013). Soft power, sports mega-events and emerging states: The lure of the politics of attraction. *Global Society*, *27*(4), 521–536. https://doi.org/10.1080/13600826.2013.827632

Han, P. (2023). Can they represent the nation? Nationalism, national identity, and naturalized athletes in Chinese football. *National Identities*, *25*(4), 339–355. https://doi.org/10.1080/14608944.2022.2125943

Han, F., & Tan, M. (2005). 中国乒乓球长盛不衰的缘由 [The reasons for Chinese table tennis to maintain prosperous over a long period of time]. *Journal of Physical Education*, *12*(3), 123–125. https://doi.org/10.3969/j.issn.1006-7116.2005.03.039

Han, P., Tang, S., & Bairner, A. (2023). Citizenship without identity? Instrumentalism, nationalism and naturalization in Chinese men's football. *International Review for the Sociology of Sport*. https://doi.org/10.1177/10126902231199580

Hargreaves, J. (1992). Olympism and nationalism: Some preliminary consideration. *International Review for the Sociology of Sport*, *27*(2), 119–133. https://doi.org/10.1177/101269029202700203

Harris, J. (2008). Match day in Cardiff: (Re)imaging and (Re)imagining the nation. *Journal of Sport & Tourism*, *13*(4), 297–313.

Hobsbawm, E. (1992). *Nations and nationalism since 1780: Programme, myth, reality* (2nd ed.). Cambridge University Press.

Hong, F., & Mangan, J. A. (2004). Will the 'Iron Roses' bloom forever? Women's football in China: Changes and challenges. In F. Hong & J. A. Mangan (eds), *Soccer, women, sexual liberation* (pp. 49–70). Routledge.

Hong, Z., & Sun, Y. (2000). The butterfly effect and the making of 'ping-pong diplomacy. *Journal of Contemporary China*, *9*(25), 429–448. https://doi.org/10.1080/713675951

Houlihan, B. (2000). Politics and sport. In J. Coakley & E. Dunning (eds), *Handbook of sports studies* (pp. 213–227). Sage.

Jarvie, G. (2017). *Sport, culture and society: An introduction* (3rd ed.). Routledge.

Jia, L. (2001). 武术运动的起源及其价值趋向 [The origin and value concept of wushu]. *Journal of Anhui Sports Science*, *4*, 42–45. https://doi.org/10.3969/j.issn.1008-7761.2001.04.010

Jiang, N. (1993). "射礼"源流考 [The origin of the rite of archery]. *Journal of Tianjin Normal University (Social Science)*, *6*, 53–55.
Jiang, K., & Bairner, A. (2019). Paolo Rossi and the origins of football fandom in China. *Asia Dialogue*. https://theasiadialogue.com/2019/04/08/paolo-rossi-and-all-that-reflections-on-the-origins-of-football-fandom-in-china/
Jiang, K., & Bairner, A. (2024). Becoming a Chinese football fan: An examination of the influence of national and local identities on the development of Chinese football fandom. *Soccer & Society*.
Jin, S., & Zhang, S. (2014). 咱京城球迷那些事儿 [Stories of our Beijing football fans]. Beijing Yanshan Publication.
Junge, M. B. (2014). *Identity and art therapy: Personal and professional perspectives*. Charles C Thomas Publisher.
Junio, E. F. L., & Rodrigues, C. (2017). The Chinese football development plan: Soft power and national identity. *Holos*, *5*, 114–124. https://doi.org/10.15628/holos.2017.5750
LaFeber, W. (1985). *America, Russia, and the Cold War*. Knopf.
Lapchick, R. E. (2000). Crime and athletes: New racial stereotypes. *Society*, *37*(3), 14–20. https://doi.org/10.1007/BF02686168
Li, Y. (2009). 论武术与军事的历史渊源 [To discuss the historically origin relationship between Wushu and the military affairs]. *Journal of Beijing Sport University*, *12*, 5–8. CNKI:SUN:BJTD.0.2009-12-003.
Li, Q. (2016). 王宗岳其人与《太极拳谱》关系之探究 [Exploration on the relationship between Wang Zong-Yue and his Tai Chi]. *Journal of the Northwest Adult Education*, *3*, 97–99. https://doi.org/10.3969/j.issn.1008-8539.2016.03.027
Li, H. (2022, February 8). 中国女足没想象中穷, 有人年入百万 [The Chinese women's football players are not as poor as imagined, someone makes millions a year]. *21st Century Business Review*. https://www.21jingji.com/article/20220208/herald/a1bab1c3544bf60e79e358c7a948b075.html
Li, G., & Fan, B. (2017). 习近平体育强国思想研究 [Xi Jinping's sport nation thinking]. *Journal of Beijing Sport University*, *4*, 1–5. https://doi.org/10.19582/j.cnki.11-3785/g8.2017.04.001
Li, R., & Xiao, H. (2012). 乒乓球在近代中国的传入及发展 [Introduction of table tennis into modern China and its development]. *Journal of Chengdu Sport University*, *38*(5), 1–6. https://doi.org/10.3969/j.issn.1001-9154.2012.05.001
Li, R., Zhang, D., Yu, J., Kong, W., & Yong, Y. (2021). 中国乒乓球的使命追溯与新时代责任 [The mission retrospect and new era responsibilities of Chinese table tennis]. *China Sport Science*, *41*(11), 69–79. https://doi.org/10.16469/j.css.202111009
Li, X., & Zhao, G. (2017). 武术的本质特征研究 [The essential characteristics of Wushu]. *Journal of Shenyang Sport University*, *36*(1), 135–138. https://doi.org/10.3969/j.issn.1004-0560.2017.01.023
Lian, Y. (2018). 民国时期羽毛球运动在上海的传播 [The diffusion and development of Shanghai badminton during the age of the Republic of China]. *Zhejiang Sport Science*, *40*(2), 66–69. https://doi.org/10.3969/j.issn.1004-3624.2018.02.013
Liang, Q. (2016). 新民说 [New democracy theory]. Beijing Institute of Technology Press.
Liu, L., & Fan, H. (2017). *The national games and national identity in China: A history*. Routledge.
Lu, X. (2004). *Rhetoric of the Chinese cultural revolution: The impact on Chinese thought*. University of South Carolina Press.
Lu, Z., & Fan, H. (2014). *Sport and nationalism in China*. Routledge.
Luo, J., & Cheng, Y. (2002). 现代羽毛球运动发展趋势及我国发展对策思考 [The development of modern badminton and the development of China]. *Sports Science*, *22*(1), 60–62. https://doi.org/10.3969/j.issn.1000-677X.2002.01.021
Lüthi, L. M. (2010). *The Sino-Soviet split: Cold War in the communist world*. Princeton University Press.
Ma, A. (2007). 殷商武术文化在中国武术史上的地位及作用 [Yinshang Wushu culture's status and foundation in China's Wushu history]. In Y. Chen (Ed.), 河洛文化与殷商文明 [Heluo culture and the civilization of Shang dynasty] (pp. 389–399). Henan People's Publishing.
MacClancy, J. (1996). Sport, identity and ethnicity. In J. MacClancy (Ed.), *Sport, identity and ethnicity* (pp. 1–20). Berg.
MacMillan, M. (2008). *Nixon and Mao: The week that changed the world*. Random House Incorporated.

Maguire, J. (1999). *Global sport: Identities, societies, civilizations*. Polity Press.
Mangan, J. A. (Ed.). (1996), *Tribal identities: Nationalism, Europe, sport*. Frank Cass.
Morris, A. D. (2004). *Marrow of the nation: A history of sport and physical culture in Republican China*. University of California Press.
Morris, D. (2016). *The soccer tribe (Reprint)*. Rizzoli.
Nielsen. (2016, October 17). *China and football*. Nielsen Holdings Plc. https://www.nielsen.com/insights/2016/china-sports-business-football-report/
Nielsen. (2022, July 2). *2022 world football report*. Nielsen Holdings Plc. https://www.nielsen.com/insights/2022/discover-what-world-cup-fans-really-want/
Olson, E. T. (2003). Personal identity. In S. P. Stich & T. A. Warfield (eds), *The blackwell guide to philosophy of mind* (pp. 352–368). Blackwell.
Olympics.com. (2022, September 27). *World table tennis championships: All-time medal table*. Olympics.com. https://olympics.com/en/news/world-table-tennis-championships-all-time-medal-table
Oonk, G., & Oonk, A. (2023). 'This is not a problem but an issue': Chinese-born table tennis players representing another country at the Olympics, 1988–2020. *International Journal of the History of Sport*, *40*(4), 350–369. https://doi.org/10.1080/09523367.2023.2186857
Peng, Q., Skinner, J., & Houlihan, B. (2019). An analysis of the Chinese football reform of 2015: Why then and not earlier?. *International Journal of Sport Policy and Politics*, *11*(1), 1–18. https://doi.org/10.1080/19406940.2018.1536075
Qi, G. (2022, July 1). 1978年世界杯转播猜想 [The conjecture of the 1978 World Cup broadcast]. *Oriental Sports Daily*. https://paper.xinmin.cn/html/dfsports/2022-07-01/A02/38016.html
Reid, H., & Croucher, M. (1983). *The way of the warrior: The paradox of the martial arts*. Overlook Press.
Riordan, J. & Jones, R. E. (Eds.). (1999). *Sport and physical education in China*. E & FN Spon.
Rizak, G. (1989). Sport in the People's Republic of China. In E. A. Wagner (Ed.), *Sport in Asia and Africa: A comparative handbook* (pp. 101–119). Greenwood Press.
Shen, W., Bao, Y., Zhang, Z., & Chen, Y. (Eds.). (1995). 中国足球的摇篮：上海足球运动半世纪 (1896–1949) [Chinese football cradle: A half-century Shanghai football (1896–1949)]. Shanghai Cultural Publication.
Shields, D. L. L., & Bredemeier, B. J. L. (1996). Sport, militarism, and peace. *Peace and Conflict*, *2*(4), 369–383. https://doi.org/10.1207/s15327949pac0204_7
Smith, A. D. (1995). *Nations and nationalism in a global era*. Polity Press.
Smith, A. (2023, August 3). Former Everton star faces prison after being charged for 'accepting and offering bribes. *Mirror*. https://www.mirror.co.uk/sport/football/news/former-everton-star-faces-prison-30619840
State Council of the PRC. (2014). 国务院关于加快发展体育产业促进体育消费的若干意见 *[Opinion on accelerating the development of sport industry and promoting sports consumption]* (Report No. 46). http://www.gov.cn/zhengce/content/2014-10/20/content_9152.htm
State Council of the PRC. (2015). 国务院办公厅关于印发中国足球改革发展总体方案的通知 *[Notice on the overall plan of Chinese football reform and development]* (Report No. 11). http://www.gov.cn/zhengce/content/2015-03/16/content_9537.htm
Stead, D., & Maguire, J. (2000). "Rite De Passage" or passage to riches? The motivation and objectives of Nordic/Scandinavian players in English league soccer. *Journal of Sport & Social Issues*, *24*(1), 36–60. https://doi.org/10.1177/0193723500241
Stride, C. B., & Vandenberg, L. (2019). The art of face-saving and culture-changing: Sculpting Chinese football's past, present and future. *Sport in Society*, *22*(5), 803–828. https://doi.org/10.1080/17430437.2018.1430487
Sugden, J., & Tomlinson, A. (1998). Power and resistance in the governance of world football: Theorizing FIFA's transnational impact. *Journal of Sport & Social Issues*, *22*(3), 299–316. https://doi.org/10.1177/019372398022003005
Sullivan, J., Ross, T., & Wu, C. (2023). Representing the nation: Exploring attitudes towards naturalized foreign football players in China. *Soccer and Society*, *24*(5), 593–606. https://doi.org/10.1080/14660970.2022.2069100

Sullivan, J., Zhao, Y., Chadwick, S., & Gow, M. (2022). Chinese fans' engagement with football: Transnationalism, authenticity and identity. *Journal of Global Sport Management, 7*(3), 427–445. https://doi.org/10.1080/24704067.2021.1871855

Tajfel, H. (Ed.) (1978), *Differentiation between social groups: Studies in the social psychology of intergroup relations*. Academic Press.

Tamir, I., Galily, Y., & Yarchi, M. (2016). "Here's hoping we get pummeled" anti-nationalist trends among Israeli sports fans. *Journal of Sport & Social Issues, 40*(1), 3–21. https://doi.org/10.1177/01937235155942

Tan, T. C., & Bairner, A. (2018). The development of football in China under Xi Jinping. *Asia Dialogue*. https://theasiadialogue.com/2018/04/05/the-development-of-football-in-china-underxijinping/

Tan, T. C., Huang, H. C., Bairner, A., & Chen, Y. W. (2016). Xi Jin-Ping's World Cup dreams: From a major sports country to a world sports power. *International Journal of the History of Sport, 33*(12), 1449–1465. https://doi.org/10.1080/09523367.2016.1243103

Tian, E., & Wise, N. (2020). An Atlantic divide? Mapping the knowledge domain of European and North American based sociology of sport, 2008–2018. *International Review for the Sociology of Sport, 55*(8), 1029–1055.

Timm, L. (2015, September 5). Cuju: 2,000 years of ancient Chinese soccer. *Epoch Times*. https://www.theepochtimes.com/article/cuju-2000-years-of-ancient-chinese-soccer-1745118

Tong, Z. (2005). *The method of Chinese wrestling*. North Atlantic Books.

Turner, J. C. (1985). Social categorization and the self-concept: A social cognitive theory of group behavior. In E. J. Lawler (Ed.), *Advances in group processes Theory and research* (pp. 77–122). JAI Press.

Venkat, R. (2022, February 6). AFC Women's Asian Cup winners: China lead the way. https://olympics.com/en/news/afc-womens-asian-cup-football-winners-champions-list

Von Mises, L. (2006). *Nation, state, and economy: Contributions to the politics and history of our time*. Liberty Fund.

Wang, Z. (1991). 王宗岳太极拳论 *[Wang Zong-Yue's theories of Tai Chi]* (Vol. 25). People's Sports Publishing House.

Wang, X. (2014). 浅谈中国羽毛球运动发展的两起两落 [On the twice up and down in the development of badminton in China]. *Sport Forum, 6*(6), 50–51. https://doi.org/10.3969/j.issn.1004-5643(t).2014.06.018

White, J. (2020, October 6). Qatar 2022 World Cup: China boss Li Tie says 'no limit' on naturalised players. *South China Morning Post*. https://www.scmp.com/sport/football/article/3104337/qatar-2022-world-cup-china-boss-li-tie-says-no-limit-naturalised

Williams, J. (2007). *A beautiful game: International perspectives on women's football*. A&C Black.

Wise, N. (2015). Maintaining Dominican identity in the Dominican Republic: Forging a baseball landscape in Villa Ascension. *International Review for the Sociology of Sport, 50*(2), 161–178.

Wise, N. (2020). Eventful futures and triple bottom line impacts: BRICS, image regeneration and competitiveness. *Journal of Place Management and Development, 13*(1), 89–100.

Wise, N. & Harris, J. (Eds.). (2019), *Events, places and societies*. Routledge.

Wu, Y. (2023, June 24). 止戈为武: 文献中记录的中华武术观 [Wu combines Zhi and Ge: Understand the value of Chinese martial arts from the classic literature]. *Guang Ming Daily*. https://epaper.gmw.cn/gmrb/html/2023-06/24/nw.D110000gmrb_20230624_1-07.htm

Yang, S. (2014). 中国寒食蹴鞠与英国忏悔节足球赛的对比研究 [A comparative study on Chinese Cuju on Hanshi Day and English Shrovetide football match in Ashbourne]. *Sports Culture Guide, 7*, 178–187. https://doi.org/10.3969/j.issn.1671-1572.2014.07.048

Young, E. P. (1977). *The presidency of Yuan Shih-k'ai: Liberalism and dictatorship in early republican China*. University of Michigan Press.

Zagoria, D. S. (2015). *Sino-Soviet Conflict, 1956–1961*. Princeton University Press.

Zhao, L. (1998). 论中国学校体育思想与实践的沿革和发展 [On the evolution and development of Chinese school physical education thinking and practice]. *China Sport Science, 5*, 5–7. https://doi.org/10.3969/j.issn.1000-677X.1998.05.002

Zhou, H. (2020). 从女权主义视角看职业女足同工同酬问题 [A feminist perspective -on the issue of equal revenue in professional women's football]. *Journal of Western, 21*, 157–160.

CHAPTER 4

CHINESE FOOTBALL FANDOM: GROWING WITH THE CHANGING CHINESE SOCIETY

Kaixiao Jiang and Liam O'Callaghan

Liverpool Hope University, UK

ABSTRACT

This chapter explores how the development of football fandom for the Chinese national team and local football clubs is strongly associated with societal changes. Although the performances of Chinese football teams, especially the national team, have failed to impress the world, football remains the most popular because of millions of supporters with loyalty and passion. Most studies related to fans mainly focus on the economic and political implications of spectatorship along with the rise of China. Nevertheless, few articles are available to answer the fundamental questions, such as 'When did these supporters come out?' and 'What were the factors of the development of fandom?'. By going through archival records and published documents over the last decades, this chapter offers a comprehensive and historical analysis of the development of football fandom in the People's Republic of China (PRC) and deals with these unanswered questions. As such, this chapter does not intend to be the most authoritative one but is one of the rare sources to lay down the foundation for research on Chinese football fandom. Furthermore, this chapter also proves that studies on football fandom can be a useful window for observing Chinese society.

Keywords: Sport history; football fandom; Chinese society; Chinese national football team; Chinese local football clubs

INTRODUCTION

Football serves as a vehicle to explore Asian societies, and its significance varies based on the distinct conditions and periods associated with each. In the case of China, as a member of the Asian family, it possesses a unique football culture that reflects the specific development of its society (Cho, 2013). A prominent example illustrating the political importance of football in China is the published Overall Plan to Boost the Development of Soccer in China (the Plan), which designates the development of football as a national strategy and highlights the political priorities of the People's Republic of China (PRC) as a driving force in shaping the Chinese football industry (State Council of the PRC, 2015). Today, it is common for countries to leverage sporting events (Tian & Wise, 2020) to have an impact on society (Wise & Maguire, 2022). Furthermore, since the Plan is a subsequent document to the Guiding Opinions of the General Office of the State Council on Expediting the Development of the Sports Competition and Performance Industry (State Council of the PRC, 2014), the evolution of Chinese football is intricately linked to the evolving needs of China's economy. Consequently, research on Chinese football, particularly those examining its political and economic significance, is experiencing substantial growth, parallelling the increased involvement of various Chinese social organisations in football (e.g. Connell, 2018; Junio & Rodrigues, 2017; Peng et al., 2019; Tan et al., 2016).

However, research on Chinese football fandom has remained relatively marginal compared to the abundance of studies on Chinese football. The investigation into Chinese football fans began in the late 1980s following Event 5.19 (Lu & Chen, 1991). On 19 May 1985, China experienced a significant loss in key qualifying games against Hong Kong for the 1986 World Cup Finals, leading frustrated fans to damage properties as an expression of their disappointment (Tan, 2004). Despite the importance of understanding the origin of fans and the dynamics between fans and teams, early studies on Chinese football fandom predominantly employed psychology to elucidate the emergence of football hooliganism in China (Shi, 2004; Song & Lu, 1997; Tan, 2004). Despite the subsequent development of a flourishing football industry catalysed by the Plan, attracting numerous scholars to delve into Chinese football-related studies, research focused on fandom remained limited. Moreover, the predominant focus of major Chinese football fandom studies has been on spectatorship's economic and political implications (Jiang & Bairner, 2020). This scarcity of knowledge regarding the development of Chinese football fandom presents a barrier to comprehending the significance of this social group within its society. Therefore, this chapter aims to shed light on how Chinese individuals perceive and identify with their football fandom, both at the national and local levels, against the backdrop of the evolving Chinese society.

THE FOUNDATION: FOOTBALL LOVERS

In the Chinese context, the original definition of football fans referred to football lovers with a strong passion for football and its games (Lu & Chen, 1991). This implies that the initial football fandom in this society did not evolve through people's emotional attachment to specific football teams (Ben Porat, 2010; Dixon, 2016; Hognestad, 2012). Nevertheless, these football lovers, initially lacking specific team affiliations, laid the groundwork for Chinese individuals to identify as fans of their football teams, both at the international and domestic levels. The following sections delineate the development of Chinese people's affinity for football and elucidate how football lovers played a pivotal role in establishing the foundation of Chinese football fandom.

THE ROOT: FOOTBALL LOVERS BEFORE 1949

Although cuju in China was recognised by the Federation Internationale de Football Association (FIFA) as one of the early forms of football in 2004 (FIFA.com, 2004; Connor, 2015), the nationwide ban on cuju during the Qing dynasty, aimed at preventing Han people from gathering and reinforcing the authority of the Manchu people, created a gap between ancient and modern football games in China (Goldblatt, 2007). Consequently, people's engagement in modern football games in the late 19th century provided Chinese football lovers with the foundation to develop their affection for this sport, serving as the origin of fandom for their national and local teams in the context of the PRC (Jones, 2004, pp. 54–66).

Due to the forced opening treaties following the Opium Wars (1839–1842; 1856–1860), British-invented sports, including football, were introduced to China (Jones, 2004, pp. 54–66; Morris, 2004). Hong Kong was the earliest location to witness modern football activities due to its status as a British colony. Subsequently, this sport also emerged in other colonial areas such as Shanghai and Tianjin (Jin & Zhang, 2014; Shen et al., 1995). However, initially, Chinese people were excluded from attending games as they were only permitted to engage in economic activities, such as trading and labour hiring, with residents of colonial areas (Balfour & Zheng, 2002). On the other hand, these individuals also refrained from playing football, identifying themselves as residents of the Celestial Empire, prioritising things from China as civilised and disparaging those from the West as barbarian (Lu & Fan, 2014; Yang, 2016).

Until the 1860s, when the Qing dynasty promoted the Self-Strengthening Movement to prioritise Western knowledge, Chinese people could engage in modern football through physical education developed by the Young Men's Christian Association (Duara, 1996; Garrett, 1970; Morris, 2004; Speak, 1999). Interschool football competitions marked the beginning of Chinese people's involvement in football, and the friendly match between Shanghai Saint John's University and Shanghai Nanyang Public School in 1902 was recognised as 'the first Chinese people's football game and the first football game between universities in China' (Shen et al., 1995, p. 8). Since then, Chinese football lovers, who developed a significant interest in this sport and its games, gradually emerged.

Football lovers at that time could be divided into the Audience and the Player. The Audience comprises people with few connections to the school teams but who love watching their games:

> Between the 1890s and the 1990s, [a football lover] worked at the canal port. Every day, he would go straight to Beijing Luhe Middle School after his daily job. While having his food, he enjoyed the school team's games and training. (Jin & Zhang 2014, p. 5)

The Audience described in the quotation never attended Luhe school as a student or had any other direct interaction with the school, such as being an employee. Therefore, his fondness for the team developed differently from the identified traditional fans worldwide who support their football teams by recognising these teams' status as representatives of their social communities (Ben Porat, 2010; Dixon, 2016; Hognestad, 2012). Without recognising these school teams as representatives of their communities, they cannot allow any established social identities in their living circumstances, such as families, neighbourhoods and workplaces, to be the factors leading them to support these school teams. In contrast, their support for these school teams results from a pure desire – to enjoy high-quality football games provided by a successful team: 'The Luhe football team was the best Beijing team with strong competitive capability... This team never lost any games' (Jin & Zhang, 2014, pp. 5–6). Luhe was a team with a strong competitive capability, and it even won 9:0 in the game against the British garrison team when Chinese people began playing football (Tang, 2004). In this respect, a team's competitive capability is the precondition allowing the Audience to develop their fondness for football games. After acknowledging this team's football performance as the channel to meet their desire to enjoy the joys brought by football, people without any connection to this team will be the followers.

The Player refers to players from different school football teams or amateur football clubs who love playing football (Jin & Zhang, 2014). However, because they are not professional players 'who played football to make a living' (p. 7), these people's passion for playing football allows them to be acknowledged as football lovers. Furthermore, the direct experience of playing football distinguishes the Player's fondness for football from the Audience's, as it guides these practical football lovers to define themselves as Chinese football founders obligated to promote football games among the Chinese people. For example, Fenglou Li, a former player at Fu Jen Catholic University in the 1930s and the first manager of the Chinese national football team after the establishment of the PRC, usually organised friendly matches among schools in North China as exhibition games and raised donations for low-income families (Li et al., 2018). Hence, the Players' passion for football is stronger than that of the Audience, who may identify games as entertainment.

Indeed, the Player's passion for football made this group the main and solid force that sustained football in the chaotic milieu from 1890 to 1949. During that time, the Chinese people experienced regime changes from the Qing dynasty to the Republic of China (ROC) and from the ROC to the PRC, which were filled with conflicts against power outside China and themselves, such as the 1911 Revolution (1911–1912), the Second Sino-Japanese War (1937–1945), and the Second Civil War (1945–1949) (Chang et al., 2002; Zhang, 1985; Zhu, 2001). Hence, playing football consistently at this age was difficult. For example, after the Shanghai Massacre of 1925, where the Shanghai Municipal Police opened fire on Chinese anti-imperialists in Shanghai's International Settlement on 30 May 1925, the annual friendly match between Saint John's University and Nanyang Public School was terminated (Shen et al., 1995). Although the termination aimed to reduce the effect of Saint John's Western background in the provoked anti-imperialist atmosphere, it also resulted in the decline of the Audience who loved watching games of Saint John's football team. Yet, the Player remained active in promoting football games, such as organising the Jiangnan Intercollegiate Athletic Association (江南各大学体育协会) and the subsequent football games among other Shanghai schools.

In terms of fondness for teams, the Player also has a different attitude from the Audience. The Player's sense of belonging to their teams helps them attach loyalty to their teams: 'At that time, [school] football players had three identities: students, players and fans' (Jin & Zhang, 2014, p. 7). In other words, this group of football lovers is similar to most original football fans of European and South American teams, meeting a status of 'participatory democracy' defined by Ian Taylor (1971). The deep connection between people and their football teams – people being the founders and initial players – helps them develop a strong sense of ownership towards their football teams. Moreover, this emotion allows the teams to be new communities that offer them new collective identities, and the affinity with their team communities also strengthens the Player's fondness for their teams (Dixon, 2013; MacClancy, 1996). As a result, the Player group's fondness for their teams is more reliable than the Audience's, which is caused by their passion for enjoying high-quality football games.

Compared with most Chinese people who lacked Western education and refused to engage with football at that time, football lovers were a minority. However, these people, especially in the Player group, carried the Chinese people's fondness for football from the chaotic age to the present PRC to develop the fandom for the Chinese football teams. The typical evidence was the first PRC nationwide football game in 1951, which was the second year after the establishment of the PRC in October 1949 (Dong & Mangan, 2001). Eventually, the spark enlightened the unique path in developing Chinese people's fondness for football.

THE TRANSITION: FOOTBALL LOVERS BETWEEN 1949 AND 1979

The first PRC archived football game was the exhibition match played by a football team from Shenyang. This game was organised as a sign: 'Modern sport is an iconic representation of modern China' (Dong & Mangan, 2001, p. 79), highlighting the PRC as a better and different Chinese regime from its forbears. It also proves that the Chinese people sustained their passion for football from a relatively chaotic age. After the end of the Second Sino-Japanese War and the Second Civil War, it is undeniable that the establishment of the PRC offered a more sustainable environment for the Chinese people to play football, such as the first National Football Championship in 1951 (Jin & Zhang, 2014, pp. 27–28):

The team that attended the first national football championship was organised based on six large administrative areas: North China, South China, East China, Northeast China, Northwest China, Southwest China, the People's Liberation Army (PLA) and the Railway Association.

Thirty-one players were selected to organise the first national football team in the PRC after this tournament (Dong & Mangan, 2001). Players were directly administered by the National Training Bureau under the direction of the National Sports Commission (a sport-focussing governmental department, today's General Administration of Sport of China) in 1952. In this respect, organising the first National Football Championship in 1951 also aimed to shape the context of Chinese elite football players' development from where schools and social communities played the leading role to a government-dominated one. Indeed, an elite football player development system with two tracks administered by the State Council of China was also established after the establishment of the national football team (see Fig. 4.1, Fan et al., 2001).

One track is from the local Sport Schools to the National Training Bureau under the direction of the National Sports Commission, while another is from the Regional PLA Sport Teams to the Sport Brigade of PLA under the direction of the General Political Ministry of PLA. Because of the emergence of this system, China had its officially recognised local and national football teams in 1952, indicating the emergence of professional football players.

Because elite football players are paid to play football, they can no longer be defined as football lovers with few interest disputes on the pitches (Jin & Zhang, 2014). This change also resulted in the decline of the Player group, who were

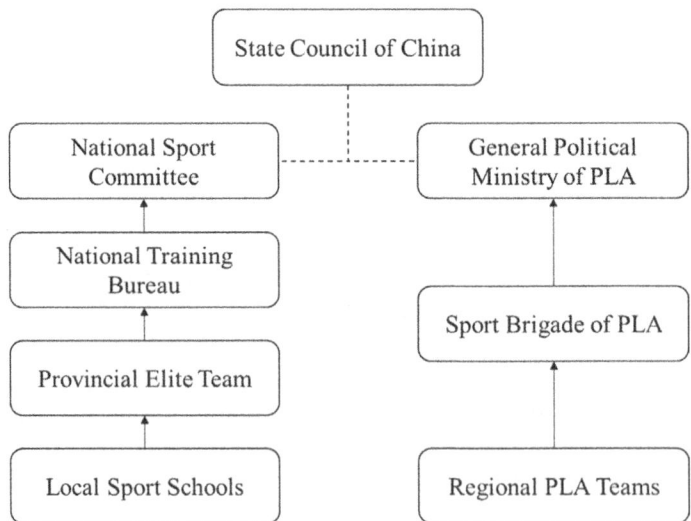

Fig. 4.1. The Administrative Structure of the Chinese Elite Football System in the 1950s.

practical football lovers and promoted football throughout China. These selected players in the official teams are the core practitioners of their Player group, as they were the main force that sustained the Chinese people's passion for football in a relatively chaotic age (Donnelly, 1981; Hebdige, 1979). Therefore, without including those professional players, the Player group is incapable of maintaining the group's leading role in developing Chinese people's fondness for football.

Hence, the Player group only consists of nonprofessional players who play football without payment. They are similar to the Audience group, fond of those official football teams and their professional fellows, such as Shengrong Qiu, the main actor in the Peking Opera Theatre Company of Beijing (Jin & Zhang, 2014). He was a football player in his workplace team while interested in the Beijing football team's games. When Beijing had a friendly match against the Japanese national football team in 1957, he even fabricated that 'his son was ill' to escape from his working slot to watch the game (pp. 42–43). Therefore, these unprofessional players can be merged into the Audience group, whose fondness for football is associated with the desire to enjoy high-quality games, indicating the beginning of the Audience group's leading role in developing Chinese people's fondness for football.

Because the establishment of the PRC ended the chaotic environment, the Audience can consistently interact with their local and national representatives on the pitches (Jin, 2012). In other words, these football lovers at this age can share the same path as the present football fans to join Crawford's defined 'Career of the Sport Supporter' (2003) and develop their original attitude towards football teams from the status of fondness – exploring the joys of high-quality football games – to the status of fandom, having a strong affinity with their teams via a long-term and constant interaction with those teams (Jiang & Bairner, 2019, 2020).

However, it appears that they do not exclusively favour their officially recognised football teams in both international and domestic contexts. Instead, they also express interest in other elite teams. In the international context, it was uncommon for Chinese football audiences between the 1950s and the 1970s to support their national team exclusively. Instead, they would 'cheer for their rival team' in the international sphere if the opposing team exhibited 'outstanding performances' (Jin & Zhang, 2014, p. 30). This mainly resulted from that China primarily played against teams from the Socialist camp, such as Hungary (Dong & Mangan, 2001). As a Socialist country, China maintained a relatively strong relationship with nations in the Socialist camp until the late 1960s when its ties with the Soviet Union deteriorated (Lüthi, 2010; Robinson, 1972; Zagoria, 2015). People in such a political atmosphere could not harbour animosity towards their identified 'comrades against Western imperialism' on football pitches, inhibiting their wholehearted support for the Chinese national football team (Jin & Zhang, 2014, p. 29).

In terms of the domestic sphere, they also pay attention to other teams in the same league as their local team if these teams are based in the same immediate place. For example, Beijing football lovers also watch games of the PLA team, which represents Chinese military troops rather than Beijing people: 'The PLA usually played games in Xiannongtan Stadium every Sunday…During the game day, you could find the stadium full of Beijing football lovers because this would be the happiest day for all of them' (p. 29). Important to note here is due to the PLA's military ownership and background, it has never had a fixed home and training base, which have used Beijing, Taiyuan in Shanxi, Shijiazhuang in Hebei, Xi'an in Shaanxi, Kunming in Yunnan, Xinxiang in Henan, Liuzhou in Guangxi and Xiangtan in Hunan as their homes. These football lovers' desire to watch high-quality football games directs them to show interest in teams with good competitive capabilities, distinguishing their Audience's identity from present fans.

Although the previous discussion also implies that celebrating local identity encouraged these Chinese people to develop their fondness for their local football teams (Jiang & Bairner, 2020, 2024), most Chinese football lovers could not develop their fandom for their local teams under this influence when local football teams emerged throughout China in the 1950s. This phenomenon is associated with the lack of a home-and-away fixture in Chinese domestic games (Fan et al., 2001; Li, 2014b). The main target of the domestic league game at that time was for the government to select the talent pool for the Chinese national football team. Without the need to attract and entertain the public, employing the tournament to organise games in major cities where local sport sectors were able to offer the stadium and hospitality was the priority (Ying, 2019). Consequently, football lovers who were not living in these major cities could not constantly interact with their official local teams. Furthermore, the regular broadcasting of domestic football games began with the establishment of professional leagues in 1994 (Yan, 2006). Before that, China Central Television (CCTV), the main national sports broadcaster, mainly focused on the national football team games. Therefore, it was unlikely for these football lovers to interact with their official local team and recognise these teams' local representative status. Without constant and consistent interaction, it was unlikely for these fans to develop their fandom by acknowledging these teams' local affinity, thereby maintaining these people's audience status from the 1950s to the 1990s.

Merging nonprofessional players into the Audience group does not decline these football lovers' role in spreading the Chinese people's passion for football. Although the establishment of the elite football player development system requires sporting governmental departments at different levels to promote football throughout China (Dong & Mangan, 2001), such a nationwide promotion mainly focuses on building the talent pool for the national football team. Eventually, public football participation is attributed to schools and workers' unions (see Fig. 4.2 to find the tracks for the Chinese school and amateur football promotions, Fan et al., 2001).

After China completed its Socialist economic reformation that altered all social organisations with private ownership to state organisations with public ownership between 1953 and 1956, it employed the planned economy to lead all economic activities to follow the plan identified by the central government, aiming to show its difference from capitalist countries that employed a marketing economy (Berki, 1975). As a result, two human resource administrative systems embedded with the planned economy, the danwei (单位, work unit) system and

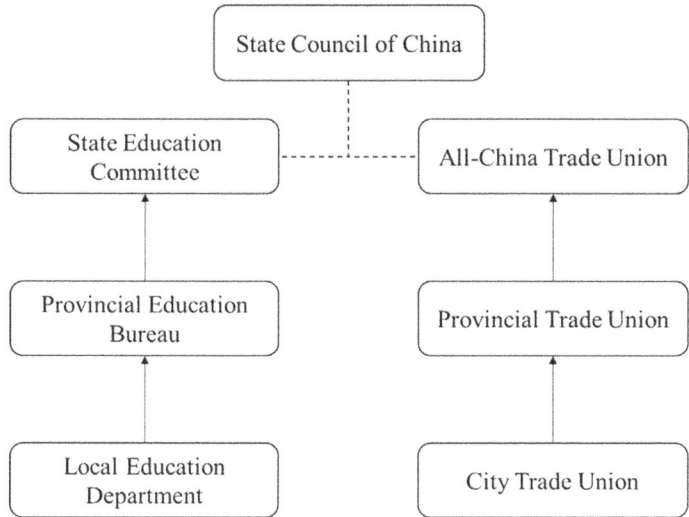

Fig. 4.2. The Administrative Structure of Chinese School and Amateur Football Games.

the Graduates' Occupational Assignment (毕业包分配, GOA), were developed and helped student players in school teams and amateur players in workers' union teams become the leading force in promoting the people's passion for football.

The danwei system is employed to ensure that every human resource can complete the plan designed by the state and meet its indicated national needs (Bray, 2005). As a result, the mobility of the population, especially people's interregional travel and accommodation, was limited by the system strictly:

> For example, to go to another danwei on business, to buy an airline ticket, or to stay in a hotel... a Chinese citizen requires a letter of introduction from his or her danwei. Members of any danwei respond to an outsider according to the status of the outsider as set out in the letter of introduction provided by his or her danwei. (Li, 1993, cited in Bray, 2005, p. 4)

Although the danwei system strictly limits the interaction between human resources in social organisations, people's mobility can still happen if a danwei is required by the governmental scheme to explore its new branch in other regions. For example, factories in major Chinese cities, such as Shanghai, Tianjin and Beijing, were required by the central government to develop their new branches in Henan province, which was a relatively underdeveloped region, to support the local economy between the 1950s and the 1970s (Chang, 2008). At that time, these factories constantly exported their employees to Henan. Because the employees at that time agreed to be the fixed human resources for their danweis when they accepted the jobs, most of them had to follow the mobility of human resources and eventually became immigrants to this place (Bray, 2005). Along with their immigration, amateur players in the workers' union teams also brought football playing to their immediate places.

The GOA is another way to realise the population's mobility and spread people's passion for football. Embedded with the planned economy, this system assigns higher education and secondary school graduates to different danweis based on the state's indicated human resource demand (Bian, 1994). That is, football players from schools can promote football to other regions once they are assigned jobs in those new places. Those players are also the fixed human resources to their danweis after accepting the jobs. They may spread the football again if their danweis are required to support the economic development in other regions via expanding their new branches.

Along with the emergence of professional players, this era witnessed the decline of the Player group. After that, the nonprofessional players were also integrated into the Audience group. Because non-professional players are the main force spreading public football playing throughout China, the Audience group has been leading in developing Chinese people's fondness for football. In addition, the peaceful environment offered by the PRC allows such passion for football to be continuous, which becomes the foundation for present fans to develop the fandom for their national and local football teams. Suppose the unprofessional players in the Audience are the spreaders of the Chinese people's passion for football. In that case, the Chinese people's experience of watching the 1978 and 1982 FIFA World Cup Finals was the catalyst that strengthened their emotions towards football (Jiang & Bairner, 2019). Furthermore, such experience inspires people to express their passion for football games and teams.

THE ENLIGHTENMENT: FOOTBALL LOVERS BETWEEN 1979 AND 1981

The 1978 Argentina World Cup was the starting point for Chinese people to begin watching football games on television (TV) and the FIFA World Cup Finals. CCTV provided the live broadcasting of the game for third place between Italy and Brazil and the final between Argentina and the Netherlands (Chen & Hu, 2008; Jiang & Bairner, 2019). Moreover, the Chinese people's experience of watching this broadcasting is accidental, and politics is the main factor behind this accident.

Before the 1970s, Chinese TV stations could not process nationwide live broadcasting because China did not have a microwave transmission system to transmit satellite data (Chen & Hu, 2008). In order to broadcast the 1972 visit by US President Richard Nixon to China, three satellite earth stations in Beijing and Shanghai were established (Qi, 2022). Nixon's visit was the result of Ping-pong Diplomacy in 1971, which aimed for China and the US to establish diplomatic relations. After the Second World War, China belonged to the Socialist camp conducted by the Soviet Union and joined the Cold War against theUS. However, the Sino-Soviet split and the American failure in the Vietnam War in the late 1960s allowed both of these political entities to seek cooperation to resist the pressure given by the Soviet Union (Fan & Xiong, 2002; MacMillan, 2008). Thus, politics laid down the foundation for the Chinese people to watch the 11th World Cup. Moreover, politics also determined the broadcasting of the FIFA World Cup finals. Due to the influence of the Cold War at that time, most international sports organisations did not compromise on the PRC's One-China policy in the China-Taiwan conflict (Homburg, 2006). Consequently, the Chinese Football Association (CFA) was not a FIFA member, while CCTV did not have the copyright to broadcast the 1978 World Cup (Chen & Hu, 2008). However, Deng Xiaoping, the vice president of the Central Committee, vice president of the Military Commission and chief of the General Staff of the PLA at that time, requested the broadcasting of that World Cup:

> When they answered the phone call, 'Can we broadcast the final of the Argentina World Cup? Comrade Xiaoping wished to watch', CCTV turned on the receiving system from the satellite earth stations to broadcast that game. (Qi, 2022)

Following Deng's requirement, China used the Hong Kong Broadcasting Company's satellite signal and CCTV also provided their first football game and the FIFA World Cup TV broadcasting (Li, 2006). The key factor of Deng's requirement was to promote the opening-up policy and Socialist market economy to reopen China (Ding, 2009). After the social disorder caused by the Great Proletarian Cultural Revolution (Cultural Revolution) – a left-wing sociopolitical campaign between 1966 and 1976 to strengthen the Chinese communist party's legitimacy, China's economy and technology were relatively underdeveloped than its Western rivals (Lu, 2004). Hence, a competitive economic environment based on the opening-up policy and Socialist market economy could reactivate and develop China because it directly allowed all Chinese industries to face the challenges brought by Western capitals. In this respect, the 1978 World Cup broadcasting can be interpreted as a sign of Deng's Socialist reformation (Qi, 2022).

Watching this tournament helped the Chinese people develop a special emotion towards football because of China's relatively poor media entertainment at that time. TV was the latest media technology for the Chinese people to accept information and enjoy entertainment between the 1970s and the 1980s (Yue & Chen, 2010). The emergence of Chinese self-developed TV was in the 1950s. However, the social disorder caused by the Cultural Revolution delayed such development (Lu, 2004). Moreover, the planned economy categorised TV as the public entertainment demand rather than their essential material needs (Yue & Chen, 2010). Consequently, a 9-inch black and white TV remained fashionable in the late 1970s, and it was unusual for a Chinese family to have a TV at that time:

> In 1978, the number of household TVs in China was very small. Most TVs were available in the urban area. It was unlikely to find a TV in suburban areas within dozens of kilometres...To watch TV, people needed to visit their neighbours, schools, and danwei's common rooms. (Chen & Hu, 2008)

Furthermore, the TV programmes offered by the TV stations were poor at that time. The Cultural Revolution also suspended all Chinese TV stations' programmes until the late 1970s (Yue & Chen, 2010). After recovering its broadcasting project in 1978, CCTV began the first Chinese regular TV programme, Xinwen Lianbo (新闻联播, News Simulcast), which is a daily news programme for important News events, government announcements, policy promotion and the activities of governmental leaders. In other words, the TV programme then was not mainly for entertainment. Watching the FIFA World Cup, the highest-quality football game in the world, therefore, was a cherished entertainment and the most memorable experience for the Chinese people (Lu, 2018).

The experience of watching the 11th World Cup heightened people's interest in football, as evidenced by their behaviour during the 1982 World Cup. CCTV broadcasted 22 games of that tournament (Wang, 2016). However, due to financial limitations, it only had live broadcasting rights for the final between West Germany and Italy. Its record broadcasting rights were jointly purchased with the Asia-Pacific Broadcasting Union in Hong Kong, so the broadcasting team recorded games with commentaries every night in Hong Kong and delivered them as broadcasting programs to Beijing the next morning. In other words, there was a 9-hour gap for Chinese people to watch games on TV after the real game time (Li, 2014a). Although people could find game information in newspapers and radio before TV broadcasting, watching TV remained the priority for most Chinese people to enjoy the 1982 World Cup (Wang, 2016). Hence, the World Cup was the most impressive and splendid TV programme for the Chinese people to enjoy, significantly contributing to football promotion throughout China.

In addition to their heightened fondness for football, people recognise it as a window to understanding the world outside China. The broadcasting of the 1978 World Cup helped the Chinese learn about the Argentine capital city, Buenos Aires, for the first time (Chen & Hu, 2008). It also allowed them to comprehend the difference between the Northern and Southern hemispheres – Argentina was in winter while China was in summer. Moreover, a few days after the World Cup, this geographical knowledge appeared on the National College Entrance Examination paper – the most significant test determining students' future direction (Zhang, 2016). Hence, only students who watched that World Cup tournament might be able to answer this question. Football has become an important channel for people to encounter the world. Furthermore, this idea was strengthened when China began its opening-up policy in 1978. China's relatively underdeveloped status compared with Western communities led people to identify everything from the Western community as advanced (Lu & Fan, 2014). As a result, football helped the Chinese encounter their recognised fashionable lifestyle, such as Rossi Mania – an idolisation of the Italian football player Paolo Rossi (Luo, 2018). After Paolo was awarded the best player in the 1982 World Cup, his hairstyle became a fashion symbol imitated by Chinese men, and a Chinese football lover even changed his name to Luoxi (罗西) – the Chinese pronunciation of Rossi.

Due to the identified social significance of football, how overseas football fans express their passion also inspires the Chinese people to articulate their enthusiasm for football games and teams. For example, the fervent demonstrations of passion by Argentinian fans for their national team during the 1978 World Cup demonstrated their legitimacy in providing unconditional support to a team, particularly their national football team (Li, 2006):

> For the first time, they witnessed coloured paper and white tape cascading down from the top of the stadium. This was how Argentinian fans celebrated Argentina's victory, and it provided them with a newfound understanding of the significance of the World Cup.

As discussed earlier, the Chinese people tempered their passion for their national football team due to the team predominantly playing games against members from its Socialist camp (Jin & Zhang, 2014). However, the experience of watching the World Cups has played a pivotal role in helping Chinese football enthusiasts identify their team preferences. Consequently, the influence of local and national identities becomes integral to the fondness Chinese football lovers have for their football teams. Their increasing loyalty to teams ultimately transforms these football enthusiasts into fans who cultivate strong affinities with their teams.

BECOMING A CHINESE FOOTBALL FAN

Since the 1980s, the Chinese people have embraced the concept of fandom – a profound connection with their national and local teams (Ben Porat, 2010; Dixon, 2016; Hognestad, 2012). Crawford's 'Career of the Sport Supporter' (2003) appears to be an apt theory for elucidating the progression of Chinese people's fan identification with their national and local football teams. It underscores the pivotal role of sustained interaction between individuals and sports teams as the crucial factor that transforms casual enthusiasts, initially seeking joy from high-quality games, into loyal fans. Nevertheless, national and local identities remain crucial factors in the realm of Chinese football fandom (Jiang & Bairner, 2024). The ensuing sections, therefore, elucidate how the Chinese people evolve into fans of their teams in the international and domestic spheres by examining how their national and local identities intersect with their interaction with these teams.

BECOMING A FAN OF THE CHINESE NATIONAL FOOTBALL TEAM

The Chinese people began interacting with the national football team in 1952 when the first national football team was established. While celebrating national identity is often cited as a motivation for developing fandom for this team (Jiang & Bairner, 2019, 2024), its significant impact appears to be more pronounced post the 1980s. Before this period, Chinese football enthusiasts primarily experienced the influence of national identity during the 1958 FIFA World Cup qualification – the inaugural step in their team's journey to the World Cup (Jin, 2012).

On the 2nd of June 1957, China hosted a home game in Beijing against Indonesia, and the intense demand for tickets reflected people's fervent passion. The extreme ticket demand was not merely for the sake of witnessing a high-quality game. Rather, it was deeply tied to people's ardent desire to support their national representative on the pitch. The ticket competition was so intense that those fortunate enough to obtain one were greatly admired: 'Everyone was looking for a ticket before the game. If someone could have a ticket, they would be envied badly' (Jin & Zhang, 2014, p. 34). Due to the overwhelming demand, individuals without tickets gathered at the Taoranting Natatorium near the Xiannongtan Stadium, which was close to a broadcasting speaker, to attentively follow the game (Jin & Zhang, 2014, pp. 32–33):

> People stood in the water throughout the game, listening attentively to the broadcast. When China scored their first goal, the entire swimming pool erupted in cheers.

As discussed in the previous section, consistently supporting their national team was challenging for Chinese football lovers due to the political environment between the 1950s and the 1970s (Jin & Zhang, 2014). However, their sense of belonging to their nation can be highlighted as a critical factor influencing their unusual behaviour during this game. After the establishment of the PRC, compulsory civic and moral education in schools and the constitution consistently highlighting national solidarity as a principle helped people grasp the meaning of nation (Jones, 1985; Maosen, 1990; Reed, 1995), which was an impossible achievement in the previous chaotic age (Luo, 2013; Zhang, 2012). Consequently, people also developed an idea to prioritise their nation over other social communities. Moreover, the game against Indonesia provided a rare opportunity for China to compete with a non-Socialist national football team at that time (Chinese Football Institution, n.d.). Thus, Chinese football lovers temporarily set aside the established idea that international football games were used to strengthen China's friendship with other Socialist entities. They acted similarly to football fans from other nations who recognised supporting their national team as a way to express their loyalty to their nation (Bairner, 2001; Sugden & Tomlinson, 1998).

Nevertheless, the effect of national identity caused by the 1958 World Cup qualification did not continue. Influenced by the Cold War, the Chinese mainland and Taiwan also had a conflict representing China in FIFA (Homburg, 2006). China's attendance in the 1958 FIFA World Cup qualification was related to the absence of Taiwan. Because FIFA rejected China's request to cancel Taiwan's legitimacy of China's representative status, the CFA notified its withdrawal of FIFA membership. After that, the Chinese national football team stopped its World Cup journey and returned to games against other Socialist national football teams (Dong & Mangan, 2001; Jones, 2004, pp. 54–66). The effect of national identity on the Chinese people's attitudes towards their national team was also suppressed.

Until 1979, when CFA restored its FIFA membership, national identity could influence Chinese people's attitude towards their national football team again.

The Chinese national team's attendance in the 1982 World Cup qualification rebegan its World Cup journey (Chinese Football Institution, n.d.). During that tournament, Chinese people claimed their strong affinity with the national team and its players for the first time (Jiang & Bairner, 2019). While having a leg injury, Zhixing Rong greatly contributed to China's 3-0 victory in a key game against Kuwait – the most powerful Asian team during the 1982 World Cup qualification. Witnessing Rong's contribution, Chinese audiences in the stadium cheered for him as a national hero: 'Your motherland thanks you, your people thank you' (Chen & Hu, 2008). As a result, the Chinese people raised the propaganda of the 'Zhixing Style' (志行风格) – a nationwide idolisation of this national team player, and people's unprecedented claim of their affinity with this player is also defined as evidence of the original fandom for the Chinese national football team (Jiang & Bairner, 2019).

Event 5.19 – the first and largest fan riot in the history of Chinese football fandom – was another typical example of the Chinese people's fandom for the national team being associated with a sense of belonging to the nation (Tan, 2004). China lost to Hong Kong in the key qualifying games for the 1986 World Cup Finals on the 19th of May 1985, which ended that national team's journey for that World Cup tournament. After the game, frustrated spectators damaged a large number of properties to vent their great disappointment at the national team's failure (Liu, 1987). With more than 100 people arrested, the Agence France-Presse identified this riot as a milestone that the Chinese finally began integrating with the world through football hooliganism (Jin, 2012).

Fans' disappointment was caused by the Chinese national team's failure to meet the target of Chinese nationalism (Jiang & Bairner, 2024). That ideology was developed as a part of Chinese people's anti-imperialism thinking in the late 19th century, and it also adopted social Darwinism that highlights the conflicts among ethnic groups as eternal (Chang, 1971). As a result, Chinese nationalism guides people to empower their nation by conquering every challenge from outside China. Moreover, China's opening-up policy in 1978 helped people realise their underdeveloped status, but sport was one of the few channels that proved people's quality to survive in the permanent conflicts among human beings (Lu & Fan, 2014). Therefore, the national team's failure against Hong Kong destroyed people's confidence in their nation. By contrast, Zhixing Rong's performance exaggerated such confidence.

However, different from this fanatic expression in the 1980s, silent watching was a common phenomenon for Chinese spectators to watch games of their national football teams (Tan, 2004, p. 88):

> Chinese spectators have usually been quite introverted and restrained... From the 1950s to the 1970s, sports-related social disorder did not occur often, probably because many of the spectators at selected matches and events had been instructed by the government to attend.

This phenomenon was deeply associated with the Chinese political atmosphere that suppressed people's emotional expression at that time. In order to avoid left-wing political persecution during the Cultural Revolution, people got used to hiding their emotions and voicing themselves (Lu, 2004). In addition, because

Ping-pong Diplomacy helped the PRC acquire the United Nations' recognition of its legitimate representative of China, the Chinese government identified international sport events as vehicles to develop its international relationships (Wise, 2020). Events have sufficient political significance, which promoted the propaganda of 'Friendship first, competition second' (友谊第一, 比赛第二) in the 1970s (Fan & Xiong, 2002). Immersed in this political atmosphere, football spectators usually suppressed their passion during the games of their national football team (Tan, 2004).

After China released its opening-up policy, the declined influence of the Cultural Revolution allowed people in the 1980s to vent their emotions freely (Jiang & Bairner, 2019). Immersed in this relatively relaxed atmosphere, the Chinese people's experience of watching two World Cups – 1978 and 1982 – helped football lovers find the validity to freely develop their fandom for their national team under the influence of national identity, especially in an extreme way (Lu, 2018). Thus, although the 1985 fan riot indicated that the Chinese people's consistent interaction with the national team allowed the national identity to develop their fandom from a non-connection status in 1952 (Jiang & Bairner, 2024), politics is a more powerful factor affecting the relationship between fans and their football teams. It is also the key factor leading the Plan to cause high expectations from Chinese football fans for their national team despite its poor record in major football events.

BECOMING A FAN OF THE CHINESE LOCAL FOOTBALL CLUB

As discussed in the previous section, most Chinese people could not develop their fandom for their local football team under the effect of their local identities until the establishment of professional football leagues in 1994 (Jiang & Bairner, 2020, 2024). The Hongshankou Conference conducted by the CFA in 1992 determined the establishment of Chinese professional football leagues with regular seasonal fixtures (Jones, 2004, pp. 54–66). Because the seasonal games announce the football clubs bearing the name of places each week throughout the nation, these teams' local representative status is promoted to the Chinese people (Bale, 1993, 2000; Jiang & Bairner, 2024). Meanwhile, these professional leagues also employ home-and-away fixtures, which allows these citizens to interact consistently with the teams bearing the name of their local communities in their immediate places. Thus, people's desire to celebrate their local identities is activated, affecting the development of the fandom for local football clubs.

The Chinese people have a strong sense of belonging to their local communities because of China's relatively long diversification in their history than the unified one. During this history, kingdoms and regimes built fortresses to claim their independent authorities in different regions, limiting population mobility and forcing people to interact with their fixed local communities (Harrison, 1969; Levenson, 1967; Townsend, 1992). As a result, people have also generated strict and clear boundaries to define their community and others (Fei, 1992). People, then, can easily recognise their team's local representative status and show a huge interest in their local football clubs when they find these teams bearing the name of their place in the Chinese domestic football leagues (Jiang & Bairner, 2024). Hence, on 17th April 1994, when the first Chinese professional football league game was organised in Chengdu, the tickets for 40,000 spectators at the Chengdu Sports Centre stadium were all sold out (Jin, 2012).

However, most people's few connections to their local football clubs at the beginning of the professional leagues caused a barrier to developing their fandom immediately. After the Hongshankou Conference in 1992, local sports bureaus and state enterprises directed by the local governments jointly organised local professional football clubs (Amara et al., 2005). Nevertheless, the establishment of local football clubs excluded fans' participation, so most Chinese football fans' connections to their local teams remained weak at that time (Jiang & Bairner, 2020, 2024). For example, the average attendance in the home stadium of Shanghai Shenhua Football Club, the Hongkou stadium, only reached half at the beginning of the Chinese professional football leagues in 1994 (He et al., 1995). By contrast, the average attendance doubled the following season after the team entitled the 1994 Jia-A League (today's Super League, He & Li, 1996). Therefore, most Chinese football fans remained consumers who wished to enjoy high-quality games initially in relation to their local football clubs:

> Initially, like many other people, that I came to watch games of Guoan Football Club at the stadium was for fun. In the 1990s, we had watched many clubs' games from other countries, such as Italy's Serie A, so we really expected to enjoy live football. (A fan of Beijing Guoan Football Club, cited in Jiang & Bairner, 2020, p. 2085)

The constant interaction between people and local football clubs, according to Jiang and Bairner (2020), is the key factor that eliminates the barrier caused by people's few connections to their local teams. Alongside the interaction, people can accumulate memories of their local football clubs, thereby allowing their football clubs to have a symbolic status to represent themselves in their living circumstances. The typical memory is people's experience of witnessing 'key moments' in the history of their local football clubs, including those special games where their clubs win uneasily or beat their identified rivals (p. 2087).

After witnessing the key moments of their local clubs, people usually define themselves as 'active participants' on the pitch who developed shared experiences with their clubs (Hognestad, 2012, p. 25). In addition, people can also accumulate 'social interactions' memories of acquiring or strengthening their social relationships with other people while watching their local football clubs' games. These experiences can usually help them define the experience of watching games as an integral part of their life, which improves their affinity with their local football clubs (Jiang & Bairner, 2020, p. 2087).

Yet, memory accumulation requires a duration of interaction. Although no previous study can offer an accurate length of this duration for Chinese people to identify themselves as loyal fans, the team's competitive capability is essential in maintaining the fans' interactions with their teams (Han, 1998; Jiang & Bairner, 2024). Because all Chinese football fans were consumers who allowed their desire to seek the joys of triumphs to affect their interaction with their local football clubs initially, these teams with strong competitive capabilities could usually maintain the size of their audiences. By contrast, the number of audiences would decline if a team cannot achieve or maintain its outstanding records:

> However, as [Shanghai Shenhua Football Club] failed more and more times, especially the game that the team lost 1-6 to the Guangzhou Apollo Football Club, you could find that a large number of fans disappeared from the stadium. (A fan of Shanghai Shenhua Football Club, cited in Jiang & Bairner, 2020, p. 2086)

Local identity also affects Chinese people's process of identifying themselves as fans of their local football clubs (Jiang & Bairner, 2024). Chinese people have an established idea of thinking highly of their local communities. They have relied on agriculture to be self-reliant for four millennia (Ho, 1969; Lin, 1990), so their emotional attachment to their places is solid. Moreover, their freedom in the Chinese context is the tolerance provided by others in the same community, and it is associated with how familiar they are with their communities (Fei, 1992). As a result, maintaining their relationship with others is important to the Chinese people's social practice. Thinking highly of the importance of their local communities also strengthens fans' affinity with their local football clubs.

People's recognition of their teams' local symbolic status is the precondition allowing local identity to jointly work with their consistent interaction with their local football clubs and affect the development of their fandom (Jiang & Bairner, 2024). At the beginning of Chinese professional football leagues, fans usually acknowledged football clubs' local affinities by examining their connection to the local teams conducted by local sport bureaus. Most initial team players and coaches of local football clubs were from those officially recognised local teams because local sports bureaus remained the supreme power to organise these local football clubs (Li, 2014b). Furthermore, the set of seasonal games with home-and-away fixtures also helped those fans recognise their teams as local symbols. The weekly team announcement during the season allowed people from other regions to recognise their football teams' local representative status in the league (Bale, 1993, 2000; Jiang & Bairner, 2024). Influenced by this phenomenon, local fans' identification of their local teams could also be strengthened.

After this, the atmosphere of celebrating local identity established by these fans can continually affect new individual fans' recognition of their teams' local symbolic status because football fandom generates a collective identity among fans to guide them to behave specifically in particular circumstances produced (Ben Porat, 2014; Jiang & Bairner, 2024; MacClancy, 1996). In this respect, local identity is the dominant factor affecting Chinese people's fandom for their local football clubs.

CONCLUSION

The chapter provides essential information about the development of Chinese football fandom and its factors across different ages. The discussion is divided into two main parts based on the Chinese people's interpretations of football fans of different ages. Before the 1980s, the concept of football fans was identified by the relationship between people and this sport, and people who showed a strong passion for football were defined as fans (Lu & Chen, 1991). By contrast, this concept has been updated to focus on the relationship between people and their football teams after that age (Jiang & Bairner, 2019). Following this dichotomy, the article discusses how football lovers and football fans in the Chinese context develop their fondness and fandom for Chinese football teams at international and domestic levels. It, therefore, further contributes to the studies of Chinese football fandom by providing a comprehensive foundation. Moreover, it also presents a channel for people to observe how the change in Chinese society affects people's social lives, especially the process of those football fans' self-identification.

The basis for the Chinese people to develop their fondness for football is the desire to enjoy high-quality games. This inclination originated in the late 19th century and was closely associated with people's experiences of playing and watching football. Hence, the original football enthusiasts are divided into two groups: the Audience and the Player. The Player group was the primary force that cultivated and sustained the Chinese fondness for football during the initial and tumultuous period. However, with the rejection of professional football players' identity as football lovers after the establishment of the PRC in 1949 (Jin & Zhang, 2014), the remaining members of the Player group merged into the Audience group because they also exhibited a strong interest in elite teams. Eventually, the Audience group became the driving force behind the development of Chinese people's passion for football. Additionally, the peaceful circumstances provided by the PRC also contributed to this shift, as it allowed football lovers to consistently interact with their teams, thereby maintaining and intensifying their passion for football and football games.

The Chinese people's experience of watching two World Cups – 1978 and 1982 – heightened their interest in football. This outcome was strongly influenced by the limited number of family-used TVs and relatively poor TV programs in China between the 1970s and 1980s (Yue & Chen, 2010). As watching TV was a cherished form of entertainment, the World Cup emerged as the most splendid TV programme for people during that period. Consequently, football captured people's attention and became a medium for them to explore the world (Jiang & Bairner, 2019). In turn, individuals also developed a special emotion for this sport. Moreover, the experience of watching the two World Cups helped them find the legitimacy to express their emotions freely towards their teams, especially their national team (Lu, 2018). Since then, the foundation for fandom – a strong emotional bond with their teams – has already been established in the Chinese football context (Jiang & Bairner, 2019).

This chapter emphasises that Crawford's 'Career of the Sport Supporter' (2003) effectively elucidates the progression of Chinese people's fan identification with their national and local football teams due to the limited connections between individuals and these teams. It underscores people's national and regional identities as crucial factors in developing Chinese football fandom. The foundation for the influence of people's national and local identities on their fandom for Chinese football teams lies in the fact that these teams, at international and domestic levels, bear the names of Chinese people's national and local communities (Jiang & Bairner, 2024). Consequently, individuals can recognise them as representatives of those communities on the pitches.

Compared with the fandom for Chinese local football clubs, the fandom for the national team emerged earlier. Chinese people's fan identification with the national football team can be traced back to the 1980s when the team embarked on its World Cup journey (Jiang & Bairner, 2019). From the 1950s to the 1980s, the shift in people's attitude towards their national team indicates that consistent interaction with the team developed their fandom. Supporting the national football team stems from people's recognition that the team can be a vehicle for empowering the nation, exemplified by the Zhixing Style during the early days of the opening-up policy when people needed sports to prove their quality for survival in the global arena (Lu & Fan, 2014). Due to compulsory civic and moral education and the constitution, the Chinese have developed an idea of prioritising the national community over local communities (Jones, 1985; Maosen, 1990; Reed, 1995). Consequently, they hold the national interest in high regard, strengthening the effect of their national identity on their fandom for the national football team (Jiang & Bairner, 2024). Moreover, the experience of watching the World Cup contributed to fandom under the influence of people's national identity, providing them with the validity to support their teams on the pitch, especially fuelling the desire to celebrate their national team's success.

Until the establishment of Chinese professional football leagues in 1994, enthusiastic fans emerged to support their local football clubs. Celebrating local identity is the primary factor in developing local football clubs' fandom (Jiang & Bairner, 2020, 2024). The long-term local interaction in their local communities helps people develop solid local identities, thereby leading them to overstate the significance of local characteristics (Fei, 1992). Consequently, they present loyalty to their local football club if they recognise the team's local symbolic status. However, the few connections between people and their local football clubs at the initial stage caused a barrier for them to develop fandom (Jiang & Bairner, 2020). Hence, the local football clubs' secure and stable competitive capacities are the critical condition that attracts audiences for consistent interaction with them. Along with the growing memories of watching games, people's affinity with these teams can be developed. After this, the effect of local identity can be activated on fans' loyalty to their local teams.

The chapter displays how Chinese society at different ages affects people's fondness and fandom for Chinese football teams, providing insights into Chinese football lovers and fans. However, the chapter does not address how the new tendency in Chinese football and its wider society affects football fandom. The previous discussion indicates that fans' attitudes towards the national and local teams change if a new tendency in Chinese football and its wider society happens. For example, the failure of the Chinese naturalised football player project and the launched corruption of the CFA in 2023 might decline people's passion for this sport and fans' loyalty to their teams because it presented a negative image of Chinese football (Leahy & Waluszewski, 2023; Sullivan et al., 2022, pp. 1–14). In other words, a fluid view is necessary to study this community. Yet, the foundation knowledge offered by this chapter can be widely applicable to understanding Chinese football fandom. Furthermore, a channel is also provided to observe the interaction between Chinese society and people.

FIVE KEY READINGS

Crawford, G. (2003). The career of the sport supporter: The case of the Manchester Storm. *Sociology, 37*(2), 219–237.

Garry Crawford presents a theoretical framework detailing the induction and behavioural patterns of sports supporters along a social and moral career path. This framework is elucidated through a case study on supporters of the Manchester Storm ice hockey team. The central concept posits that the development of fandom is a consequence of ongoing interaction between individuals and their sports teams or athletes. While the article does not specifically focus on football, its insights can be broadly applied to understand the evolution of fandom for Chinese football.

Dong, J., & Mangan, J. A. (2001). Football in the new China: political statement, entrepreneurial enticement and patriotic passion. *Soccer & Society, 2*(3), 79–100.

In this article, Dong and Mangan display the development of football in the PRC based on both Chinese archival records and published documents. This article is a rare source about how modern football evolved in China from the establishment of the PRC to the age when China professionalised local football teams.

Jiang, K., & Bairner, A. (2020). Chinese football fandom and civic identities: a study of the fans of Shanghai Shenhua and Beijing Guoan. *Sport in Society, 23*(12), 2078–2098.

Studying fans of the Shanghai Shenhua Football Club and the Beijing Guoan Football Club, Jiang and Bairner present how Chinese people develop their fandom for their local football clubs and how the relationship between Chinese football fans and their clubs has contributed to the local symbolic status of clubs. As a rare source to explore the relationship between fans and football clubs in the Chinese context, this article also demonstrates a mode of football fandom development which has not been influenced to the same extent as in Europe and South America by family inheritance.

Jones, R. (2004). Football in the People's Republic of China. In J. Horne & W. Manzenreiter (Eds.), *Football Goes East: Business, culture and the people's game in East Asia* **(pp. 54–66). Routledge.**

In this chapter, Robin Jones presents Chinese football from the Chinese, Asian and interactional contexts. While introducing how football develops in China, he also highlights that the football culture in a specific community is a result of people's interaction with their environment. Moreover, this interaction is an ongoing process.

Tan, H. (2004). Football "Hooligans" and Football Supporters Culture in China. In W. Manzenreiter & J. Horne (Eds.), *Football Goes East: Business, culture and the people's game in China, Japan and South Korea* (pp. 87–101). Routledge.

Hua Tan's article presents Chinese football hooliganism as a distinctive character through its difference from the wider background of Chinese society and culture. As one of the early studies of Chinese football hooliganism and football supporters' culture in the Chinese context, it is a supplement to the research on global football hooliganism.

REFERENCES

Amara, M., Henry, I., Liang, J., & Uchiumi, K. (2005). The governance of professional soccer: Five case studies – Algeria, China, England, France and Japan. *European Journal of Sport Science, 5*(4), 189–206. https://doi.org/10.1080/17461390500344503

Bairner, A. (2001). *Sport, nationalism, and globalization: European and North American perspectives.* State University of New York Press.

Bale, J. (1993). *Sport, space and the city*. Routledge.

Bale, J. (2000). The changing face of football: Stadiums and communities. *Soccer and Society, 1*(1), 91–101. https://doi.org/10.1080/14660970008721251

Balfour, A. H., & Zheng, S. (2002). *Shanghai*. Wiley-Academy Press.

Ben Porat, A. (2010). Football fandom: A bounded identification. *Soccer and Society, 11*(3), 277–290. https://doi.org/10.1080/14660971003619594

Ben Porat, A. (2014). Who are we? My club? My people? My state? The dilemma of the Arab soccer fan in Israel. *International Review for the Sociology of Sport, 49*(2), 175–189. https://doi.org/10.1177/1012690212458506

Berki, R. N. (1975). *Socialism*. J.M. Dent & Sons Ltd.

Bian, Y. (1994). *Work and inequality in urban China*. State University of New York Press.

Bray, D. (2005). *Social space and governance in urban China: The danwei system from origins to reform*. Stanford University Press.

Chang, L. (2008). 行政区划与区域经济发展河南省案例分析 *[The administrative regionalization and the development of the regional economy case analysis of Henan province]*. Science Press.

Chang, C. C., Chen, C. C., & Chang, P. (2002). 晚清民國史 *[History from the Late Qing Dynasty to the Republic of China]*.

Chang, H. (1971). *Liang Chi-chao and intellectual transition in China, 1890-1907*. Harvard University Press.

Chen, Z., & Hu, Y. (2008). 复刻回忆: 世界杯与中国球迷的三十年 [World Cup memories since 1978]. *NetEase News*. http://news.163.com/special/00014DRO/worldcup78.html. Accessed on 5 January 2023.

Chinese Football Institution. (n.d.). 中国国家男子足球队比赛 *(1957) [The record of the Chinese national football team (1957)]*, Retrieved January 5, 2023 from http://www.cfadata.com/. Accessed on 5 January 2023.

Cho, Y. (2013). Introduction: Football in Asia. *Soccer and Society, 14*(5), 579–587. https://doi.org/10.1080/14660970.2013.792478

Connell, J. (2018). Globalisation, soft power, and the rise of football in China. *Geographical Research, 56*(1), 5–15. https://doi.org/10.1111/1745-5871.12249

Connor, N. (2015, December 23). China opens a shrine to mark its love affair with disgraced former FIFA president Sepp Blatter. *The Telegraph*. https://www.telegraph.co.uk/sport/football/sepp-blatter/12065899/China-opens-a-shrine-to-mark-its-love-affair-with-disgraced-former-Fifa-president-Sepp-Blatter.html

Crawford, G. (2003). The career of the sport supporter: The case of the Manchester Storm. *Sociology, 37*(2), 219–237. https://doi.org/10.1177/0038038503037002001

Ding, X. (2009). The socialist market economy: China and the world. *Science & Society*, *73*(2), 235–241. https://doi.org/10.1521/siso.2009.73.2.235

Dixon, K. (2013). Learning the game: Football fandom culture and the origins of practice. *International Review for the Sociology of Sport*, *48*(3), 334–348. https://doi.org/10.1177/1012690212441157

Dixon, K. (2016). Sports fandom. In B. Houlihan & D. Malcolm (Eds.), *Sport and society: A student introduction* (3rd ed., pp. 438–459). Sage.

Dong, J., & Mangan, J. A. (2001). Football in the new China: Political statement, entrepreneurial enticement and patriotic passion. *Soccer and Society*, *2*(3), 79–100. https://doi.org/10.1080/714004853

Donnelly, P. (1981). Toward a definition of sport subcultures. In M. Hart & S. Birrell (Eds.), *Sport in the sociocultural process* (3rd ed., pp. 565–588). William C.

Duara, P. (1996). *Rescuing history from the nation: Questioning narratives of modern China*. University of Chicago Press.

Fan, L., Li, Y., Wang, Z., & Tan, F. (2001). 中国足球后备人才培养历史回顾与探讨. [Review and discussion on the history of the football talent pool in China]. *Journal of Capital University of Physical Education and Sports*, *13*(4), 72–75. https://doi.org/10.3969/j.issn.1009-783X.2001.04.021

Fan, H., & Xiong, X. (2002). Communist China: Sport, politics and diplomacy. *International Journal of the History of Sport*, *19*(2–3), 319–342. https://doi.org/10.1080/714001751

Fei, X. (1992). In G. G. Hamilton & W. Zheng (Eds.), *From the soil: The foundations of Chinese society*. University of California Press.

FIFA.com. (2004, October 19). The cradle of football. *Fédération Internationale de Football Association*. https://www.fifa.com/news/the-cradle-football-94490

Garrett, S. S. (1970). *Social reformers in urban China: The Chinese YMCA, 1895-1926*. Harvard University Press.

Goldblatt, D. (2007). *The ball is round: A global history of football*. Penguin.

Han, Y. (1998). 中国足球内幕 *[Insight of Chinese professional football clubs]*. China City Press.

Harrison, J. P. (1969). *Modern Chinese nationalism*. Hunter College of the City University of New York.

He, Z., & Li, Y. (1996). 95 全国足球甲 A 联赛上海赛区观众人数剧增的原因探析 [An analysis of the dramatic increase in the number of spectators in the Shanghai area in 1995 Jia-A League season]. *Journal of Shanghai University of Sport*, *20*(2), 11–16. CNKI:SUN:STYB.0.1996-02-003

He, Z., Li, Y., Gong, X., & Cui, S. (1995). 对增加上海市足球比赛现场观众人数的对策研究 [Strategy to increase the number of audiences in Shanghai football competition sites]. *Journal of Shanghai Physical Education Institute*, *S2*, 42–15. http://www.cnki.com.cn/Article/CJFDTotal-STYB1995S2013.htm

Hebdige, D. (1979). *Subculture: The meaning of style*. Routledge.

Ho, P. (1969). The loess and the origin of Chinese agriculture. *The American Historical Review*, *75*(1), 1–36. https://doi.org/10.1086/ahr/75.1.1

Hognestad, H. K. (2012). What is a football fan? In R. Krøvel & T. Roksvold (Eds.), *We love to hate each other: Mediated football fan* (pp. 25–44).

Homburg, H. (2006). FIFA and the "Chinese question", 1954–1980: An exercise of statutes. *Historical Social Research/Historische Sozialforschung*, *69*–87. https://doi.org/10.12759/hsr.31.2006.1.69-72

Jiang, K., & Bairner, A. (2019). Paolo Rossi and the origins of football fandom in China. *Asia Dialogue*. https://theasiadialogue.com/2019/04/08/paolo-rossi-and-all-that-reflections-on-the-origins-of-football-fandom-in-china/

Jiang, K., & Bairner, A. (2020). Chinese football fandom and civic identities: A study of the fans of Shanghai Shenhua and Beijing Guoan. *Sport in Society*, *23*(12), 2078–2098. https://doi.org/10.1080/17430437.2020.1835859

Jiang, K., & Bairner, A. (2024). *Becoming a Chinese football fan: An examination of the influence of national and local identities on the development of Chinese football fandom*. Soccer & Society.

Jin, S. (2012). 当代北京足球史话. Contemporary China Publishing House. [The Contemporary History of Beijing Football].

Jin, S., & Zhang, S. (2014). 咱京城球迷那些事儿 *[Stories of our Beijing football fans]*. Beijing Yanshan Publication.

Jones, W. C. (1985). The constitution of the People's Republic of China. *Washington University Law Review*, *63*(4), 707–735. https://openscholarship.wustl.edu/law_lawreview/vol63/iss4/4

Jones, R. (2004). Football in the People's Republic of China. In J. Horne & W. Manzenreiter (Eds.), *Football goes east: Business, culture and the people's game in East Asia*. Routledge.

Junio, E. F. L., & Rodrigues, C. (2017). The Chinese football development plan: Soft power and national identity. *Holos*, *5*, 114–124. https://doi.org/10.15628/holos.2017.5750

Leahy, J., & Waluszewski, K. (2023, February 15). China launches corruption probe into football association chief. *Financial Times*. https://www.ft.com/content/5df6157d-05e3-4005-810b-59c5e7013923

Levenson, J. R. (1967). *Liang Chi-chao and the mind of modern China* (Vol. 34). University of California Press.

Li, H. (1993). 中国单位现象与城市社区的整合机制 [China's Danwei phenomenon and the mechanisms of conformity in urban communities]. *Sociology Research*, *5*, 23–32. CNKI:SUN:SHXJ.0.1993-05-003

Li, E. (2006). 宋世雄解说世界杯回忆 [Memories of Shixiong song's commentary on World Cup]. *CCTV*. http://www.cctv.com/tvguide/20060615/102301.shtml. Accessed on 5 January 2023.

Li, M. (2014a). Shixiong Song: There was no culture for the Chinese to watch football, even the World Cup broadcasting right was jointly purchased. *Sohu Sport*. http://sports.sohu.com/20140527/n400109596.shtml. Accessed on 5 January 2023.

Li, Y. (Ed.). (2014b). 上海足球半世纪 *(1949–1999)* *[The half century of Shanghai football: 1949–1999]*. Shanghai Educational Publishing House.

Li, K., Zhang, X., Bai, J., & Xu, M. (Eds.). (2018). 津门足坛双百颂 *[Football stories in Tianjin]*. Tianjin Renmin Press.

Lin, J. Y. (1990). Collectivization and China's agricultural crisis in 1959–1961. *Journal of Political Economy*, *98*(6), 1228–1252. https://doi.org/10.1086/261732

Liu, X. (1987). *5.19 长镜头 [The insight into the fan riot on May 19th, 1985]*. Sichuan Literature and Art Publishing House.

Lu, X. (2004). *Rhetoric of the Chinese cultural revolution: The impact on Chinese thought*. University of South Carolina Press.

Lu, Y. (2018). 中国人的足球思维: 作为视觉艺术的足球 [Football thinking of Chinese people: Football as a visual art]. *Journal of Hebei Sport University*, *32*(6), 1–7. https://doi.org/10.3969/j.issn.1008-3596.2018.06.001

Lu, Y., & Chen, E. (1991). 论球迷 [On fandom]. In Z. Wang (Ed.), 球迷之友 *[The friend of fans]* (pp. 1–24). Beijing Sport University Press.

Lu, Z., & Fan, H. (2014). *Sport and nationalism in China*. Routledge.

Luo, Z. (2013). 乱世潜流: 民族主义与民国政治 *[Underflow in chaos China: Nationalism and the politics of the Republic of China]*. China Renmin University Press.

Luo, X. (2018). 万物天缘: 球迷罗西自传 *[The Autobiography of fan Luo Xi]*. People's Literature Publishing House.

Lüthi, L. M. (2010). *The Sino-Soviet split: Cold War in the communist world*. Princeton University Press.

MacClancy, J. (1996). Sport, identity and ethnicity. In J. MacClancy (Ed.), *Sport, identity and ethnicity* (pp. 1–20). Berg.

MacMillan, M. (2008). *Nixon and Mao: The week that changed the world*. Random House Incorporated.

Maosen, L. (1990). Moral education in the People's Republic of China. *Journal of Moral Education*, *19*(3), 159–171. https://doi.org/10.1080/0305724900190302

Morris, A. D. (2004). *Marrow of the nation: A history of sport and physical culture in Republican China* (Vol. 10). University of California Press.

Peng, Q., Skinner, J., & Houlihan, B. (2019). An analysis of the Chinese football reform of 2015: Why then and not earlier? *International Journal of Sport Policy and Politics*, *11*(1), 1–18. https://doi.org/10.1080/19406940.2018.1536075

Qi, G. (2022, July 1). 1978年世界杯转播猜想 [The conjecture of the 1978 World Cup broadcast]. *Oriental Sports Daily*. https://paper.xinmin.cn/html/dfsports/2022-07-01/A02/38016.html

Reed, G. G. (1995). Moral/political education in the People's Republic of China: Learning through role models. *Journal of Moral Education*, *24*(2), 99–111. https://doi.org/10.1080/0305724950240201

Robinson, T. W. (1972). The Sino-Soviet border dispute: Background, development, and the March 1969 clashes. *American Political Science Review*, *66*(4), 1175–1202. https://doi.org/10.2307/1957173

Shen, W., Bao, Y., Zhang, Z., & Chen, Y. (Eds.). (1995), 中国足球的摇篮: 上海足球运动半世纪 (1896–1949) [*Chinese football cradle: A half-century Shanghai football (1896–1949)*]. Shanghai Cultural Publication.

Shi, Y. (2004). 球场观众暴力的理论阐释和因素分析 [The theoretical explanation and analysis of the riots of stadium spectators]. *Journal of Xi'an Institute of Physical Education*, *21*(1). https://doi.org/10.3969/j.issn.1001-747X.2004.01.002

Song, K., & Lu, Y. (1997). 国内外球迷现象研究 (综述) [Research on ball game fan phenomena in China and abroad]. *Journal of Beijing Sport University*, *20*(4), 5–10. CNKI:SUN:BJTD.0.1997-04-001.

Speak, M. (1999). China in the modern world: 1840–1949. In J. Riordan & R. E. Jones (Eds.), *Sport and physical education in China* (pp. 70–89). E & FN Spon.

State Council of the PRC. (2014). 国务院关于加快发展体育产业促进体育消费的若干意见 [*Opinion on accelerating the development of sport industry and promoting sports consumption*] (Report No. 46). http://www.gov.cn/zhengce/content/2014-10/20/content_9152.htm

State Council of the PRC. (2015). 国务院办公厅关于印发中国足球改革发展总体方案的通知 [Notice on the overall plan of Chinese football reform and development] (Report No. 11). http://www.gov.cn/zhengce/content/2015-03/16/content_9537.htm

Sugden, J., & Tomlinson, A. (1998). Power and resistance in the governance of world football: Theorizing FIFA's transnational impact. *Journal of Sport & Social Issues*, *22*(3), 299–316. https://doi.org/10.1177/019372398022003005

Sullivan, J., Ross, T., & Wu, C. (2022). *Representing the nation: Exploring attitudes towards naturalized foreign football players in China*. Soccer & Society. https://doi.org/10.1080/14660970.2022.2069100

Tan, H. (2004). Football "hooligans" and football supporters culture in China. In W. Manzenreiter & J. Horne (Eds.), *Football goes east: Business, culture and the people's game in China, Japan and South Korea* (pp. 87–101). Routledge.

Tan, T. C., Huang, H. C., Bairner, A., & Chen, Y. W. (2016). Xi Jin-Ping's World Cup dreams: From a major sports country to a world sports power. *International Journal of the History of Sport*, *33*(12), 1449–1465. https://doi.org/10.1080/09523367.2016.1243103

Tang, L. (2004). 中国吃 [*Chinese food*]. Guangxi Normal University Press.

Taylor, I. (1971). Soccer consciousness and soccer hooliganism. In S. Cohen (Ed.), *Images of deviance* (pp. 134–164). Pelican.

Tian, E., & Wise, N. (2020). An Atlantic divide? Mapping the knowledge domain of European and North American based sociology of sport, 2008–2018. *International Review for the Sociology of Sport*, *55*(8), 1029–1055.

Townsend, J. (1992). Chinese nationalism. *The Australian Journal of Chinese Affairs*, *27*(4), 97–130. https://doi.org/10.2307/2950028

Wang, Y. (2016). 中国看世界: 刻骨铭心的直播史 [China's view of the world: An unforgettable live broadcasting history]. *Sohu*. https://www.sohu.com/a/114611655_162197. Accessed on 5 January 2023.

Wise, N. (2020). Eventful futures and triple bottom line impacts: BRICS, image regeneration and competitiveness. *Journal of Place Management and Development*, *13*(1), 89–100.

Wise, N., & Maguire, K. (Eds.). (2022), *A research agenda for event impacts*. Edward Elgar.

Yan, D. (2006). 盘点 CCTV 足球报道的历史与现状 [The history of football reports and broadcastings on the China Central Television]. *Broadcasting Realm*, *3*, 45–49. http://www.cnki.com.cn/Article/CJFDTotal-STJZ200603018.htm

Yang, Y. (2016). 从'天下主义','民族国家'到'新天下主义' – 中国民族主义特质流衍论略 [From Tianxialism, nation state to new Tianxialism – The discussion of the nature of Chinese nationalism]. *Journal of the History of Political Thought*, (02), 21–40. https://doi.org/10.3969/j.issn.1674-8662.2016.02.002

Ying, Y. (2019). 足球经济学 *[Football economics]*. Scientific Research Publishing.

Yue, M., & Chen, Q. (2010). 中国电视新闻 50 年发展史论略 [The history of Chinese TV programmes in the past 50 years]. *Southeast communication*, *3*, 76–78. https://doi.org/10.3969/j.issn.1672-9579.2010.03.025

Zagoria, D. S. (2015). *Sino-Soviet Conflict, 1956–1961*. Princeton University Press.

Zhang, K. (1985). 辛亥革命与近代社会 *[The 1911 Revolution and the modern Chinese society]*. Tianjin Renmin Press.

Zhang, C. (2012). 近代中国知识分子的民族主义思想研究 *[The study of nationalism of the modern Chinese intellectuals]*. China Minzu University Press.

Zhang, Y. (2016). History and future of the National College Entrance Exam (NCEE) in China. In Y. Zhang (Ed.), *National College Entrance Exam in China* (pp. 1–15). Springer.

Zhu, Y. (2001). 辛亥革命与近代中国社会变迁 *[The 1911 Revolution and the change of Chinese society]*. Central China Normal University Press.

CHAPTER 5

THE COMMERCIALISATION OF CHINESE PROFESSIONAL FOOTBALL: TRANSITION AND EVOLUTION

Yang Ma

University of Bayreuth, Germany

ABSTRACT

The chapter articulates the transition to and evolution of the commercialisation of Chinese professional football. It is periodised based on major turning points. The research yielded two major findings. First, there exists a distinct 'Chinese way' of commercialising football. However, it does not indicate that Chinese football doggedly avoided the Western governance model. For the club governance, Chinese football authorities set about recommending privately operated enterprises, large and medium-sized state-owned enterprises. Second, the commercialisation transitions of professional football in China were triggered by exogenous policy shifts, rather than endogenous changes in market structures, resulting in higher horizontal financial fragility than is associated with the commercialisation model adopted in more developed Western markets. The applicability to voluntary football clubs is assessed as well.

Keywords: China; Soccer; commercialisation; professional football; sport governance

INTRODUCTION

Under the great pressure of the global economic downturn, the People's Republic of China (PRC) has sought to undergo a complete transformation from manufacturing-led model to service-centred one (Liu et al., 2017; Sullivan et al.,

2019). The sport industry has been affirmed as a new pillar (Junior & Rodrigues, 2019; Liu, 2017, p. 3; Zheng, Chen, et al., 2019). Obviously, the recent developments in sport policy are interrelated to economic policy and try to make economic gains from privately operated enterprises and greater commercialisation. This connection is labelled as a 'policy mix' and is similar to the German approach to sport governance (Kurscheidt & Deitersen-Wieber, 2011; Ma & Kurscheidt, 2019a). Major sporting events are playing an important role in this development and transformation to lend to greater competitiveness (Wise, 2020). Notably, echoing the point view of Tan et al. (2016), football is always a barometer of sport industry and is a main focus area is sociology of sport research (Tian & Wise, 2020).

Despite the rapid commercialisation growth of Chinese football, this topic is rarely mentioned inside academia. Fragmented descriptions are limited to a certain and individual commercialisation phases of Chinese football (Gerrard, 2014; Hong & Zhouxiang, 2013; Jinxia & Mangan, 2001). For instance, the seminal work of Hong and Zhouxiang (2013) remains the starting point for any study of commercialisation in and around Chinese professional football from 1993 to 2013. Newspapers are replete with details of the penetration of the commercialisation elements that have come to characterise professional football in China, but few of these articles contain any type of scholarly critique. To date, the only two volumes to solely target the commercialisation of sport and provide scholarly analyses are *Power Play* (Lawrence & Rowe, 1986) and *The Commercialisation of Sport* (Slack, 2004). Unfortunately, neither incorporate any Chinese cases or examples.

This chapter seeks to fill a gap in this literature by first periodising the evolution of the commercialisation of Chinese football. It is always difficult to attempt a full-scale undertaking of study on the evolution of the commercialisation of football, and Chinese professional football is no exception. Concerns can be raised not only about producing an ambiguous analysis but also about missing key phases. To minimise criticism of the latter type and to present a relatively complete commercialisation evolution, phases are periodised based on turning points. Hence, four phases are demarcated: the pre-communist era, the planned economy era, the reforms and opening-up era and Xi's era. Notably, this periodisation also accords with the suggestions of Sullivan et al. (2019, p. 494) and Liang (2014, 2017).

The understanding of 'commercialisation' within this research is rooted in the generalised definition proposed by Ma and Kurscheidt (2022); that is, commercialisation may be interpreted as a transformation in the systems of resource distribution towards greater adoption of the market logic. The precise and defining characteristics of each era and the key transition points are identified. This is followed by a comprehensive interpretation of the commercialisation of Chinese football. The article concludes with an evaluation of the applicability of voluntary football clubs in the Chinese context.

THE PRE-COMMUNIST ERA: WESTERNISATION OF FOOTBALL

The Opium War, which started in 1840, was widely recognized as an important watershed in Chinese history (Mangan & Fan, 2003, p. 170). Rulers of the poor, weak and underdeveloped China of the 19th and early 20th centuries were eager to reform the outdated social, economic and political systems. As indicated by Trott (2017), the Qing government (last dynasty) opted for the wholesale replacement of the old institutions with modern ones inspired by Western models. The Westernisation process covered various domains. For instance, in the political domain, the imperial boards were replaced with modern-style line ministries.

Modern sport was perceived to be the best instrument to cultivate citizens for a new China through enhancing physical strength, increasing intelligence and elevating morality (Kang, 2005). By contrast, most traditional Chinese sports were criticised because of the lack of competitive elements. Historically, *Chuju*, traditional Chinese football, was an aggressive game with original competitive spirit and forms (Baker et al., 1993; Mangan & Fan, 2003). To exploit its high competitiveness, during the Han (206 BC–220 AD) and Tang (618 AD–907 AD) dynasties, *Chuju* was employed to train soldiers (Mangan & Fan, 2003). However, under the long-standing influence of Confucian ethics, *Chuju* gradually lost its competitive attribute and declined into a highly ritualised '*Chuju* ceremony' (Mangan & Fan, 2003). With the arrival of modern sport as a representative of Western culture, traditional Chinese sports including *Chuju* were neglected and excluded from the curricula of modern schools (Mangan & Fan, 2003).

In the pre-Communist era, China embarked on the process of Westernising football when the sport was imported to Hong Kong by the Britons after the Opium War (Liang, 2017). In 1897, football matches were first organised by the Britons in Hong Kong (Mangan & Fan, 2003). In 1908, the first Chinese non-governmental football association was established in Hong Kong (Mangan & Fan, 2003). In 1915, five non-governmental regional sport associations (North, South, East, West and Central) were founded (Mangan & Fan, 2003).

Every regional sport association took charge of the sporting issues of several provinces. To organise and supervise national and international sporting competitions, another non-governmental national sport organisation, namely, the *China National Amateur Athletic Federation*, was created in Nanjing, the then capital of the Nationalist Government in China (Mangan & Fan, 2003). This organisation was the official representative in all international sport organisations including the International Olympic Committee (IOC) (Mangan & Fan, 2003). Moreover, football was incorporated into the school curriculum (Mangan & Fan, 2003). Football matches between college teams gradually became regular football events (Mangan & Fan, 2003).

In the pre-Communist era, led by the non-governmental sport associations, football clubs adopted a community-based structure with amateur status (Liang, 2017). Local amateur football leagues were organised regularly during this period (Liang, 2017). The supporters of local football clubs were mainly college students and residents (Liang, 2017). Notably, the national football team of the Republic of China was so strong that its dominance of the now-defunct Far Eastern Games was never challenged between 1915 and 1934 (Sullivan et al., 2019).

THE PLANNED ECONOMY ERA: GOVERNMENT-OWNED WORK UNION

Political leaders perceived football as a symbol of modernity that provided an international platform on which the ideological supremacy of the Communist system could be manifested (Connell, 2018; Fei et al., 1992; Jinxia & Mangan, 2001, p. 83). In the planned economy era, Chairman Mao Zedong's brand of revolutionary politics and social mobilisation sought to transform the material conditions of peasants and the proto-working class under the Soviet model of industrialisation (Lin & Blanchard, 2017). The PRC's desire for a Soviet-style governance structure was also reflected in the sports domain. As argued by Zheng (2015), in the planned economy era, the governance structure of PRC's sport was largely the outcome of the transfer of the Soviet model.

In 1952, imitating the States Sports Ministry in the Soviet Union, a governmental ministry, namely, the State Physical Education and Sport Commission (SPESC), was established, which signalled the salient status of sport as an official governmental responsibility (Fan, 2008, p. 28). In 1956, 'The Competitive Sports System of the PRC' was enacted, in which 43 sports or disciplines including football were officially affirmed as competitive sport and full-time teams were set up at the provincial and national levels (Fan, 2008). Liang (2014, p. 431) underlined that during the planned economy era, there was no signal of the emergence of professionalisation. Consistent with Hu's (2019) insight, the more accurate term is quoted as 'Zhuanye athletes' (i.e. sporting civil servants rather than professional athletes). Against this backdrop, the non-governmental sport associations and local football clubs that emerged in the pre-Communist era with a community-based structure were thoroughly disbanded (Liang, 2017). Under the planned economy, sport was centralised and solely controlled and governed by governmental agencies (Fan, 2008).

The political elite of the PRC thoroughly understood that spectacular sporting results would clearly be a prerequisite to realise non-sporting objectives injected into sport. The PRC long dreamt of becoming a football power, resembling what was achieved by the predecessor Republic of China regime in the pre-Communist era (Sullivan et al., 2019). Despite the damage to the centralised elite sport system inflicted by the catastrophic Great Lead Forward and Cultural Revolution, football was still incorporated into the 10 key sports or disciplines selected from the previous 43 sports or disciplines (Fan, 2008).

Under this centralised elite sport system, which adheres to a top-down logic, work-union structured provincial elite teams were initiated (Liang, 2017). Financing for the provincial football teams did not rely on the local communities (Liang, 2017). Specifically, provincial football players and coaches were offered permanent contracts by corresponding Provincial Sports Bureaus (PSBs) (Hong

& Zhouxiang, 2013; Liang, 2017). In the planned economy era, the 'Zhuanye' football teams were perceived to be government-owned work unions that did not differ from work unions in other industries (Liang, 2017). It is noteworthy that in the planned economy era, in contradiction to the dominance of socialism and the central role of proletariats, any form of commercialisation of football was closely associated with 'capitalist disease', which was strongly castigated by the PRC (Grix et al., 2019; Hong, 1997). Therefore, in the planned economy era, there was no room for football broadcasting, football sponsors and football ticket sales (Hong, 1997).

THE REFORMS AND OPENING-UP ERA: RESTRICTED CAPITALISM

In 1979, the Nagoya Resolution was passed by the IOC (Zheng et al., 2018), and the PRC's memberships in the IOC and other organisations of the international sporting community were reinstated (Tan & Bairner, 2010). Since then, the PRC has been committed to its catch-up journey in the world of elite sport and concomitantly the pursuit of Olympic (gold) medal success at the Summer Olympics was officially prioritised with the issuance of the 'Olympic Strategy' in 1985 (Hu & Henry, 2017). However, in an attempt to promote PRC's medal achievement, government authorities strategically centred efforts on selected sports or disciplines. The importance of 'heavy cost of investment' sports or disciplines was intentionally compromised. Against this backdrop, the development of many collective ball sports has been held up (Zheng & Chen, 2016, p. 159).

As the recognised 'strong-hold of Western countries' (Dubal, 2010; Zheng et al., 2018, p. 52), football was compelled to choose an alternative approach for survival in China (Liang, 2017, p. 4). In 1978, the PRC started to conduct reform projects on a national scale, gaining a harmonious blend of Chinese economy and global economy (Yu et al., 2017, p. 715). Numerous protectionist policies were abrogated (Yu et al., 2017), and the commercialisation elements finally shed the notorious label 'capitalist disease'. Chinese football was 'encouraged' to conform to the market-led principle. The implied message of the word 'encourage' is that the traditional centralised elite sport system remained stable (Zheng, Lau, et al., 2019) while the governance structure of football was pushed into the forefront of reform. The view is also shared by Zheng (2015), who found the centralised sport governance structure of most Olympic sports largely remains intact in the reforms and opening-up era. Football was expected to support itself by its own labour and relieve the financial burden borne by the sport authorities, which shouldered the responsibility for implementing the 'Olympic Strategy' efficiently and perfectly (Brownell, 2008; Liang, 2017).

Interestingly, Deng Xiaoping's campaign of 'getting rich first' was clearly targeted at major socio-economic groups, including private enterprise owners, workers and managers at state-owned enterprises, workers employed in the private sector, professionals, students and farmers (see Zheng, 2017). Chinese football could not be classified into any of the aforementioned categories. More importantly, concerning 'getting rich first', while previously financially backed by the governmental agencies, the reforms and opening-up initiative managed to lift Chinese football out of 'affluence' instead.

Arguably, the harsh reality was that, in the reforms and opening-up era, Chinese football was immune to large-scale reform initiatives both at the league and club levels (Zheng, 2017). At the league level, the not-so-hidden governmental hand remained. Although the professional football league, namely, Jia-A League, was established in 1992 and had its inaugural season in 1994, the Chinese Football Association (CFA), remained a governmental entity directly supervised and monitored by the General Administration of Sport (GAS) (Peng et al., 2019; Zheng, 2017), the successor of the SPESC. Moreover, in the reforms and opening-up period, at the club level, the professional football clubs were managed by PSBs or collectively governed by PSBs and privately operated or state-owned enterprises (Amara et al., 2005). The PSBs continued to exercise pressure on the daily operation of professional football clubs (Hong & Zhouxiang, 2013). With regard to the state-owned enterprises, Amara et al. (2005) pointed out that soft loans by state-owned enterprises can be equated with public subsidy. Hence, in the reforms and opening-up period, the commercialisation process of professional football in China can be interpreted as 'restricted capitalism' (Amara et al., 2005).

XI'S ERA: THE WESTERNISATION OF FOOTBALL AGAIN?

Confronted with the economic downward pressure, the PRC re-examined its traditional economic policy, which depended heavily on the manufacturing industry and massive exportation (Sullivan, 2018). The sport industry has been affirmed as a new pillar (Liu et al., 2017, p. 3; Zheng, Chen, et al., 2019). Obviously, the recent developments in sport policy are interrelated to economic policy and try to make economic gains from privately operated enterprises and greater commercialisation (Liu et al., 2019). Compared to the aforementioned reforms and opening-up era, Chinese football clubs have rid themselves of the *not-so-hidden* governmental control from PSBs and have been permitted and acquired by state-owned or privately operated enterprises, primarily in the real-estate field (Giulianotti, 2002, 2015; Sullivan et al., 2019, p. 506). Obviously, at the club level, the 'capitalism' attribute has been deepened with the introduction of privately operated enterprises, large and medium-sized state-owned enterprises (Ma & Kurscheidt, 2019b, p. 14; Yu et al., 2017, p. 719).

A COMPREHENSIVE INTERPRETATION OF THE COMMERCIALISATION OF PROFESSIONAL FOOTBALL IN CHINA

The first commercialisation transition of professional football in China was identified as occurring during the transition from the planned economy era to the reforms and opening-up era. Resonating with the argument of Ma (2020), this first transition to commercialisation adheres to a politically-led logic. It is worth noting that the logic implies that the first-wave commercialisation was triggered by an exogenous policy prioritisation towards 'low investment and high return' sports or disciplines rather than an endogenous change in market structures. The second commercialisation transition of professional football in China took place during the transformation from the reforms and opening-up era to Xi's authoritarian era. Propelled by the policy rhetoric of positioning professional football as a potential wealth generator in the service-led industry, the second-wave commercialisation witnessed incremental reform at the club-governance level. The defining characteristic of the latest era is the 'Footballisation of China'. Xi's three wishes concerning Chinese football profoundly have incentivised the political use of modern football. It is arguable that similar to the first transition, the second commercialisation transition was meant to be driven by the politically-led logic. Undoubtedly, within the Chinese context, throughout the commercialisation process of professional football, there is no sign of an endogenous change in market structures.

The commercialisation of professional football in China also reflects the dynamic process of Chinese elite sport governance. The first-wave commercialisation of Chinese professional football accompanied the initial divergence of Chinese elite sport governance into two separate logics, the centralised model of sport governance for Chinese Olympic elite sport and the more liberal and commercialised model of professional football in China (Ma, 2020). The second-wave commercialisation was expected to accentuate the divergence of the aforementioned two logics. However, the two logics have not continued to diverge. Chinese football authorities are believed to employ a gradualist approach to institutional reform, which greatly serves commercialisation. To date, only incremental reform at the club-governance level has been fulfiled (Liu & Schwarz, 2020; Ma & Kurscheidt, 2019a).

CONCLUSIONS

Following politically-led logic, the distinct 'Chinese way' of commercialising football has already experienced two transitions during the process. For the first transition, the not-so-hidden governmental hand took charge of professional football in China at both the club- and league-governance levels. In the passing decades, successive presidents of the CFA have consistently promised to provide a better governance framework and more effective government support. It is arguable that compared with the wholesale institutional replacements in Qing's era, a gradualist approach was employed by the CFA. Notably, in Xi's era, the development of football has been advanced to the national level, and this second transition witnessed the initial achievement of incremental reform. Following Guangzhou Evergrande, most professional clubs in China have been fully acquired by private enterprises. However, in light of the fact that the commercialisation transitions of professional football in China were mainly triggered by exogenous policy shifts, rather than endogenous change in market structures, it can be expected that the Chinese Super League (CSL) clubs will be more fragile than their Western counterparts (Franck, 2011).

To date, the commercialisation of professional football has not improved the performance of Chinese national football team directly and effectively. The Chinese football authorities do realize that Chinese football is at risk in light of the deficiency of grassroots support. In the football history of most European countries, voluntary football clubs have been the foundation upon which both the popularity and commercialisation of football is based. However, in the case of the Chinese context, it is impossible for the Chinese Communist Party (CCP) to be tolerant of the large-scale emergence of the voluntary football clubs. Voluntary football clubs were positioned as the cornerstones of democracy, teaching members democratic ways of acting (Ma, 2020). The 'bottom-up' approach that pumps money into voluntary football clubs and enables football to be a sport that is truly accessible for the masses to partake in is unlikely to be employed by the Chinese football authorities. It would be very difficult for the CCP to tolerate football evolving into a forum for anti-state mobilisation, as it has in other emerging states, such as Brazil, despite sharing similar social conditions such as inequality and corruption (Ma, 2020). Voluntary sport clubs do exist in the PRC. However, all of them must be registered in the local sports bureau and accept any form of monitoring and guidance. Despite the fog of gloom sitting over the country, Chinese football authorities seek to determine a developmental approach with Chinese characteristics.

Finally, it is worth mentioning that in Xi's era, Chinese women's football embraces the marvellous opportunity to steer for greater commercialisation under the context of policy mix of sport and economic policy. The lack of studies on Chinese women's football in international academia can be interpreted from at least two perspectives. First, starting at the Red Mountain Valley conference held in 1992 and continuing to the present, Chinese football has embarked on the path of a 29-year reform process. However, the reform results are unsatisfying because the CSL, the top-tiered professional football division, remains under the full control of a governmental organisation, namely, the CFA. Regarding the PRC, which features a one-party political system, organisational change from the old template to the new template will be absolutely accelerated through the intervention of the central government. Hence, the advent of the current political backing, especially from President Xi Jin-Ping, stimulates the resumption of time-consuming football reform. Such a revolutionary reform draws academic attention directly to the supply side (on the league and/club level) and policy issues. Second, it is not always feasible for international researchers to conduct quantitative or qualitative studies targeted at Chinese women's football. Extra resources are inevitably required, such as a Chinese version of questionnaires and a Chinese version of the semi-structured interview protocol. In addition, most of the information available to Chinese women's football has seldom been reported on by any foreign media. Thus, it is understandable that many of the studies on women football are Western-biased, and very little research has included samples from non-Western societies.

FIVE KEY READINGS

Chen, S., & Henry, I. (2016). Evaluating the London 2012 games' impact on sport participation in a non-hosting region: A practical application of realist evaluation. *Leisure Studies, 5,* 686–707. https://doi.org/10.1080/02614367.2015.1040827

Chen Shushu and Ian Henry deal with the formal evaluation of policy implementation where assertions of potential policy impact are based on untested assumptions. Drawing support from a Realist Evaluation framework, this study shows that the programme represented a positive approach to fostering regular engagement with sport and physical activities.

Peng, Q., Chen, S., Li, J., Houlihan, B., & Scelles, N. (2023). The new hope of Chinese football? Youth football reforms and policy conflicts in the implementation process. *European Sport Management Quarterly, 6,* 1928–1950. https://doi.org/10.1080/16184742.2022.2083649

In this paper, Peng et al. draw attention to the implementation of youth football policies in China following the 2015 national football reform. The authors argue that policymakers, implementers and the overall society, even if they are willing to foster a positive youth sport development, can also generate an adverse effect if they do not work together.

Zheng, J., Lau, P., Chen, S., Dickson, G., De Bosscher, V., & Peng, Q. (2023). Interorganisational conflict between national and provincial sport organisations with China's elite sport system: Perspectives from national organisations. *Sport Management Review, 5,* 667–681. https://doi.org/10.1016/j.smr.2018.10.002

In this paper, Zheng et al. scrutinise inter-organisational conflict between Chinese national and provincial sport organisations. The authors argue that whilst famed for the top-down bureaucratic system, there is considerable inter-organisational conflict within the Chinese sport system.

McLeod, C. M., Pu, H., & Newman, J. I. (2018). Blue skies over Beijing: Olympics, environments, and the People's Republic of China. *Sociology of Sport Journal, 35*(1), 29–38. https://doi.org/10.1123/ssj.2016-0149

McLeod, Pu and Newman take the case of the environmental objectives attached to the 2008 Beijing Olympics to explore how environmental objectives are achieved through sport. Employing Latour's object-oriented political ecology, they argue that environmental objectives are possible when environments are made public.

Leite Junior, E., & Rodrigues, C. (2024). China, football, and development: Socialism and soft power. Routledge.

This book delves into the Chinese Football Development Plan, offering fresh insights into hegemony, soft power, socialism with Chinese characteristics, and China's ascent to geopolitical prominence. Through a critical Marxist lens and drawing from Gramsci's theory of hegemony, it argues that football serves as a tool for persuasion and seduction, contributing to the 'hegemonic clash'. Contrary to Western perspectives, it portrays football as integral to China's national rejuvenation, illuminating the state's role in fostering development and innovation.

REFERENCES

Amara, M., Henry, I., Liang, J., & Uchiumi, K. (2005). The governance of professional soccer: Five case studies – Algeria, China, England, France and Japan. *European Journal of Sport Science*, 5(4), 189–206.

Baker, J. A. W., Cao, X.-J., Pan, D. W., & Lin, W. (1993). Sport administration in the people's republic of China. *Journal of Sport Management*, 7(1), 71–77.

Brownell, S. (2008). *Beijing's games: What the Olympics mean to China*. Rowman & Littlefield.

Connell, J. (2018). Globalisation, soft power, and the rise of football in China. *Geographical Research*, 56(1), 5–15.

Dubal, S. (2010). The neoliberalization of football: Rethinking neoliberalism through the commercialization of the beautiful game. *International Review for the Sociology of Sport*, 45(2), 123–146.

Fan, H. (2008). China. In B. Houlihan & M. Green (Eds.), *Comparative elite sport development: Systems, structures and public policy* (pp. 26–52). Butterworth-Heinemann.

Fei, X., Hamilton, G. G., & Zheng, W. (1992). *From the soil, the foundations of Chinese society: A translation of Fei Xiaotong's Xiangtu Zhongguo, with an introduction and epilogue*. University of California Press.

Franck, E. (2011). Private firm, public corporation or member's association governance structures in European football. *International Journal of Sport Finance*, 5(2), 108–127.

Gerrard, B. (2014). Media ownership of teams: The latest stage in the commercialisation of team sports. In T. Slack (Ed.), *The commercialisation of sport* (pp. 240–257). Routledge.

Giulianotti, R. (2002). Supporters, followers, fans, and flaneurs: A taxonomy of spectator identities in football. *Journal of Sport & Social Issues*, 26(1), 25–46.

Giulianotti, R. (2015). The Beijing 2008 Olympics: Examining the interrelations of China, globalization, and soft power. *European Review*, 23(2), 286–296.

Grix, J., Brannagan, P. M., & Lee, D. (2019). *Entering the global arena: Emerging states, soft power strategies and sports mega-events*. Palgrave Macmillan.

Hong, F. (1997). Commercialism and sport in China: Present situation and future expectations. *Journal of Sport Management*, 11(4), 343–354.

Hong, F., & Zhouxiang, L. (2013). The professionalisation and commercialisation of football in China (1993–2013). *International Journal of the History of Sport*, 30(14), 1637–1654.

Hu, X. R. (2019). Ideological conflicts behind mutual belief: The termination of the 'dual-registration policy' and the collapse of an effective elite diving system in China. *Sport in Society*, 22(8), 1362–1381.

Hu, X., & Henry, I. (2017). Reform and maintenance of Juguo Tizhi: Governmental management discourse of Chinese elite sport. *European Sport Management Quarterly*, 17(4), 531–553.

Jinxia, D., & Mangan, J. A. (2001). Football in the new China: Political statement, entrepreneurial enticement and patriotic passion. *Soccer and Society*, 2(3), 79–100.

Junior, E. L., & Rodrigues, C. (2019). The Chinese plan for football development: A perspective from innovation theory. *Sport, Business and Management: An International Journal*, 9(1), 63–77.

Kang, Y. (2005). *Datongshu*. Shanghai Guiji Press.

Kurscheidt, M., & Deitersen-Wieber, A. (2011). Sport governance in Germany. In C. Sobry (Ed.), *Sports governance in the world: A socio-historic approach* (pp. 259–306). Editions Le Manuscrit.

Lawrence, G., & Rowe, D. (1986). *Power play: Essays in the sociology of Australian sport*. Hale & Iremonger.

Liang, Y. (2014). The development pattern and a clubs' perspective on football governance in China. *Soccer and Society*, 15(3), 430–448.

Liang, Y. (2017). Marketization impact on the relationships between supporters and football clubs. *International Journal of the History of Sport*, 34(17–18), 1835–1853.

Lin, K.-C., & Blanchard, J.-M. F. (2017). Governance, domestic change, and social policy in China in historical perspective. In J.-M. F. Blanchard & K.-C. Lin (Eds.), *Governance, domestic change, and social policy in China: 100 Years after the Xinhai revolution* (pp. 1–20). Palgrave Macmillan.

Liu, H. (2017). The regulation of Chinese professional football: Review and prospects. *International Journal of the History of Sport, 34*(17–18), 1950–1963.

Liu, Z., Chen, R., & Newman, J. I. (2019). The football dream of a sleeping dragon: Media framing(s), east–west geopolitics, and the crisis of the Chinese men's national team. *Communication & Sport, 9*(1), 55–87.

Liu, D., & Schwarz, E. C. (2020). Assessing the community beliefs about the corporate social responsibility practices of professional football clubs in China. *Soccer and Society, 21*(5), 584–601.

Liu, D., Zhang, J., & Desbordes, M. (2017). Sport business in China: Current state and prospect. *International Journal of Sports Marketing & Sponsorship, 18*, 1–19.

Ma, Y. (2020). *Governance of Olympic elite sport and professional football in China: Studies on the national games of China and the Chinese Super League*. PhD Thesis, Bayreuth University, Germany.

Ma, Y., & Kurscheidt, M. (2019a). 'Governance of the Chinese Super League: A struggle between governmental control and market orientation', in 'football and its shifting global powerbase', eds. Paul Widdop, Simon Chadwick, and Dan Parnell. *Sport, Business and Management: An International Journal, 9*(1), 4–25.

Ma, Y., & Kurscheidt, M. (2019b). The national games of China as a governance instrument in Chinese elite sport: An institutional and agency analysis. *International Journal of Sport Policy and Politics, 11*(4), 679–699.

Ma, Y., & Kurscheidt, M. (2022). Doing it the Chinese way: The politically-led commercialization of professional football in China. *Journal of Global Sport Management, 7*(3), 355–371.

Mangan, J. A., & Fan, H. (2003). *Sport in Asian society: Past and present*. Frank Cass.

Peng, Q., Skinner, J., & Houlihan, B. (2019). An analysis of the Chinese football reform of 2015: Why then and not earlier? *International Journal of Sport Policy and Politics, 11*(1), 1–18.

Slack, T. (2004). *The commercialization of sport*. Routledge.

Sullivan, J. (2018). *China's football dream*. University of Nottingham.

Sullivan, J., Chadwick, S., & Gow, M. (2019). China's football dream: Sport, citizenship, symbolic power, and civic spaces. *Journal of Sport & Social Issues, 43*(6), 493–514.

Tan, T. C., & Bairner, A. (2010). Globalization and Chinese sport policy: The case of elite football in the people's Republic of China. *The China Quarterly, 203*(203), 581–600.

Tan, T. C., Huang, H. C., Bairner, A., & Chen, Y.-W. (2016). Xi Jin-Ping's world cup dreams: From a major sports country to a world sports power. *International Journal of the History of Sport, 33*(12), 1449–1465.

Tian, E., & Wise, N. (2020). An Atlantic divide? Mapping the knowledge domain of European and North American based sociology of sport, 2008–2018. *International Review for the Sociology of Sport, 55*(8), 1029–1055.

Trott, S. (2017). Grassroots governance reform in urban China. In J. M. F. Blanchard & K. C. Lin (Eds.), *Governance, domestic change, and social policy in China: 100 Years after the Xinhai revolution* (pp. 129–148). Palgrave Macmillan.

Wise, N. (2020). Eventful futures and triple bottom line impacts: BRICS, image regeneration and competitiveness. *Journal of Place Management and Development, 13*(1), 89–100.

Yu, L., Newman, J., Xue, H., & Pu, H. (2017). The transition game: Toward a cultural economy of football in post-socialist China. *International Review for the Sociology of Sport, 54*(6), 711–737.

Zheng, J. (2015). *A comparative analysis of the policy process of elite sport development in China and the UK (in relation to three Olympic sports of artistic gymnastics, swimming and cycling)*. PhD Thesis, Loughborough University, UK.

Zheng, S. (2017). China's political stability: Comparisons and reflections. In J. M. F. Blanchard & K. C. Lin (Eds.), *Governance, domestic change, and social policy in China: 100 years after the Xinhai revolution*. Springer.

Zheng, J., & Chen, S. (2016). Exploring China's success at the Olympic Games: A competitive advantage approach. *European Sport Management Quarterly, 16*(2), 148–171.

Zheng, J., Chen, S., Tan, T. C., & Lau, P. W. C. (2018). Sport policy in China (Mainland). *International Journal of Sport Policy and Politics*, *10*(3), 469–491.

Zheng, J., Chen, S., Tan, T. C., & Houlihan, B. (2019). *Sport policy in China*. Routledge.

Zheng, J., Lau, P. W. C., Chen, S., Dickson, G., De Bosscher, V., & Peng, Q. (2019). Interorganisational conflict between national and provincial sport organisations within China's elite sport system: Perspectives from national organisations. *Sport Management Review*, *22*(5), 667–681.

CHAPTER 6

JACK AND THE VISITING GIANTS: THE DEVELOPMENT OF CHINESE BASEBALL

Xiaoqian Richard Hu

Tsinghua University, China

ABSTRACT

In contrast to other Chinese sports, which attract enormous commercial interests and relates to a kind of political kudos and ideological significance, Chinese baseball represents a singular case for the author to investigate the way in which China responds to sport globalisation due to its peripheral position in, and limited resource from, the domestic sport system and powerful stakeholders from the global society. The study examines the development of Chinese baseball and its interplay with the global sport giants and international events (i.e. the Olympic Games and the Major League Baseball [MLB]). Given the influence of sport globalisation, the author also identifies the consistent dominance of Chinese sport authorities and the spectrum of local stakeholders' reaction towards globalisation. The chapter ends with a discussion of the relationship between marginal position of Chinese baseball in the local sport system and the rationale of its response to sport globalisation.

Keywords: Chinese sport; Zhuanye sport; Olympic glory; Chinese sport reform; MLB China; Olympic baseball

INTRODUCTION

Despite its English origin, the fairy tale of *Jack Spriggins and the Enchanted Bean* is widely enjoyed by kids around the world. May it be Jack's logic of trade, his adventurous spirit or a mere mortal's victory over (or escape from if you like) a frenzy giant. The last part is usually narrated or illustrated as the climax of not only the original story but also its various adaptations, one of which even runs a spoiler with its title: *Jack the Giant Slayer*.

From another perspective, it could also be argued that such imaginations of an underdog vs the giants of the world are commonly played out and realised. When we think about Chinese baseball, this becomes *déjà vu*, especially in this era of globalisation where local communities encounter global visions, trends, and expectations. This kind of interplay between the local and the global is evidenced in a number of domains, including sport, and has been well discussed by scholars from diverse perspectives (Callinicos, 2007; Maguire, 1994; Rosenberg, 2000; Roudometof & Robertson, 1995), and represents important geographical framing in sports research (Tian & Wise, 2020).

Modern sports, the foci of our discussion in this book, is well recognised as one of these domains. Here, local communities respond diversely to global phenomena from many facets, such as the transnational broadcasting of sport events (Hu et al., 2022; Kanchana, 2017), global marketing strategies of sport clubs (Hayton et al., 2017; Huang, 2013) as well as sport nationalism, the topic that never age, in the era of globalisation (Carroll & Bairner, 2019; Tomlinson & Young, 2006). Important to note is the role of developing a large-scale and mega-events portfolio to develop a strategy to increase the image of sport and China's competitiveness internationally (Wise, 2020).

During the interplay between the local and the global, which is recognised as the process of the globalisation of human society, sport is also assigned with various roles (Wise, 2015). For instance, thanks to the association between the global diffusion of modern sport and the expansion of the British Empire and subsequently the American soft power, modern sport has long been recognised as a consequence of globalisation to which the different local societies' reactions vary across a spectrum with total acceptance and total rejection sitting at respective ends (Elias & Dunning, 1993; Houlihan, 1994; Huizinga, 1970). In contrast, the global distribution of modern sport has also been recognised as one of the key drives of globalisation (Galtung, 1991) or a cultural transfer mechanisms which privileges the culture of the West (Bale, 1994) which is an important area of work concerning sociological and geographical dimensions of sport (Wise & Kohe, 2020).

Despite the various perspectives in respect of the role of modern sport in the globalisation of human society, it is well acknowledged that there has been a trend of homogenisation of sport, in cultural terms particularly, in the era of globalisation. Nevertheless, the degree of the aforementioned homogenisation, or Westernisation as some would argue, varies from the international to local level. Specifically speaking, at international level, there has been a consistent dominance of the West, even though some peripheral or semi-peripheral states that are in a disadvantaged position in the 'Western-ruled' international sport community have sometimes gained success and/or become constant dominance, such as Chinese table tennis players and Latino baseball players, in international championships and the Olympics (Grix, 2013; Lucidarme et al., 2018). Nonetheless, at national and regional level, local stakeholders are more able 'to resist or, at the very least, to domesticate globalising impulses' (Bairner, 2001).

Moreover, the power of the local stakeholder is considerably reinforced in the domain of sport, which is recognised as nationalist behaviours (Kellas, 1991; Wise, 2015) and is widely employed as imagined communities to connect people across the nation (Jarvie, 1993).

Academic attention has been paid accordingly to each side of this two-folded role of sport in the globalisation. This is to say, sport scholars have consistently investigated and discussed the role of sport in promoting a global market, culture and governance structure (Bodet et al., 2010; Hayton et al., 2017; Nauright & Zipp, 2020). On the other side of coin, there are also literature studies focussing on the function of sport as a means employed by nation state to stimulate its domestic economic growth to establish national identity and to negotiate with the trend of globalisation (Bowes & Bairner, 2018; Devlin & Billings, 2016; Gong, 2020; Yu et al., 2019).

This function of sport is also evidenced in China's engagement and interaction with the global sport community, which has attracted great academic interests. For instance, thanks to China's increasing interests in, and engagement with, the international Olympic movement, its relationship with the IOC and the international Olympic movement has been studied from a variety of perspectives (Brownell, 2008; Cha, 2009; Fan, 1998; Hu, 2015a; Luo & Huang, 2013; Price & Dayan, 2008; Xu, 2008). Moreover, academic effort has also been remarkably invested by either Chinese or non-Chinese speaking scholars in examining the interplay between China and the international community in specific domains within sport, such as football, namely reportedly a personal hobby of Xi Jinping (Connell, 2017; Hu, 2015b; Tan et al., 2016), basketball, through which China sent one of its most significant single piece export to the US (Houlihan et al., 2010; Lane, 2004; Li, 2018), volleyball, with which considerable political connotation has been associated (Fan & Lu, 2019; Hu & Liang, 2019) and doping (Tan et al., 2018; Vidar Hanstad & Houlihan, 2015).

The aforementioned instances are well recognised as either crucial issues in sport or major sports to which highly political significance is assigned in the Chinese society (Fan et al., 2005; Hu, 2015a). Great attention has consequently been paid to these domains by China's government-run sport system, which is skilfully managed by the government and its agencies with the prioritisation of their own needs and preference, especially during their interaction with the international community (Chen et al., 2019; Tan & Bairner, 2010, 2011; The Office of the Joint Meeting of the Football Reform and Development Department of the State Council, 2015).

In contrast to the academic enthusiasm on the relationship between China and sport globalisation in these vital areas, there are far less studies, particularly in English, examining China's interaction with global sport within those sports that are deemed as less significant in its government-run sport system. Inspired by such curiosity, this paper is sought to examine how China interplays with sport globalisation with a marginal sport, which makes hardly any difference to its political task of winning glory for the country and the consequential political kudos of sport bureaucrats.

Baseball, a minor sport in China, is thus selected for the study. In contrast to the aforementioned Chinese sports, which attract enormous commercial interests and/or embrace ideological significance in the local society, baseball in the Chinese sporting landscape is peripheral and therefore attracts limited resources from the domestic sport system. Furthermore, the development of Chinese baseball is also affected by the moves of powerful international stakeholders, such as the Major League Baseball (MLB) and the IOC. Given the IOC's remarkable power over the agenda of the Olympic-accentuating Chinese elite sport system and the MLB's 20-year business campaign with Chinese baseball since the beginning of the 21st century, it could be argued that, this time, it is very difficult for Jack Spriggins to stop the visiting giants from chopping off the beanstalk for they have already been in the house.

THE POLITICISATION OF CHINESE BASEBALL

Baseball was introduced to China in the second half of the 19th century. It was Chinese students studying overseas during the Qing Monarchy that brought attention to the sport after returning from the US and Japan. Western colonisers also had their endeavours to bring baseball along with other modern sports, such as football, basketball and tennis to China (Brownell, 2008; Carter & Sugden, 2012). It is not so difficult for us to notice the thread of global influence in the early spread of baseball in China. For instance, European and American residents in Shanghai founded the first baseball club in China, Shanghai Baseball Club, no later than 1863 (Reaves, 2022). Decades later, on the 2nd of June 1905, the first baseball game between two teams composed of only Chinese players offered sound evidence of such Western influence because, ironically, the teams competing did not have 'Chinese names' but St. John's School and YMCA Shanghai (Song & Chen, 2005). It is therefore argued that the earliest stages of baseball's development in China could be recognised as a consequence of early globalisation, which was realised through the process of the colonisation of China in the hand of both Western powers and its neighbour, Japan. Those from these colonising nations used the proactive promotion of the sport, as this was an attempt to convince local elites that China could strengthen their nation by competing in modern sport (Brownell, 2008).

In spite of its endeavour and eventual achievement in the campaign of anti-imperialism, the Communist Party of China (CPC) had proactively embraced and accentuated baseball. They did this, despite the byname of baseball as the American pastime – even before the establishment of the People's Republic of China (PRC) in 1949. This is because the sport was viewed by the Party leaders as a useful military drill for a solider. They could refine their marksmanship by seeing pitches in the batter's box (Wang, 1953) or improve grenade-throwing skills by pitching and throwing baseballs (Chen et al., 1990; Gu, 1989). In line with the military usefulness of the sport trusted by the CPC, the first national event of baseball in the PRC was organised as a part of the inaugural Military Games of the People's Liberation Army in 1952 (People's Daily, 1952). After this event, the sport gained in popularity and the number of teams increased from eight to fourteen in the second Military Games of the People's Liberation Army in 1959 (Sha, 2014).

Sharing the fate of other sports in the communist regime, baseball is associated with political functions and ideological connotation. This sport was also significantly influenced by the political climate. Before the outburst of the Culture Revolution in 1966, there had been more than 10 national baseball championships in China, despite the fame and popularity of the American pastime at the opposite side of the Iron Curtain (Gu, 1989). One of the main purposes of these baseball events was to 'showcase the development of all kinds of sports in the socialist regime to intellectuals and returned overseas Chinese' (The Sport Council of Luwan District, 1958). There was thus social and political semblance here, as the intellectuals and returned overseas Chinese were valued by the CPC and many of them learnt how to play baseball during their university days either in China or overseas, baseball was therefore employed as an apparatus to unite them with the new-born regime. It turned out that this strategy was so effective that the target group soon became the other main part of Chinese baseball population besides the aforementioned baseball players in the military force (Sha, 2014). For instance, most players of the two teams from Shanghai in the National Baseball Division Series in 1958 were musicians from Shanghai Orchestra and university graduates who were working in research institutes and hospitals (Sha, 2014). One year later, the Beijing baseball team won the baseball event in the first National Games with nine Japanese Chinese on its active roster (Li, 2003).

The political climate domestically in China soon became unfavourable to the American pastime. A great proportion of the Chinese baseball population, marshals and intellectuals for instance, were politically stigmatised and/or persecuted as 'rightists' and 'revisionists' in the Cultural Revolution. Moreover, the sport was also perceived as diplomatically unproductive by the leaders of the PRC, as it was very difficult to find another baseball-loving country at the ideologically east side of the Iron Curtain except Cuba, which ironically sits, geographically, in the west side.

Consequently, the number of baseball teams in China had shrunk dramatically since the early 1960s. In June 1963, the Shanghai baseball team, which was the last baseball team in the government-run elite sport system in China, was dismissed (Li, 2003). Two years later, there were no elite-level baseball players left in the country, as they had been 'suggested' to move across to other sports. It took nearly 10 years for the national baseball tournament to be reinstated in 1974, which was, interestingly, just two years after China restored the diplomatic relationship with its baseball-zealous neighbour, Japan.

If we take the official elimination of the sport during the Cultural Revolution as a watershed in the history of Chinese baseball, it could be argued that, in the first stage of the development of baseball in China, the ancient empire accepted the import from the West while experiencing a series of swift but radical changes in its status from a feudal kingdom to a semi-colonial country, a capitalist republic and finally to a communist land. Despite the unfavourable position of the local society against external powers during this period, local actors have proactively and variously interpreted this symbol of modernity and Western lifestyle with nationalist, political and ideological accounts. It was also such local narrative, the ideological ones in particular, that resulted in the decade-long extinction of the sport with strong capitalist background in the Communist state.

THE OLYMPIC TASK AND THE GIANT IN THE HOUSE OF CHINESE BASEBALL

As mentioned above, the restoration of the National Baseball Championship in 1974 was also influenced by the local political environment and diplomatic affairs, in particular the establishment of the diplomatic relationship between the PRC and Japan (Sha, 2014). This is not the sole case in which the fate of a sport in China, or that of Chinese sport in general, is influenced by the political climate in the country. For instance, mass sport and elite sport had been alternately prioritised in the government agenda after 1949 due to the ideological oscillation in the early days of the communist regime (Wu, 1999). Paramount emphasis has constantly been placed on the latter by the government since 1979, when the PRC obtained the right to represent China in the IOC from its political rival, *i.e.* the ROC in Taiwan (Hu, 2015a; The Chinese Olympic Committee, 2004; Wu, 1999).

Thanks to the aforementioned political connotation of sport in China, the shift in the priority of the Chinese government's sport agenda led to a rapid development of Chinese elite sport, the dominant form of which is known as Zhuanye sport, a planned-economy-based and government-financed and controlled elite sport system (Hu et al., 2021). For instance, more than 30 years after the announcement of the first reform policy of Chinese sport, which is planned to be directed towards a civil-society-based mode, government funding still takes up to 94.8% of the 2022 budget of the General Administration of Sport (GAS), which is the government body holding the responsibility for sport issues in China and financing all national squads (The GAS, 2022).

The GAS also holds a non-governmental identity as the All-China Sports Federation, which is commonly utilised during its interaction with international community (Yu & Huang, 2015). This institutional setting, known as two banners shared by one group, is also commonly witnessed in the relationship between Chinese NGBs (such as the Chinese Baseball Association [CBA]) and the Administration Centres of Sports (such as the Administration of Handball, Hockey, Baseball and Softball), the latter of which are pubic institutions directly affiliated to the GAS and works as the GAS's puppet line controlling the NGBs (Hu & Henry, 2017).

The political significance of sport in China results in an extreme emphasis on elite sport performance and the consequential political task, *i.e.* winning glory for the country, of the government-run Zhuanye system (Fan & Lu, 2013). Given the importance of the Olympic Games in the global sport calendar and the aforesaid nationalist and political significance that the Chinese society assigns to the modern edition of the ancient Greek religious event, Olympic performance is not only highly valued in the Chinese society but also closely associated with the political kudos of sport bureaucrats and the financial interests and career development of Zhuanye athletes and coaches (Brownell, 2008; Chen et al., 2019; Hu & Henry, 2017).

THE OLYMPICS, THE GIANT TURNING THE WHEEL OF FATE

The Olympic Games is also significant for Chinese baseball though there is only slim, if not none, chance for the Chinese team to win the Olympic glory because it never had any baseball team from mainland China advanced to the Olympic Games nor been the top two in either the Asian Baseball Championship or the baseball event in the Asian Games due to their consistent defeats in the hands of the Asian baseball powers, *i.e.* Japan, Korea and Chinese Taipei. Consequently, Beijing's successful bid for the 2008 Games led to a significant shift in the status of Chinese baseball, at least in the Zhuanye system, from a sport with rarely any hope to qualify for the Olympics to one that will participate in the Games. A former outfielder of the national squad elaborates the importance of such shift for Chinese baseball through a vivid, but rather miserable, metaphor and states:

> the Olympics is significant for a peripheral sport to the Zhuanye system ... athletes and coaches of Olympic sports are like the GAS's own flesh and blood, but we ... were like a group of orphans.

Beijing's successful bid for the 2008 Games provided the newly-adopted orphan with an unprecedented opportunity to have a taste of the privilege enjoyed by 'the GAS's own flesh and blood'. Not only had players who would form the Chinese team but also the Zhuanye baseball system in general received greater attention and benefits from the GAS. Taking the scenario of the status of the national squad, it was recalled by a senior baseball administrator that there had never been a permanently established Team China before Beijing was awarded the 2008 Olympics, as the national team was always temporarily formed one or two months in advance of an international event and dismissed afterwards. This was contrastingly different with the setting of the sports in which Chinese athletes are dominant, such as table tennis, badminton and diving, because elite athletes of these sport have been gathered and accommodated in the Training Bureau of the GAS for most of the time, if not always. Subsequent to the successful bit for the 2008 Games, the environment for Chinese baseball had been dramatically changed. For instance, extra financial support was granted to the national team for a roster of 20 players though it took 25 players to form an Olympic baseball team, and there were also improvements in facilities and services provided by the Chinese sport government.

Similar to most of the sports played by the Chinese at the Beijing Olympics, Chinese baseball also achieved a historical breakthrough in 2008. China secured their first victory against its blood relative, yet political rival, Chinese Taipei. Nevertheless, this unprecedented achievement led to rarely any impact on the post-2008 development of Chinese baseball, which has rather been influenced essentially by the elimination of baseball from the Olympic programme. For instance, the government funding for the CBA was decreased by 75% after the Beijing Games and the domestic baseball league, the China Baseball League, had also been terminated since 2012 due to insufficient funds (Hu, 2015a). It is explained by a senior official of the CBA that

> we are not in the era of Norman Bethune, in which resources are provided [to you] for free...For a [sport] association, it doesn't work if we only focus on Zhuanye teams or on whether or not it could participate in the Olympics... [We] have to find more option, at least for survival.

Henry Norman Bethune was a Canadian physician who is best known in the PRC for his service to the Chinese communist military force in the second Sino-Japanese war (the Asian part of the WWII). He was a member of the Communist Party of Canada. After refusing the invitation from Chiang Kai Shek, he went to Yan'an to join Mao Zedong's communist side. He died in 1939 of septicaemia, which he contracted through a finger cut in an operation. Mao wrote a famous article aftermath, in Memory of Norman Bethune (Mao, 1939), in which he was portrayed as a devoting, kind-hearted internationalist without any thought of himself. Therefore, employing the metaphor, Norman Bethune, in the above quote embraces strong communist connotation in China. The official constructs a link between the communist era which has been gone in her opinion and the severe situation with which Chinese baseball, in particular the planned-economy-based Zhuanye baseball, was confronted. In addition to the above quotation, she also admits that it was subsequent to the 'de-Olympic-isation' of baseball that the CBA started to seriously explore diverse ways of the civil-society-based development, 'at least for the survival' of Chinese baseball. The causal relationship between the Olympic fate of baseball and the direction of development of the sport in China is also acknowledged by a number of stakeholders of Chinese baseball.

This elaboration of the shift in the focus of Chinese baseball ascribes the expansion of the horizon of sport bureaucrats to the removal of baseball from the Olympic sport roster. Such dramatic change in the Olympic fate of baseball is recognised as a fundamental shock to the Zhuanye baseball system by a senior director of MLB China, who was the former director of the Olympic programme of one of the TOP sponsors of the 2008 Olympics before his career in the business of baseball. The sport marketing veteran further remarks that

> the exclusion of baseball from the Olympics ... is good in short terms, as the privilege (for Zhuanye baseball) terminates ... no glory no money. ... Then, the nature (of the post-2008 development of Chinese baseball) is how to reform the system.

His indication of the elimination of the privilege for Chinese baseball is in line with not only the aforementioned statement portraying baseball as an orphan in the Zhuanye system but also the dramatic cut of the government funding of Chinese baseball in the post-2008 era, the reason of which is explicitly acknowledged in the quotation as 'no glory no money'. It is however interesting to note his positive attitude towards the 'relegation' of Chinese baseball in the power hierarchy of the Zhuanye sport system, which, as we would argue, is consistent with his expectation of the new priority in the development of Chinese baseball, *i.e.* the reform of the system. And, as revealed previously by the official from the CBA, the reform is driven by the CBA's need of 'find[ing] more option, at least for survival' and is sought to establish the civil-society-based development mode of Chinese baseball.

It could therefore be argued that the development of Chinese baseball since Beijing was awarded the 2008 Olympic Games has been significantly influenced by the Olympic fate of the sport, which resulted in a temporary surge in the attention paid to Zhuanye baseball as well as its return to the orphanage after the 2008 Olympics. Moreover, due to the second elimination of baseball from the Olympic programme after the Tokyo Games, the situation has been even worsened for Chinese baseball as it is well believed and mentioned by a number of our interviewees, including senior officials of the CBA and coaches and players from Zhuanye provincial baseball teams, that the GAS is considering seriously about removing the sport from the National Games of China. The dim future of baseball in the domestic version of the Olympic Games is recognised as a direct threat to its development at local level because of the political and financial significance of the National Games to provincial sport governments, which share a similar principle with the GAS namely 'no glory no money' (Ma & Kurscheidt, 2019).

As a rundown of the way in which Chinese baseball is impacted by the move of the Greek giant from Olympia, we would argue that it is the Olympic fate of baseball rather than the Olympic baseball event in Beijing that works as the de facto driving force of the post-2008 development of Chinese baseball, which is expected to move towards a civil-society-based mode. This trend, as demonstrated in this part, is perceived variously by different stakeholder. On the one hand, actors from Zhuanye baseball, in particular those at the elite level, have been negatively impacted by the global factor, *i.e.* the wobbling Olympic fate of baseball, and have thus been driven towards the civil society due to its limited and reducing resource provided by the traidiational Chinese elite sport system. On the other hand, the withdrawal of baseball from the greatest spectacle in global sport is nonetheless appreciated by other stakeholders for the perception that the change may strengthen the link between Zhuanye baseball and the civil society, in which, as demonstrated subsequently, there has already been another global giant in the house.

THE MLB: THE GIANT IN THE HOUSE

When China collected the last piece of the puzzle of its Olympic dream at the beginning of the 21st century, there were also other global actors increasingly involving with Chinese baseball. The interaction between Chinese baseball and the MLB presents an interesting case of the interplay between a local community with various stakeholders but limited resource and one of the most dominant actors in a specific global sport.

The American baseball giant and its Chinese counterpart started their cooperation with a specific focus on the Chinese national team. Since 2001, the MLB had hosted Team China for annual training camps in the States and provided coaches and consults (such as Jim Lefebvre, 1965 Rookie of the Year and the manager of Seattle Mariners from 1989 to 1991, who had been the head coach of Team China from 2003 to 2009) for the Chinese team after Beijing was granted the 2008 Olympics (Yu & Zhang, 2006).

It was recalled by a senior official in the CBA during our interview that the cooperation was initiated by the MLB as a friendly gesture after one Major League club mistakenly signed a minor league contract with a Chinese player who was still under contract with a Zhuanye team at the time of signing. Nonetheless, there are also other drives of the American side to establish the cooperation, such as to find one player good enough to play in the Majors, thus seeking a star athlete to become the Yao Ming of baseball (Donohue, 2008). Nevertheless, the support from the States has been highly appreciated on the communist side of the Pacific for its remarkable effect in elite sport performance, which is accentuated throughout the Zhuanye system.

For instance, not only does the then Chair of the CBA acknowledge that 'the efforts in those years had strong relationship with our victory in the Beijing Games' but also a provincial sport bureau official we interviewed indicate that 'the training camps means a lot... also for provincial teams, particularly those with many players in the national team'.

While working with (or working for, if you like) Zhuanye baseball in the training camps, the MLB has also conducted other business initiatives in China. In 2006, the MLB opened its China office (hereafter, the MLB China) to direct and implement its business strategy in China (CBS News, 2006). Different with the elite-level-focused Team China project, the task of the MLB China is to promote baseball, or more precisely to develop the fan base of the MLB, in China through, for instance, exhibitions in Chinese shopping malls and the nationwide 'Playball' championships for primary school students.

In contrast to the general appreciation of stakeholders from the Zhuanye system towards the Team China project, their perception of the effort made by the MLB China varies noticeably. For instance, a senior official of the CBA expresses his gratitude through indicating that:

> we sincerely appreciate their help, with which the development of Chinese baseball cannot be separated... we tried to get eggs from a hen borrowed from our neighbour.

In the quotation, the CBA official acknowledges the extrinsic nature of the assistance from the MLB China through employing a common Chinese idiom, *i.e.* 'get(ting) eggs from a hen borrowed from neighbour'. Moreover, this idiom also indirectly constructs the indispensability, or inseparability if we follow his term in the quotation, between the foreign assistance and the realisation of the goal of local stakeholders, who 'tried to get eggs' *or to promote* the development of Chinese baseball due to their struggles with resource and support in the post-2008 era.

In contrast to the indebted account from the NGB of Chinese baseball, it is addressed by a senior manager from the MLB China that their promotional campaigns have been '"criticised" or "sneered"' at by those from the Zhuanye system. However, the negative reaction of stakeholders from the Zhuanye system is positively perceived by the MLB China as the evidence of the fruitfulness their business strategy and/or, as he remarks, as the result that 'makes me feel happy and that (proves) I am correct'. It is further explained that:

> [Increasing the number of fans as many as possible] is the ultimate benchmark of our work in the promotion campaign, as [those fans] could continuously consume baseball... Thus, I don't care so much about the serious fans and Zhuanye baseball, who love and are involved with baseball anyway.

In the quotation, the MLB China's indifference to Zhuanye baseball is ascribed to its business priority, *i.e.* market development rather than performance development, the latter of which, as previously demonstrated, is the predominant task of the Zhuanye system. It could therefore be argued that the criticism from Zhuanye baseball, which is neglected by the MLB China, is an expectable, if not intended or planned, outcome of the business strategy of the MLB China.

Furthermore, the divergent reaction of local stakeholders, who though are all associated with Zhuanye baseball, to the American giant's strategic choice namely neglecting 'the serious fans and Zhuanye baseball' could be recognised as the consequence of their respective identities in Chinese baseball and diverse ways through which their interests are realised. More specifically, despite the CBA's role as the *de facto* leader of the Zhuanye system and its political task of winning glory for the country, it is also responsible for the general development of baseball in the country and, as previously mentioned, had to 'find more option, at least for survival' after the Beijing Olympics. It is therefore benefited directly by the MLB China's campaigns, which promote grassroot baseball with rarely using any resource from the CBA except the NGB's official endorsement during their negotiation with local governments. In contrast, other stakeholders from Zhuanye baseball, in particular from provincial Zhuanye teams, are less profited in these campaigns due to their concentration on elite performance.

Along with their mockery of campaigns of the MLB China, the reaction of Zhuanye baseball at provincial level soon became more radical after the establishment of the MLB Development Centre (DC) in 2009. Different with the Zhuanye system, which have long been criticised for the sacrifice of education of young athletes (Liu et al., 2020), the DC, which is a baseball training institute attached to a local middle school, recruits students aged between 12 and 19 with a hope for a chance to play pro in the US or to continue of their academic pursuits with baseball at universities globally (Brudnicki, 2020). The local middle school provides education of the trainees/students of the DC, while the MLB pays all their expenses at the DC and sends an international group of instructors for their training, which is conducted in English.

At the time of writing, there have been more than 100 graduates from the three DCs. Some head to universities in China or the States, while some others continue their baseball careers as coaches in the DCs. Recently, there have been a few numbers of DC graduates registered in the Zhuanye system. And it is worth noting that there have been eight DC alumni signed by MLB franchises though none of them had made to the Majors yet (Li, 2022).

However, the DCs had been strongly against by the Zhuanye system at the early stage of its establishment. Because the student athletes enroled by the DCs are also prospects for Zhunaye baseball, their new choices (of playing pro or continuing studies overseas) is thus viewed as a significant threat to the already shattered talent poll of the Zhunaye system, which has long been competing with the domestic education sector for resource and talents (Hu, 2019). Therefore, rarely any primary school and mid-school baseball coaches, most of whom are close with the Zhunaye system, would recomand their players to go to the DCs, which were portrayed as a talent thief and hopeless destination, at least before Ray Chang was appointed as the director and headcoach of the DCs in 2017. Ray Chang, an American Chinese who played Minor League Baseball in the San Diego Padres system and was inch close to the Majors, was the cornerstone of Team China's victories in the World Baseball Classic, the baseball equivalent of the FIFA World Cup, respectively over Chinese Taipei and Brazil in 2009 and 2013. When Ray took his directorship in the DC, most of his teammates in the national squad have retired and become coaches or officials in either the Zhuanye system or the local education sector. Therefore, Ray has enjoyed a much closer relationship with, and greater influence in, Zhuanye baseball, if not Chinese baseball in general, than the business executives in the MLB China and the American coaches in the DC, both of whom were viewed as outsiders by the Zhuanye system.

It was since Ray's tenure in the DCs that there have been DC graduate registered in Zhuanye provincial teams, which is recognised as a significant step for the American giant. Five years later, a team from Shanghai, the city in which the first baseball club in China established and the first baseball game between two Chinese teams played, won the title of the 2022 U18 National Championship. *Coincidentally*, 10 out of the 15 players of the national champion of the next generation of Zhuanye baseball come from the DC (Han, 2022). At the very moment, when an outburst of laughter was shared by the 15 new champions of Chinese baseball, Jack shakes the hand of the giant again, and this time, with less scepticism.

CONCLUSION

Similar to other modern sports in China, Chinese baseball is a consequence of early globalisation related to Western colonialism and the consequential expansion of Western leisure culture, which were accompanied with unfavourable memories of the Chinese nation particularly when the sport was brought to the country by foreign powers. In the local narrative, modern sport is associated with, and is accentuated for, extrinsic functions, such as to strengthen the nation that was mocked as the sick man of East Asia and/or to unite the ideological others before the Cultural Revolution. Such extrinsic functions, which are the consequences of the local interpretation of a global phenomenon namely modern sport, have also been the constant theme in the Chinese elite sport discourse since the initial acceptance of modern sport by the elites in the Chinese society in the mid-18th century.

In line with this local disposition of modern sport, of elite sport in particular, baseball is employed by the Chinese government as an apparatus to interact with global sport following its own agenda. Nevertheless, thanks to the strong government will and control, Chinese baseball itself has limited power over its own choice in the communication with the global community of sport and has been therefore negatively affected by the unfavourable climate in global sport. This is evidenced in its decadal disappearance in the government-run sport system for its unproductivity in diplomatic terms and the potential exclusion of the sport from the National Games after its second removal from the Olympic roster (The IOC, 2020).

Though Chinese baseball has more to say when dealing with global actors at its homecourt, the attitude of local stakeholders varies dramatically in accordance to their evaluation of the consistency between the practice of external stakeholders and their own interests. This is particularly the case in the various attitudes of stakeholders at diverse levels of the Zhuanye system towards the MLB, the MLB China and the DC. We would argue that the heterogeneity of local actors results in a spectrum of reaction towards sport globalisation, while local stakeholders' respective position is related to the degree at which the realisation of their interests is interpreted as a dependant of the resource provided by, or related to, global actors.

However, such position shall not to be taken as an over-exaggeration of powerful global actors because this link between local interests and global resource is, to a certain degree, a construct of local community in regard to the globalisation and its position in this trend. In return for the influence of globalisation, local construct may also significantly affect human community or a global phenomenon. Evidence of these impactful local narrative may include the conservatism and right-wing populism tendency in recent Western politics, which result in a variety of Trumpism/neo-nationalism and the proclamation that 'globalisation is almost dead. Free trade is almost dead' (Cheng, 2022, p. 1).

Under such circumstance, the advantage position of powerful global actors, including those with dominant power and lavish resource, become not-so-secured even in the situation when the interest of local stakeholder is closely associated with their resource. Though it may seem strange, in the case of the Olympic fate of baseball, it could be argued from the perspective of the nature of Zhuanye sport that, although the interest of Chinese baseball is remarkably influenced by the IOC's decision, the post-2008 development of Chinese baseball is, in essence, the inevitable outcome of the extreme emphasis that the Chinese sport government places on the Olympic performance rather than the termination of baseball in the Olympics.

Essentially, it also is such strong government power over elite sport discourse that results in the prioritisation of Olympic performance and the consequential dominance of the Zhuanye system in Chinese sport for its effectiveness in securing Olympic success. This relationship between the NGB's dominant voice, which originates from the other banner it holds behind the non-governmental one, and the stability of the Zhuanye system in Chinese sport is well understood and acknowledged by the aforementioned sport marketing guru, who states that

I told [the CBA] ... neither were you nor I able to [develop Chinese baseball] alone; I would like to help you, what I asked was only a share of it... [we have to let the CBA know that] it is the master [in Chinese baseball], and it is the government, which means it will always be the master.

So, it seems that there is nothing could stop Master Jack Spriggins from swinging his axe to the beanstalk, even though the falling giant may crash the poor orphan himself, except his visitor chooses to lay golden eggs for him as does the hen.

FIVE KEY READINGS

Brownell, S. (2008). *Beijing's games: What the Olympics mean to China.* **Rowman & Littlefield.**

Brownell provides an in-depth demonstration of the development of modern sport in China since the phenomenon of modernity was introduced to the Mid-Kingdom in the early 18th century. The work also remarkably enlightens the readers with abundant information regarding the connotation associated with elite sport in the communist regime.

Sha, Q. (2014). Playing baseball in the New China: The changes in the circumstance and the various identities of a sport [在新中国打棒球：一项体育运动的 境遇变迁及其多重角色]. *Research of the History of the CPC [中共党史研究]*, **(2), 45–54.**

In this paper, which is published in a Journal specifically focussing on the history of the CPC, Sha explicitly demonstrates the dramatic fate of the American pastime in the PRC and the relationship between the development of Chinese baseball with the ever-changing political climate in early stage of the country that consistently upholds its claim of communist ideology.

Klein, A. M. (2006). *Growing the game: The globalization of major league baseball.* **Yale University Press.**

This book delves into the globalisation of baseball, exploring its expansion and evolution worldwide. Klein examines the sport's cultural, social and economic impacts, highlighting its significance as a global phenomenon. Through case studies and analysis, the book explores soccer's baseball's role in various societies and its intersection with politics, identity and commercialisation. Klein sheds light on the challenges and opportunities faced by soccer's growth, offering insights into how the sport navigates issues of tradition, modernity and globalisation. This book offers a comprehensive examination of the sport of baseball and globalisation.

Kelly, W.W. (2007). Is baseball a global sport? America's 'national pastime' as global field and international sport. *Global Networks*, **7(2), 187–201.**

In the 19th century, numerous sports and leisure activities emerged, spreading rapidly from the West to other regions through imperial and mercantile networks. Notably, soccer, cricket and baseball gained widespread popularity, undergoing adaptation through what I've termed 'uncanny mimicry'. This article examines baseball's unique development in the USA and its expansion into the Caribbean and western Pacific. Unlike soccer and cricket, baseball didn't originate in elite schools but rather became commercialised and professionalised early on without ideological ties to a 'character' ethic. Despite being embraced as America's pastime, it faced both emulation and resistance abroad, exemplified by Japan's 'samurai' baseball. This paper lies the foundation for looking at baseball in the context of other cultures.

Tan, T., & Bairner, A. (2011). Managing globalization: The case of elite basketball policy in the People's Republic of China. *Journal of Sport Management*, **25, 408–422.**

As one of the serial papers looking at Chinese elite sport policy, Tan and Bairner demonstrate the scenario concerning the interplay between Chinese elite basketball and sport globalisation. It elaborates the constraints and possibility the Chinese government confronted with in basketball, which is more popular and more significant than Chinese baseball, while there has also been a powerful global stakeholder, i.e. the NBA, at the gate, if not in the house, of Chinese elite sport.

REFERENCES

Bairner, A. (2001). *Sport, nationalism, and globalisation*. State University of New York.
Bale, J. (1994). *Landscapes of modern sport*. Leicester University Press.
Bodet, G., Chanavat, N., & Bodet, G. (2010). *Building global football brand equity Lessons from the Chinese market*. https://doi.org/10.1108/13555851011013155
Bowes, A., & Bairner, A. (2018). England's proxy warriors? Women, war and sport. *International Review for the Sociology of Sport*, *53*(4), 393–410. https://doi.org/10.1177/1012690216669491
Brownell, S. (2008). *Beijing's Games: What the Olympics mean to China*. Rowman & Littlefield.
Brudnicki, A. (2020). *MLB China offers development and learning centers*. https://www.mlb.com/news/mlb-china-development-learning-center. Accessed on 18 December 2022.
Callinicos, A. (2007). Globalization, imperialism and capitalism. In D. Held & A. McGrew (Eds.), *Globalisation theory*. Bookmarks.
Carroll, G., & Bairner, A. (2019). In from the side: Exile international rugby union players in Britain, blood ties and national identities. *National Identities*, *21*(4), 417–433. https://doi.org/10.1080/14608944.2018.1491542
Carter, T. F., & Sugden, J. (2012). The USA and sporting diplomacy: Comparing and contrasting the cases of table tennis with China and baseball with Cuba in the 1970s. *International Relations*, *26*(1), 101–121. https://doi.org/10.1177/0047117811411741.
CBS News. (2006, November 3). Baseball to open office in China. *CBS News*. https://www.cbsnews.com/news/baseball-to-open-office-in-china/. Accessed on 19 February 2024.
Cha, V. D. (2009). *Beyond the final score : The politics of sport in Asia*. Columbia University Press.
Chen, S., Preuss, H., Hu, X. (Richard), & Keyon, J. (2019). Sport policy development in China: Legacies of Beijing's 2008 Summer Olympic Games and 2022 Winter Olympic Games. *Journal of Global Sport Management*, *6*(3), 234–263. https://doi.org/10.1080/24704067.2019.1566756.
Chen, X. [陈显明], Liang, Y. [梁友德], and Du, K. [杜克和]. (1990). *The history of Chinese baseball [中国棒球运动史]*. Wuhan Press.
Cheng, T.-F. (2022). TSMC founder Morris Chang says globalization 'almost dead'. https://asia.nikkei.com/Business/Tech/Semiconductors/TSMC-founder-Morris-Chang-says-globalization-almost-dead. Accessed on 18 December 2022.
The Chinese Olympic Committee (Ed.). (2004). *Reinstatement in the Olympic movement*. http://en.olympic.cn/china_oly/history/2004-03-27/121827.html
Connell, J. (2017). Globalisation, soft power, and the rise of football in China. *Geographical Research*, *56*(1), 5–15. https://doi.org/10.1111/1745-5871.12249.

Devlin, M. B., & Billings, A. C. (2016). Examining the World's Game in the United States: Impact of nationalized qualities on fan identification and consumption of the 2014 FIFA World Cup. *Journal of Broadcasting & Electronic Media*, *60*(1), 40–60. https://doi.org/10.1080/08838151.2015.1127243.

Donohue, M. (2008). *Fastball to nowhere*. https://www.thenationalnews.com/uae/fastball-to-nowhere-1.506829. Accessed on 12 December 2022.

Elias, N., & Dunning, E. (1993). *The quest for excitement: Sport and leisure in the civilizing process*. Basil Blackwell.

Fan, H. (1998). The Olympic movement in China: Ideals, realities and ambitions. *Culture, Sport, Society*, *1*(1), 149–168. https://doi.org/10.1080/14610989808721805

Fan, H., & Lu, Z. (2013). *The politicisation of sport in modern China: Communists and champions*. Routledge.

Fan, H., & Lu, Z. (2019). China's sports heroes: Nationalism, patriotism, and gold medal. *International Journal of the History of Sport*, *36*(7–8), 748–763. https://doi.org/10.1080/09523367.2019.1657839

Fan, H., Wu, P., & Xiong, H. (2005). Beijing ambitions: An analysis of the Chinese elite sports system and its Olympic strategy for the 2008 Olympic Games. *International Journal of the History of Sport*, *22*(4), 510–529. https://doi.org/10.1080/09523360500126336

Galtung, J. (1991). The sport system as a metaphor for the world system. In F. Landry, M. Landry, & M. Yerles (Eds.), *Sport ... the third millennium*. University of Laval Press.

Gong, Y. (2020). Reading European football, critiquing China: Chinese urban middle class fans as reflexive audience. *Cultural Studies*, *34*(3), 442–465. https://doi.org/10.1080/09502386.2019.1633370.

Grix, J. (2013). Sport politics and the Olympics. *Political Studies Review*, *11*(1), 15–25. https://doi.org/10.1111/1478-9302.12001

Gu, S. (1989). *The history of sport in China [中国体育史]*. Beijing. [谷世权].

Han, L. (2022) The U18 National Baseball Championship finishes, *Shanghai flyes highly with assistance from the MLB DC [2022年全国青年棒球锦标赛落幕, MLB DC少年助力上海队夺冠]*. http://life.ynet.com/2022/12/07/3559363t978.html. Accessed on 18 December 2022.

Hayton, J. W., Millward, P., & Petersen-Wagner, R. (2017). Chasing a Tiger in a network society? Hull City's proposed name change in the pursuit of China and East Asia's new middle class consumers. *International Review for the Sociology of Sport*, *52*(3), 279–298. https://doi.org/10.1177/1012690215588526

Houlihan, B. (1994). *Sport and international politics*. Harvester Wheatsheaf.

Houlihan, B., Tan, T., & Green, M. (2010). Policy transfer and learning from the West: Elite basketball development in the People's Republic of China. *Journal of Sport & Social Issues*, *34*(1), 4–28. https://doi.org/10.1177/0193723509358971

Hu, X. R. (2015a). *An analysis of Chinese Olympic and elite sport policy discourse in the post-Beijing 2008 Olympic Games era*. Loughborough University. https://dspace.lboro.ac.uk/2134/17458

Hu, X. R. (2015b). Chinese football and its number one fan: The political influence on China's emerging interest and new moves in football. http://www.policyforum.net/chinese-football-and-its-number-one-fan/

Hu, X. R. (2019). Ideological conflicts behind mutual belief: The termination of the 'dual-registration policy' and the collapse of an effective elite diving system in China. *Sport in Society*, *22*(8), 1362–1381. https://doi.org/10.1080/17430437.2019.1587410

Hu, X. R., & Henry, I. (2017). Reform and maintenance of Juguo Tizhi: Governmental management discourse of Chinese elite sport. *European Sport Management Quarterly*, *17*(4), 531–553. https://doi.org/10.1080/16184742.2017.1304433

Hu, X. R., & Liang, J. (2019). The nationalist construction of Chinese Olympians: Media, change, reform. In T. Ren, K. Ideda, & C. W. Woo (Eds.), *Media, sport, nationalism: East Asia: Soft power projection via the modern Olympic Games* (1st ed., pp. 17–48). Logos Verlag.

Hu, X. R., Liang, J., & Bairner, A. (2021). A rebel and a giant: Change and continuity in the discursive construction of Chinese sport heroes. *Sport in Society*, *24*(12), 2199–2221. https://doi.org/10.1080/17430437.2021.1991319

Hu, X. R., Zhao, J., Li, J., & Bairner, A. (2022). Why join the navy when you can be a pirate? A study of Chinese audience's willingness to pay for the live streaming of the premier league. *Sport in Society*, *0*(0), 1–20. https://doi.org/10.1080/17430437.2022.2137406.

Huang, F. (2013). Glocalisation of sport: The NBA's diffusion in China. *International Journal of the History of Sport*, *30*(3), 267–284.

Huizinga, J. (1970). *Homo ludens: A study of the play element in culture*. Temple Smith.

Jarvie, G. (1993). Sport, nationalism, and cultural identity. In L. Allison (Ed.), *The changing politics of sport* (pp. 58–83). Manchester University Press.

Kanchana, K. (2017). Copyright and live streaming of sports broadcasting. *International Review of Law, Computers & Technology*, 1–24.

Kellas, J. G. (1991) *The politics of nationalism and ethnicity*. Macmillan Education.

Lane, D. C. (2004). From Mao to Yao: A new game plan for China in the era of basketball globalisation. *Pacific Rim Law & Policy Journal Association*, *13*(1), 127–162. https://doi.org/10.1525/sp.2007.54.1.23

Li, M. [李敏宽] (2003). Chanting in my fatherland [放歌在祖国的天地间]. In *Returning home for 50 years, collection of works of Japanese Chinese and Chineses oversea students returned from Japan in the early stage of the PRC* (pp. 231–239). [回国五十年：建国初期回国旅日华侨留学生文集]. Taihai Press.

Li, W.-Y. (2018). Interview with Yu (Lucy) Huang, Coordinator, Data Strategy & Fan Loyalty, National Basketball Association China. *International Journal of Sport Communication*, *11*(2), 193–199. https://doi.org/10.1123/ijsc.2018-0073

Li, J. (2022). Another young bat signing with the major league. *Aiming to Change the 'Minor' Sport [又一位「棒少年」将签约MLB，能否助力棒球摘掉「小众」标签]*. http://sports.ifeng.com/c/8IrIQK9jHbk. Accessed on 18 December 2022.

Liu, B., Guo, Z., Wang, S., Chen, Y., & Zhang, B. (2020). Dual career: The demand, dilemma and exploration of the competitive sports reserve talents cultivation with Chinese characteristics in the new era [体教融合：新时代中国特色竞技体育后备人才培养的诉求、困境与探索]. *Journal of Physical Education*, *27*(6), 12–19.

Lucidarme, S., Babiak, K., & Willem, A. (2018). Governmental power in elite sport networks: A resource-dependency perspective. *European Sport Management Quarterly*, *18*(3), 348–372. https://doi.org/10.1080/16184742.2017.1405998

Luo, S., & Huang, F. (2013). China's Olympic dream and the legacies of the Beijing Olympics. *International Journal of the History of Sport*, *30*(4), 443–452.

Ma, Y., & Kurscheidt, M. (2019). The national games of China as a governance instrument in Chinese elite sport: An institutional and agency analysis. *International Journal of Sport Policy and Politics*, *11*(4), 679–699. https://doi.org/10.1080/19406940.2019.1633383

Maguire, J. A. (1994). Sport, identity politics, and globalisation diminishing contrasts and increasing varieties. *Sociology of Sport Journal*, *11*(4).

Mao, Z. (1939). Jinian Baiqiuen [in memory of Norman Bethune]. *Selection of the Works of Mao Zedong*, *2*, 1991. http://news.xinhuanet.com/ziliao/2004-06/24/content_1545030.htm

Nauright, J., & Zipp, S. (2020). *Routledge handbook of global sport*. Routledge. https://doi.org/10.4324/9781315714264

People's Daily. (1952, July 22). Military Games of the People's Liberation Army is taking place on 1st August. *People's Daily*.

Price, M. E., & Dayan, D. (2008). *Owning the Olympics: Narratives of the new China*. University of Michigan Press: University of Michigan Library. http://www.loc.gov/catdir/enhancements/fy0809/2008002887-d.html

Reaves, J. A. (2022). *Taking in a game: A history of baseball in Asia*. University of Nebraska Press.

Rosenberg, J. (2000). *The follies of globalisation theory: Polemical Essays*. Verso.

Roudometof, V., & Robertson, R. (1995). Globalisation, world-system theory, and the comparative study of civilisations: Issues of theoretical logic in world-hisotrical sociology. In S. K. Sanderson (Ed.), *Civilisations and world system*. (pp. 273–300). Alta Mira.

Sha, Q. (2014). Playing baseball in the New China: The changes in the circusmtance and the various identities of a sport [在新中国打棒球：一项体育运动的 境遇变迁及其多重角色]. *Research of the History of the CPC [中共党史研究]*, (2), 45–54.

Song, X., & Chen, J. (2005). A brief research on the development road of the baseball in P.R.C [浅析棒球运动在中国的发展之路]. *Journal of Harbin Physical Education Institute*, *23*(5), 83–85.

Tan, T., & Bairner, A. (2010). Globalisation and Chinese sport policy: The case of elite football in the People's Republic of China. *The China Quarterly*, *203*(September), 581–600. https://doi.org/10.1017/S0305741010000603

Tan, T., & Bairner, A. (2011). Managing globalization: The case of elite basketball policy in the People's Republic of China. *Journal of Sport Management*, *25*, 408–422.

Tan, T., Bairner, A., & Chen, Y. (2018). *Managing compliance with the World Anti-Doping Code: China's strategies and their implications.* https://doi.org/10.1177/1012690218805402

Tan, T., Huang, H. C., Bairner, A., & Chen, Y. (2016). Xi Jin-Ping's world cup dreams: From a major sports country to a world sports power. *International Journal of the History of Sport*, *33*(12), 1449–1465. https://doi.org/10.1080/09523367.2016.1243103

The GAS. (2022). The 2022 budget of the general administration of sport. https://www.sport.gov.cn/n315/n332/c24214199/content.html. Accessed on 15 June 2022.

The IOC. (2020). *Official programme of the Olympic Games PARIS 2024.* https://stillmed.olympics.com/media/Documents/Olympic-Games/Paris-2024/Paris-2024-Event-Programme.pdf. Accessed on 7 October 2022.

The Office of the Joint Meeting of the Football Reform and Development Department of the State Council. (2015). *Guowuyuan Zuqiu Gaige Fazhan Bu Lianxi Huiyi Guanyu Yinfa Zhongguo Zuqiu Xiehui Tiaozheng Gaige Fangan de Tongzhi [Notification from the Office of the Joint Meeting of the Football Reform and Development Department of the State Council].*

The Sport Council of Luwan District. (1958). *The baseball and softball development plan of Luwan District of Shanghai [卢湾区体委关于市垒棒球训练打算]*. The Sport Council of Luwan District.

Tian, E., & Wise, N. (2020). An Atlantic divide? Mapping the knowledge domain of European and North American based sociology of sport, 2008–2018. *International Review for the Sociology of Sport*, *55*(8), 1029–1055.

Tomlinson, A., & Young, C. (2006). *National identity and global sports events: Culture, politics, and spectacle in the Olympics and the football.* World Cup.

Vidar Hanstad, D., & Houlihan, B. (2015). Strengthening global anti-doping policy through bilateral collaboration: The example of Norway and China. *International Journal of Sport Policy and Politics*, *7*(4), 587–604. https://doi.org/10.1080/19406940.2015.1014394

Wang, K. (1953, November 28). Sport in the People's Liberation Army of China [中国人民解放军的体育运动]. *People's Daily*. [王克].

Wise, N. (2015). Geographical approaches and the sociology of sport. In R. Giulianotti (Ed.), *Routledge handbook of the sociology of sport* (pp. 142–152). Routledge. (pp.

Wise, N. (2020). Eventful futures and triple bottom line impacts: BRICS, image regeneration and competitiveness. *Journal of Place Management and Development*, *13*(1), 89–100.

Wise, N., & Kohe, G. Z. (2020). Sports geography: New approaches, perspectives and directions. *Sport in Society*, *23*(1), 1–10.

Wu, S. (1999). 中国体育史 *[The history of sport in the People's Republic of China]. (S Wued.)*. China Book Press.

Xu, G. (2008). *Olympic dreams: China and sports 1895–2008*. Havard University Press.

Yu, D., & Huang, Y. (2015). Analysis of the weakening in the administration role of the ACSF [中华全国体育总会职能弱化的历史探析]. *Journal of Xi'an Physical Education University [西安体育学院学报]*, *32*(2), 146–151.

Yu, L., Newman, J., Xue, H., & Pu, H. (2019). The transition game: Toward a cultural economy of football in post-socialist China. *International Review for the Sociology of Sport*, *54*(6), 711–737. https://doi.org/10.1177/1012690217740114

Yu, C., & Zhang, J. (2006). Combination of sports and education and construction of college top level sport teams. *China Sport Science*, *26*(6), 79–84.

CHAPTER 7

FROM AN EXPATRIATE-ONLY SPORT TO AN ASIAN GAMES SPORT: THE DEVELOPMENT OF CRICKET IN CHINA

Boyang He[a], Dominic Malcolm[b] and Chunyang Xu[c]

[a]*Xi'an Jiaotong University, China*
[b]*Loughborough University, UK*
[c]*Tongji University, China*

ABSTRACT

This chapter provides an exhaustive analysis on the development of cricket in China in order to advance existing theories of cricket's development and consider future implications for the international game. Adapted from two journal articles of He and Malcolm (2021) and He et al. (2023), it structures the development of cricket in China according to two key historical era: cricket as an 'expatriate-only' game and cricket as an 'Asian Games sport'. The first era, cricket as an 'expatriate-only' game, is constructed according to three key phases: early development; post-war and the 'opening-up' era. The second era, cricket as an 'Asian Games sport', is constructed according to five periods: budding period (2003–2005), peak period (2006–2010), stable period (2011–2014), trough period (2015–2018) and revival period (2019–present). This paper offers a broadened examination of cricket's development in China, contending that cricket in the country (specifically the mainland) manifests itself in two distinct forms, that is, first, it survives as a grassroots sport, sustained by a resilient expatriate diaspora community. Second, it exists as a sport primarily directed by the state and bolstered by the Asian Games and deeply integrated into the Chinese educational system. It concludes that the degree to which the co-existed motives of multiple stakeholders aligned and misaligned, and the interdependence with the unstable 'Asian Games sport status' will serve as the cornerstone for cricket's future in China and contribute significantly to the international sport's global development.

Keywords: China; cricket; expatriate; education; Asian games

INTRODUCTION

Recent news that India men's and women's cricket squads both won gold medals at 2023 Hangzhou Asian Games (International Cricket Council, 2023; Wisden, 2023) not only reflects India's predominance of cricket in Asia, it can be also seen as an encouraging sign of progress for the promotion of the game in the continent through sports mega events, as it is the first time that India send teams to Asian Games since cricket was introduced to the event in the 2010 Guangzhou Games (Wisden, 2023).

While the much-awaited participation of India in Asian Games have been realized, it is quite surprizing that both China's men's and women's cricket teams missed the Hangzhou Games given that the Chinese men's cricket squad played in the ICC (International Cricket Council) Men's T20 World Cup Asia B Qualifier in July, Malaysia (ESPNcricinfo, 2023a), whilst the women's played Women's T20 East Asia Cup 2023 in May (ESPNcricinfo, 2023b) and subsequently the ICC's T20 World Cup Asia Region Qualifier in September (ESPNcricinfo, 2023b). It should be noted that Women's East Asia Cup 2023 was played at Pingfeng Campus Cricket Field in Hangzhou (Cricket Hong Kong, 2023), a purpose-built cricket stadium for the Hangzhou Asian Games, where China Women performed reasonably well that only lost to Hong Kong Women in the one-over eliminator of the final match.

The absence of China's cricket squads in the Asian Games that held in their own country indeed seems puzzling, particularly considering China's huge investment to spend approximately US$20 million to construct the brand new Pingfeng Cricket Stadium (Lavalette, 2021), which is seen as 'an unprecedented move for an associate member of the [ICC] whose national men's team has barely played any international cricket matches in recent years (He et al., 2023, p. 830). In this regard, China provides a highly illustrative case study that enables us to broaden our comprehension of the modern evolution of cricket on a global scale.

Adapted mainly from two journal articles of He and Malcolm (2021) and He et al. (2023), this chapter aims to provide a most comprehensive analysis on the development of cricket in China according to two key historical eras: *Cricket as an 'expatriate-only' game* and *Cricket as an 'Asian Games sport'*. The first era, Cricket as an 'expatriate-only' game, is constructed according to three key phases: early development; post-war and the 'opening-up' era. Based on the interview data, the second era, Cricket as an 'Asian Games sport' is constructed according to five periods: budding period (2003–2005), peak period (2006–2010), stable period (2011–2014), trough period (2015–2018) and revival period (2019–present). This chapter offers a comprehensive analysis of cricket's development in China, reflecting upon and enriching current theories regarding its diffusion process and also emphasises several crucial processes that can enable and/or constrain the future development of the global game.

CRICKET AS AN 'EXPATRIATE-ONLY' GAME
The Early Development of Cricket in China

A map of Macau created in 1834 shows a cricket ground and is considered the earliest record of such a sporting space in China (Ljungstedt, 2004). The sport of cricket in Macau and China is linked to colonisation. In 1842, the British Crown Colony in Hong Kong in 1842 saw the development of sports from Britain expand, and cricket saw an increase after the Opium War and subsequent post-war agreements (Bridges, 2017). By 1851, Hong Kong Cricket Club (HKCC) was formerly established, and a pitch to play cricket was designated on a military parade ground (Hall, 1999). From a colonial standpoint, this displayed a semblance of power through military presence and a sport commonly played in Britain, as these were spaces for military teams to compete on. As the 20th century rolled around, the establishment of a cricket league in Hong Kong was created for those stationed in the region representing the British Empire. This league was established for those in the police, civil service, university staff and armed forces (Bridges, 2017). Soon after, educational institutions established their own cricket clubs as a way of integrating sporting culture into university life. The Chinese Recreation Club did field a cricket team from 1911 to 1926; however, there were only a few Chinese players representing Hong Kong University. During the time from World War I to the end of World War II, the number of ethnic Chinese on these cricket clubs were scarce (Bridges, 2017).

The presence of the British military and the British influence in university education in Hong Kong created a foundation for cricket's diffusion into China. To this regard, cricket was viewed as a 'civilising mission', and evidence found in Hong Kong can be considered similar to that in other parts of the world where the British had an established Empire presence, including India in South Asia and the Caribbean in the Americas. It can also be noted that the sport of rugby followed similar patterns in parts of the world with British influence (see Harris & Wise, 2020). Power relations at play were seen as displays of 'white' British sporting culture, as characteristics were also deemed uniquely lined to English governance and law (Malcolm, 2021). Nevertheless, it becomes apparent that the capacity of cricket to shape character and instil a specific ethos of adhering to rules was experienced by the local Chinese population encountering the game for the first time (see He & Malcolm, 2021).

By the end of the 1850s, by 1858, the city of Shanghai saw the emergence of the Shanghai Cricket Club (the SCC). The cricket club and grounds were situated right in the heart of Shanghai with a large playing field and a turf wicket comparable that was comparable to any grounds found across the British Empire at the time (Dutta, 2015). This description hints at the significant role nostalgia played in the club's establishment. Records pertaining to the SCC's inaugural game indicate that its organisation was also militarily facilitated.

Cricket, therefore, served as a medium for the colonisers to forge mutually supportive relationships. Like in Hong Kong, the presence of the military was there to safeguard British trade interests and with this presence you would find sports commonly played in Britain.

Cricket in Post-War China

Since the establishment of 'New China' in 1949, expatriate-run cricket clubs were disbanded, effectively bringing cricket to a halt in mainland China. This shift occurred partially due to the ascendancy of anti-imperialistic and anti-colonial sentiments that became integral to the new regime's ideological framework and legitimacy (Fan & Lu, 2015). Furthermore, the anti-elitist fervour of the Great Proletarian Cultural Revolution from 1969 onward further discouraged the sport's continuance in China. Once the mutual relationships associated with trade lessened, this impacted the nurturing of cricket's development.

In Hong Kong, cricket was still played by many and leading to the formation of the Hong Kong Cricket Association (HKCA) in 1968. Nevertheless, cricket in Hong Kong encountered numerous challenges during this period. Hong Kong did maintain membership in cricket's international community and associations but was unable to participate in an ICC tournament until 1982 (Bridges, 2017). Much of this issue faced with not being able to participate was tied to there not being enough skilled players qualified to compete at a higher level internationally. A legacy of ICC affiliation became merely symbolic and lacked a level of play and competition that was functionally viable. In this regard, territorial peculiarities within the vast array of British imperial relations exerted a distinct influence on the evolution of cricket.

Cricket and the 'Opening Up' of China

As stipulated in the agreement that established Hong Kong as a Crown Colony, the territory was due to be back to Chinese sovereignty in 1997. This would be a turning point economically and politically seen through the lens of a constitutional transition and economic liberalisation. Some argue this helped the sport of cricket catalyse from Hong Kong into the mainland (Bridges, 2017). Further to this point, the post-colonial residents of Hong Kong presented mixed emotions: apprehension about how reunification might curtail their autonomy, yet optimism that the territory could serve as a gateway for global engagement with China (Bridges, 2017). Analogously, the sentiment surrounding cricket appeared intertwined with a blend of perceived challenges and fresh prospects. Consequently, in 2001, a league for primary school playground cricket commenced in Hong Kong, accompanied by the establishment of various age-group leagues for Chinese teams (Bridges, 2017).

This broader political context also facilitated the re-establishment of the SCC in 1994 (Dutta, 2015). These Commonwealth expatriates who work in Shanghai garnered initial support from the Shanghai Sports Federation, which enabled the visit from Hong Kong's Craigengower Cricket Club (HKCCC). One way to open up exposure to sport is through network coverage, and this was done by showing matches between HKCCC and SCC on Saturday evening programs in China (Dutta, 2015). Showcasing cricket on the news was also like to social and political sanding, and developing the sport with British ties resonated with influential individuals in the public spotlight.

The expatriate cricket's unique growth patterns during this era were similarly apparent in the subsequent significant milestone: the emergence of Sixes Cricket tournaments. Introduced as a fresh format, Sixes tournaments (a shorter version of the game) commenced in Hong Kong in 1992. With growing support and a potential new fan base, this was hindered by a few years later in 1997 by the Asian financial crisis until 2001, but many argue this financial impact impacted development for over another decade. Meanwhile, a comparable Shanghai Sixes competition surfaced shortly afterwards in 1994 and persisted until 2004. When it came to attracting external support, the Shanghai event parallelled its Hong Kong counterpart, gaining endorsement from the ICC and Asian Cricket Council (ACC), thereby drawing numerous renowned international cricketers.

In 2012, a third prominent Cricket Sixes tournament emerged in China, spearheaded by the successor of the PCC, Beijing Cricket Club (BCC) (He & Malcolm, 2021). Regularly, 16 teams representing Australia, Singapore, Hong Kong, Malaysia and the Philippines grace this tournament. While primarily catering to the expatriate community, the Beijing event also demonstrates a considerable domestic focus, pulling teams from various Chinese cities, particularly Beijing, Shanghai, Guangzhou and Wuxi. It should be noted that the Shenyang Sunbirds, a team entirely comprising local Chinese cricketers, made their debut in this tournament in 2012 (Dutta, 2015).

From the standpoint of using events to develop cricket, a Sixes tournaments signify a unique aspect within the broader evolution of cricket. The observed level of collaboration reflects the historical significance of trade ties. These tournaments underscore the relevance of modern developmental influences, including television, corporate sponsorships and the utilization of sport as a medium for exerting soft power and gaining global recognition. Although this format is particularly prevalent in certain regions, the modifications to the number of participants and the emphasis on sixes echo some of the adjustments made to differentiate baseball from cricket. This not only exemplifies how a cultural product can undergo adaptation while preserving its identity but also highlights the pivotal role of the Commonwealth diasporic community in shaping the future of cricket in mainland China.

CRICKET AS AN ASIAN GAMES SPORT
Budding Period (2003–2005)

It is noted that the ACC made efforts to push cricket to the local Chinese population in the early 2000s. The ACC's major motives for this, according to Wagg, were 'geo-political and global commercial interest(s)' (Wagg, 2010, p. 225). An international administrator echoed Wagg's points, observing that 'the ACC was trying to stimulate regional interest in cricket as a way of challenging the power balances between the ICC and the ACC itself, to obtain a greater say in how cricket will be managed and promoted' (Roy). Similarly, Cricket Australia 'held multiple training camps for native coaches and primary school students since 2005 to expand its influence' (Steve). Indeed, commercial interests are closely intertwined with geo-political considerations, as evidenced by the eagerness of these international cricket bodies to align themselves with both.

From the perspective of China as a receiver, however, Chinese cricket administrators view the sport authorities' open attitude towards cricket as primarily a practical reaction to geo-political developments. For instance, a former official from the Small Ball Sports Management Centre (SBSMC) mentioned that China was aware of Guangzhou's forthcoming hosting of the 2010 Asian Games due to being the sole applicant, and the ACC had been advocating for cricket's inclusion in the Asian Games. To this end, China 'needed to take actions to get prepared' (John).

As the specialist official bureau to oversee a variety of non-Olympic sports, the SBSMC supervises cricket and its management organisation, the Chinese Cricket Association (CCA). The CCA has gained widespread acknowledgement as the cricket authority in China. This recognition extends across platforms such as the official websites of the ICC and ACC, influential media (Hogg, 2010; Maidment, 2005) and academic papers published in both English and Chinese (Dutta, 2015; Feng & Liu, 2011; Ren & Chen, 2013; Wagg, 2010). These references portray the CCA as a well-structured organisation to outsiders as they establish international relationships to build collaboration and interaction. One critical point to address is the CCA lacks registration with the China Civil Affairs Bureau. Nonetheless, the CCA gained recognition from global cricket authorities and was registered with the ACC circa 2003. Being registered enabled CCA to be eligible for financial assistance and support to develop the sport (Chinese Cricket Annual, 2003). Bridges (2017) notes that China's affiliate membership resulted in US$5 million grant to develop cricket.

Support through such grants was a step towards bringing China into the cricket community. However, to Chinese sports officials, there is a lack of interest in developing sports that are not featured in the Olympics, so CCA needed to focus on attracting external support. Nevertheless, these endeavours culminated in the formal introduction of cricket to the native Chinese population, with the Guangzhou Asian Games serving as a pivotal momentum.

Peak Period (2006–2010)

One break that benefited the development of cricket was the inclusion of the sport in the Asian Games. The Guangzhou Asian Games saw the sport featured and was a paramount success for the GAS. For the newly formed national teams, the Asian Games was an opportunity to showcase their place in the region. To develop a venue, Guangzhou's city government provided US$5 million to build a professional cricket stadium. This was constructed at Guangdong University of Technology.

China was met with competition at this event as other Test nations included Bangladesh, India, Pakistan and Sri Lanka, competing in T20 matches (a shorter version of the game). However, there was no broadcasting of cricket matches on television and herein lies the challenge for developing different versions of the game and a limited opportunity to seek new revenue and funding sources.

To advance the sport China needed to seek skilled players and coaches who could develop and grow the sport, and this meant recruiting internationals to play in China as a way of enabling the players to become exposed to elite players and enhance the quality of play. Notable figures such as a former Pakistani Test cricketer, the ex-captain of the Indian women's team and Bangladesh's inaugural Test centurion, Aminul Islam came to China. Their role was a mentoring one (Chinese Cricket Annual, 2006). In 2006, Shenyang Sport University (SSU) established cricket teams (Chinese Cricket Annual, 2007), and this would become a talent hub for developing the sport over the next decade. Meanwhile, in Shanghai where expatriate cricket had flourished since the 1990s, Chinese administrators capitalised on this opportunity and collaborated with local universities and schools. This led to the formation of the Shanghai Cricket Association (SCA) in 2008 and played an integral role in connecting local Chinese players with expatriate clubs.

Training camps and organising regularly schedule cricket matches were arranged. For instance in December 2006, SSU hosted the inaugural National Championship (Chinese Cricket Annual, 2006). This would become the only annual cricket tournament in China. Then in 2008, a dedicated talent-scouting team comprised both Chinese and internationals focused on preparing a squad for the Asian Games (Chinese Cricket Annual, 2008). Participants were recruitment from 25 schools across four cities. A pool of 500 players competed for a spot after the first phase of skills training and simulated games, and competitions followed until 14 were selected for the national teams. This team would travel to international matches as a way of strengthening the team and to gain exposure, and this allowed the players to gain recognition.

The Chinese men's team faced significant challenges at the Guangzhou Games. They were drawn against tough opponents like Pakistan in the group stage and ultimately failed to secure a win (Felix). Players would note that they had a limited opportunity to practice in turf pitches instead of artificial grass football pitches.

Incheon Games Period (2011–2014)

The performance of the Chinese men's squad meant that the limited resources invested in them were further cut. While many Chinese male cricketers have left cricket, the women's cricket team maintained a remarkable level of consistency during this era (Gel). This stability was primarily due to their ample playing chances. In October 2012, the ACC hosted the Women's T20 Asia Cup at the Guanggong International Cricket Stadium, marking the venue's first tournament since the 2010 Guangzhou event (He et al., 2023). Although the competition was primarily for ICC associate/affiliate members, it still garnered participation from second- or third-tier teams of several test-playing nations, including India, Pakistan, Sri Lanka and Bangladesh (Gel). China was defeated against Bangladesh and Sri Lanka but showed promise in their opening match against Bangladesh, nearly clinching victory through their strong fielding efforts. The final match vsNepal also provided encouragement as Nepal stood among Asia's top non-test nations.

The women's team further demonstrated their prowess during a July 2014 tour to England where they competed in different matches. They played several matches, suffering only one loss against an invitational Marylebone Cricket Club (MCC) XI at Lord's (Felix; SCA's report to the ICC 2017). In addition to these international opportunities, local sports authorities in Shandong Province, China, began to extend their support to the women's side. That same year, the Shandong SBSMC and Linglong Tire Company sponsored a two-month training tour to New Zealand for the women's team, preparing them for the upcoming Asian Games (Young).

The coach and captain of the women's squad believed that this preparation would get the team a medal at the Incheon Asian Games. China's performance in group matches demonstrated their confidence as they would go on toto defeat Japan in the quarterfinals. However, while the semi-final loss to Pakistan was expected, the heartbreaking defeat in the bronze medal match against Sri Lanka left a profound sense of disappointment (He et al., 2023). Their previous loss to Thailand in the 2013 ACC Women's Championship final also cost them the chance to compete in the global qualifier for the 2015 Women's T20 World Cup in Ireland. The significance of this setback was immense, as Thailand received significant funding from the ICC for participating in the global qualifier, enabling them to invest in cricket facilities, hire international coaches and provide player salaries, thereby ensuring the sustained growth of their women's cricket team. This observation aligns with a report tracing Thailand's women's cricket development, where the team manager, Kader, identified 2013 as a pivotal year due to their qualification for the global event (Rego, 2019).

Negative news continuously befell to Chinese cricket since 2013. It is noted that the ACC no longer considered China as a priority for cricket development in the region (Dutta, 2015). It was evident that the Chinese cricket authorities were well-informed of the ACC's dwindling interest in their cricket development. As Amber noted that 'The actual support is declining... for example, four job positions for retired Chinese cricketers as ACC Development Officers were not extended after the first term' (Amber).

Trough Period (2015–2018)

The ACC's reversal on its plan for cricket development in China posed additional challenges to the sport's future in the country. Nonetheless, the exclusion of cricket from the 2018 Asian Games held in Indonesia dealt a final blow to Chinese cricket, according to most cricket enthusiasts in the country. This exclusion had a significant impact on various planned initiatives and led to several skilled players withdrawing from cricket (He et al., 2023)

Cricket's absence from the 2018 Asian Games was the alteration of the event's location. While Hanoi (Vietnam) originally held the hosting rights, they relinquished them to Jakarta (Indonesia), which proved inadequate in providing the necessary infrastructure for cricket matches (He & Malcolm, 2021). However, several interviewed players and coaches revealed that they were conscious that cricket might be excluded from the 2018 Asian Games after the Incheon games. This realization was presumably not surprizing to Chinese cricket administrators, as Felix notes, there are 'few countries would invest heavily to build a stadium for a relatively unknown sport'.

The exclusion of cricket from the 2018 Asian Games dealt a severe blow to the national teams. Following the 2010 Guangzhou games, certain players had persevered by securing coaching positions or embarking on Master's programs at SSU to keep honing their cricket skills, all in anticipation of participating in the 2018 Games (Gel). The announcement of cricket's absence in 2018 Asian Games left the players in a state of confusion and disappointment. Consequently, quite a few national players have abandoned the cricketing career (Gel). Nevertheless, the Chinese women's squad won the East Asia Cup in 2015 and played in the 2015 ICC Women's World T20 Qualifier, where they defeated Netherlands and Thailand (Gel).

This trough period of Chinese cricket bears similar features to the first two periods; the precarious status of cricket within the Asian Games framework has profoundly impacted its growth trajectory in China. Remarkably, neither the domestic sports administration nor the global cricket bodies seem to exert much control over this aspect. This trend persists in the subsequent phase as cricket makes a comeback in the Hangzhou 2022 Asian Games, sparking both optimism for a renewal and scepticism regarding the sustainability of its developmental prospects.

Revival Period (2019–Present)

The majority of sports disciplines slated for inclusion in the 2022 Asian Games had already been determined prior to Hangzhou's designation as the host city (Butler, 2015). This highlights the unique circumstances surrounding cricket, as it was only after a subsequent decision by the OCA and ACC in April 2019 that the sport was reinstated for the upcoming games in Hangzhou (Felix). As the decision being made, the ACC and the OCA sent officials to Hangzhou and located Zhejiang University of Technology as an appropriate place for building a new cricket ground for the Asian Games. It is noted that the University covers 20% of the total budget of 170 million Chinese Yuan while the Hangzhou local government pays for the most 80% (He et al., 2023)

Unlike the sluggish advancement of cricket in China, the construction of the stadium progressed at a typically rapid Chinese rate, culminating in its inauguration in February 2022.

Indeed, the reintroduction of cricket to the Asian Games reactivates the stilted development of cricket in China, but the key thing is developing the sport early in the schools. It is noted that in 2019, the first Belt and Road International Cricket

Tournament was held in Shandong and Shanghai, and the China-Afghanistan-Pakistan Youth Cricket Friendship Games was played in Jinan and Beijing. Both tournaments were 'supported by China's Ministry of Foreign Affairs' because they are seen as 'conducive to, and good practices of China's broader Belt and Road Initiative that facilitated the friendship between China and her cricket-playing neighbours' (John). It should be highlighted that all the women's Under-19 matches were umpired by Chinese female national players, arguably a positive sign for the Chinese players as it makes their cricketing careers more sustainable.

By contrast, the male team underwent a complete reorganization, welcoming new players primarily recruited from two local colleges in Shanghai: Shanghai Communications Polytechnic and Shanghai Jiaotong School. This reorganization aligns with the collaborative efforts between the SBSMC of the GAS and the SCA to jointly establish a 'talent hub' in Shanghai (Felix). Likewise, the SBSMC forged a partnership with the Shandong Small Ball Union and the Jinan Cricket Association (JCA) to jointly develop the national women's team (Young). These strategic alliances have reinforced the SCA and JCA's (as well as Shandong Small Ball Union's) prominent role in Chinese cricket, granting them greater authority and autonomy in selecting national players.

This enhanced autonomy is expected to facilitate stronger ties with local educational institutions and attract more sponsorships from local businesses. Given the challenges faced by Chinese cricket governing bodies in securing broadcasting agreements and gaining mainstream media attention, securing local sponsorships emerges as a critical factor for the sustainable growth of regional cricket. For instance, the financial backing provided by the Shandong Linglong Tire Company has been instrumental in the rapid and robust development of cricket in Shandong in recent years (He et al., 2023).

CONCLUSION

Given the geopolitical and postcolonial dynamics of the relationships between China and Britain, what is found today are two distinct cricketing strands in China: one as an expatriate sport sustained by a resilient diasporic community and the other as an Asian Games sport, sponsored by the state, integrated into the educational system and aligned with the broader framework of Chinese sports.

A closer examination reveals that cricket in China has been shaped by multiple stakeholders with sometimes divergent motivations and interests. Specifically, international cricket organisations have viewed China as a potential opportunity for commercial and geopolitical expansion; expatriate communities have leveraged cricket as a medium for social networking and trade facilitation; key Chinese coaches and cricket administrators have perceived an opportunity for career advancement through this under-developed international sport in China and Chinese cricketers have derived a sense of pride and excitement from their newfound status as national athletes. Therefore, the degree to which these co-existed motives aligned/misaligned and the interdependence with the unstable 'Asian Games sport status' are likely to continually impact on the future development of cricket in China.

FIVE KEY READINGS

Kaufman, J., & Patterson, O. (2005). Cross-national cultural diffusion: The global spread of cricket. *American Sociological Review, 70*(1), 82–110.

In this article, Jason Kaufman and Orlando Patterson explore the dynamics of cross-national cultural diffusion through the study of a case in which a symbolically powerful cultural practice, the traditionally English sport of cricket, successfully diffused to most but not all countries with close cultural ties to England. This article highlights a key process that the diffusion of cultural practices can be promoted or discouraged by intermediaries with the power to shape the cultural meaning and institutional accessibility of such practices.

Malcolm, D. (2013). *Globalising cricket: Englishness, empire and identity.* **Bloomsbury.**

This book is an excellent guide to understanding the historical development of cricket from its earliest beginnings to the recent past. It is a very well written and readable historical sociology of cricket that covers the emergence of the game in England to its globalisation in the 21st century. Underpinned by the figurational sociology of Norbert Elias, this book brings together discussions of the influence of social class, commercialisation, violence, formal innovation, national consciousness and the projection of empire on cricket in its formative years.

Zheng, J., Chen, S., Tan, T., & Lau, P. (2018). Sport policy in China (Mainland). *International Journal of Sport Policy and Politics, 10*(3), 469–491.

This article reviews China's sport policy at different periods since its inception, analyses the rationale for, and form and extent of, government intervention, presents the sport structure in China and identifies the dominant characteristics of its sport policy. It covers various sport policy areas, ranging from elite sport and mass sport to sports mega-events, and sports professionalisation is discussed, and their relative policy significances are compared. The degree of balance between these areas and policy priorities are thus defined.

Mustafa, F. (2013). Cricket and globalisation: Global processes and the imperial game. *Journal of Global History, 8,* 318–341.

This article aims to redefine the role of sports within the context of global historical phenomena. Focussing on the spread of cricket throughout the British Empire, its adoption by colonised regions, and subsequent commercialisation, it delves into the transformation of an initially elite English pastime into a sport dominated by former colonies, particularly India. Central to its inquiry is the question of how such a shift occurred. Through this investigation, the article endeavours to offer theoretical insights into the dynamics of global processes and cultural exchanges during the 20th century and the role the sport played in these exchanges. The paper argues these processes led to a discernible reconfiguration of the 'cultural economy' of sports, shifting influence from the developed nations of the West to the developing nations.

Gupta, A. (2004). The globalisation of cricket: The rise of the non-West. *International Journal of the History of Sport, 21*(2), 257–276, at 259.

Globalisation in sports mirrors broader international relations dynamics, with wealth and technology predominantly controlled by the West, leading to their dominance in major events like the Olympics. Commercial success hinges on Western-friendly time zones. European football exemplifies this, with UEFA and European teams monopolising the sport globally, even recruiting talent from non-Western regions. In contrast, cricket bucks this trend, as non-Western nations not only excel on-field but also wield significant economic and political influence. This shift is attributed to globalisation processes fostering transnational fan communities, technological advancements in coverage and declining influence in host countries, allowing alternative power centres to emerge.

REFERENCES

Bridges, B. (2017). Maintaining a minority sport: Cricket in post-colonial Hong Kong. *International Journal of the History of Sport, 33*(11), 1242–1253.

Butler, N. (2015). *Hangzhou confirmed as host of 2022 Asian Games.* https://www.insidethegames.biz/articles/1030204/hangzhou-confirmed-as-host-of-2022-asian-games. Accessed on 2 December 2023.

Cricket Hong Kong. (2023). *Exciting Hangzhou 2023 Women's East Asian Cup.* https://www.hkcricket.org/events/east-asia-cup-2023. Accessed on 2 December 2023.

Dutta, S. (2015). China. In T. Wigmore & P. Miller (Eds.), *Cricket in its outposts crick* (pp. 179–202). Pitch Publishing.

ESPNcricinfo. (2023a). Syazrul Idrus becomes the first man to take a seven-for in T20Is. https://www.espncricinfo.com/story/syazrul-idrus-of-malaysia-breaks-the-record-for-best-bowling-figures-in-men-s-t20is-1389414. Accessed on 5 December 2023.

ESPNcricinfo. (2023b). CHN-W vs MYA-W, ICC Women's T20 World Cup Asia QLF 2023, 19th match, group B at Bangi, 4 September 2023 – Full scorecard. https://www.espncricinfo.com/series/icc-women-s-t20-world-cup-asia-qlf-2023-1394741/china-women-vs-myanmar-women-19th-match-group-b-1394769/full-scorecard. Accessed 6 December 2023.

Fan, H., & Lu, Z. (2015). *The politicisation of sport in modern China: Communists and champions.* Routledge.

Feng, J., & Liu, W. (2011). Woguo Banqiu Yundong Fazhan de Kexingxing Fenxi [Analysis on development feasibility of Chinese cricket]. *Journal of Nanjing Institute of Physical Education, 10*(4), 84–85.

Hall, P. (1999). *150 years of cricket in Hong Kong.* The Book Guild Ltd.

Harris, J., & Wise, N. (Eds.). (2020). *Rugby in global perspective: Playing on the periphery.* Routledge.

He, B., & Malcolm, D. (2021). The development of cricket in China. *Sport in Society, 24*(8), 1372–1387.

He, B., Yang, J., & Malcolm, D. (2023). 'Cricket is perfectly suited to the Chinese people': The contemporary development of Chinese cricket. *International Journal of the History of Sport, 40*(9), 830–850.

Hogg, C. (2010). China catches cricket bug ahead of Asian Games debut. https://www.bbc.co.uk/news/world-asia-pacific-11718145. Accessed on 2 January 2024.

International Cricket Council. (2023). India clinch their first-ever Gold medal in cricket at the Asian games. https://www.icc-cricket.com/news/3700322. Accessed on 5 December 2023.

Lavalette, T. (2021). As focus intensifies on rising U.S., cricket in China remains a work in progress. http://www.forbes.com/sites/tristanlavalette/2021/11/27/as-focus-intensifies-on-rising-us-cricket-in-china-remains-a-work-in-progress/?sh=24ce55df66be. Accessed on 10 January 2023.

Ljungstedt, A. (2004). *An historical sketch of the Portuguese settlements in China*. Adamant Media Corporation.

Maidment, P. (2005). China's cracking cricket. *Forbes*. https://www.forbes.com/global/2005/1031/102A.html#40911a964429. Accessed on 2 January 2024.

Malcolm, D. (2021). Cricket, Brexit and the Anglosphere. *Sport in Society*, *24*(8), 1274–1290.

Rego, N. (2019). The smiling assassins: How Thailand built a formidable women's national cricket team. https://emergingcricket.com/insight/the-smiling-assassins-how-thailand-built-a-formidable-womens-national-cricket-team-part-2/. Accessed on 2 January 2024.

Ren, X., & Chen, C. (2013). Banqiu zai Zhongguo de Fazhan Tanjiu [Research on the development of cricket in China]. *Sport*, *8*, 155–156.

Wagg, S. (2010). It's just not shen shi yun dong: The prospects of cricket in China. In C. Rumford & S. Wagg (eds), *Cricket and globalization*. Cambridge Scholars Publishing.

Wisden. (2023). Explained: Why India Men won Asian Games gold medal, despite final washout. https://wisden.com/series-stories/asian-games-2023/explained-why-india-men-won-asian-games-gold-medal-despite-final-washout. Accessed on 2 January 2024.

CHAPTER 8

ESPORTISATION: THE INCLUSION OF ESPORTS IN THE HANGZHOU ASIAN GAMES

Jianping Hong[a] and Jiandong Yi[b]

[a]Beijing Sport University, China
[b]Wenzhou University, China

ABSTRACT

The inclusion of esports as an official event in the Hangzhou Asian Games is an important step towards the institutionalisation of esports. The significance of this event marks that Asia once again takes a lead in the global esportisation. This chapter investigates a series of history events in the inclusion process of esports into the comprehensive Games in Asia using process sociology and actor network theory (ANT). This study will analyse the type characteristics of esports events in Hangzhou Asian Games, whilst examining how key stakeholders' interact and balance in the network composed of international sports organisations, host of the event, emerging esports organisations and esports game companies. The chapter also examines the functions of global game industrial economic geography, local cultural politics, esports geopolitics and Olympic values in esports sportization, aiming to reveal the implications of esports inclusion in the Asian Games on the debate of whether esports meets the criteria to be classified as a 'sport' and its enlightenment of digital strategy to the inclusion esports in the Olympics.

Keywords: Esportisation; Hangzhou Asian Games; figurational sociology; acting network theory; stakeholder interaction; institutionalisation

INTRODUCTION

On 16 December 2020, the 38th Olympic Council of Asia (OCA) General Assembly approved esports as a medal event for the 2022 Asian Games in Hangzhou (Cui et al., 2023). This is an important step in the institutionalisation of esports and marks that Asia is once again at the forefront of global esportisation development. It is not difficult to discover from the history of the Asian major sporting events that the inclusion of esports as an official competition is not an isolated event. How did the phenomenon of esports becoming a general game event in the Asian context gradually occur over the past two decades? Which key stakeholders have decided that esports became an official event at the Asian Games? What factors determine the setting of esports events for the Hangzhou Asian Games? What is the implication for the Olympic Games from esports becoming a medal event of the Asian Games? These are the questions that this article aims to explore.

Socialists Elias and Dunning (1986) examined the civilization of Western European societies from the Medium Ages to the early 20 century by researching the control of violence and aggression closely related to the Modern sports, thus generating the sociology of the process, which was different from the static research of structural functionalism. They also proposed the concept of 'sportisation' in the research of modern British fox hunting and provided a persuasive explanation of how the sport developed from an obscure game to a modern form. These conceptualizations among others as noted by Tian and Wise (2020) have profoundly influenced sociology and the sociology of sport (Lu, 2010). In the historical turn of sociology, 'process events' analysis, which emphasises dynamics, fluidity and the relationships and interactions of participants in the process of events, has been widely used in social science research (Guo, 2016; Wise & Maguire, 2022). Esports offer new sociological dimensions for sport, and these are also geographical as we move into virtual environments (Wise, 2015; Wise & Kohe, 2020). Diving deep into sociological theory, scholars from the Paris school, represented by the French sociologist Bruno Latur and Michel Caron, proposed actor network theory (ANT) in the 1980s. This particular theory considers society as an intricate network of connections between heterogeneous 'actors', which include human and non-human actors (such as ideas, technological objects creatures, etc.). ANT uses translation to analyse the generation of social networks (Latour, 1987). Translation analysis emphasises the heterogeneity of actors and the non-determinism of network generation. It follows what actors say and think and examines which actors are involved and given specific shapes, as well as the operations of translators and mediators in the process of social practice. This new research agenda has been widely applied as an analytical framework for sociological research on technological innovation. In this paper, we will comprehensively adopt the perspective of process-analysing and ANT to examine the milestones in the way of the esports inclusion in the Asian Games, summarise the logics behind the formation and evolution of the esportisation in the glocalisation context, explore the impact of Hangzhou Asian Games esports strategic exploration on the institutionalisation in esports and evaluate its innovative significance.

ESPORTISATION IN ASIA: A PROCESS – EVENT ANALYSIS

For the so-called 'process event analysis', Chinese sociologist Sun Liping (2010) once had a graphic illustration: 'for example, we go to a village studying the social relations of villagers with each other. How could we know how intimate they are? The villagers themselves made their best answer: only when there is one thing happens, do we know who is your best friend and who is just a stranger to whom. 'When there is one thing happens' is an eventing process which shows the logic. The Chinese old saying goes

> Fighting the tiger with brothers and going into battles with father and son (Should be a dear brother, his soldiers it means one family unity, of one mind, be of one heart and one mind, to do things easily succeed!).

From this saying, 'fighting the tiger' and 'going into battles' are the eventing process which shows the real relationships like brothers and father and son. Focussing on, describing, analysing such events and processes, and dynamically interpreting the logic within them is what we said here 'process event analysis' research strategy and narrative approach' (Sun, 2010). Compared to Europe and America's professionalisation of esports development path (Taylor, 2014), the sportisation, inclusion of esports in the mega sporting events is an Asian Phenomenon and also draws insight from social aspects that are data-driven (Tian, 2020). These followings, from the Asian Indoor Games/Asian Indoor and Martial Arts Games and the Southeast Asian Games to the Asian Games, are descriptions of the eventing process related to esports inclusion in the Asian Games.

Korea's Dominant Period

As early as 2000, International Cyber Marketing hosted the World Cyber Games (WCG). In the following years, WCG became the most well-known international event in the esports industry under the support of the top-tier Olympic Games sponsor Samsung Group. With the demonstration of Korea, esports also developed rapidly in China and was approved as the 99th sport by the General Administration of Sport of China at the end of 2003 (Hong, 2021). In 2005, the Asian Electronic Sports Federation (AESF) was founded, and in 2007, the OCA made esports an official event at the second Asia Indoor Games (AIM) in Macau. 'AIM' is a comprehensive sporting event established by the OCA that focuses on non-Olympic, non-winter sports with high spectator and commercial value. In Macau 'AIM', three esports events 'Need for Speed', 'FIFA 2007' and 'NBA 2007' are all simulated sport games.

In 2008, the International Esports Federation (IeSF) was established in South Korea. The third 'Asian Indoor Games' was held in Hanoi, Vietnam, and

VIRESA, the Vietnam esports Association, was in charge of organising the event with the assistance of KeSPA. KeSPA was founded in 1999 and is affiliated with the Ministry of Culture and Tourism of Korea. Three previous simulated sport games were retained, and three non-simulation sports games 'StarCraft', 'Warcraft' and 'Counter-Strike' were added. Korea held a dominant position in the competition of 'StarCraft'. At the end of this game, Korea won two gold medals and one silver medal in a total of six events, including the first and the second place in 'StarCraft' and the championship in 'Counter-Strike', while China achieved one gold, one silver and four bronze medals (Titan, 2018b).

Later, in 2013, the fourth Asian Indoor Games and the Asian Martial Arts Games were combined to form the Asian Indoor and Martial Arts Games (AIMAG), held in Incheon, Korea (Titan, 2018b). Esports became the official event in the fourth AIMAG, and the OCA authorised IeSF to formulate the rules of esports events. Finally, six esports titles were set: 'League of Legends', 'StarCraft', 'FIFA2013', 'Need for Speed', 'Special Force' and 'Tekken'. Among them, 'League of Legends' is another overwhelming superior esports game in Korea. Starting from S3 2013, South Korea has won the 'League of Legends' Global Finals for five consecutive years (Titan, 2018b). Eventually, Korea gripped four gold medals, including two solo events to sweep the first and second places. The Chinese team won only two silver and one bronze.

China's Dominant Period

In December 2015, Tencent wholly acquired Riot Games, the US game company that developed 'League of Legends'. In January 2017, Hangzhou-based Alibaba became a TOP sponsor of the International Olympic Committee (IOC) (Titan, 2018b). In April 2017, the OCA reached a strategic partnership with Ali Sports and announced that esports would be added to the 2017 'AIMAG', the 2018 Asian Games and become an official sport of the 2022 Hangzhou Asian Games at the same time (Titan, 2018b). In Turkmenistan's capital Ashgabat in 2017, esports held as a performance event in the fifth 'AIMAG', 'DOTA2', 'StarCraft', 'Hearthstone: Heroes of Warcraft' and 'KOF XIV' were set as the official events, but 'League of Legends' was excluded, which Tencent owns the copyright and Koreans have an overwhelming advantage.

Then KeSPA announced to quit the 'AIMAG' for two main reasons: first, it objected to the failure of 'League of Legends', as the most popular esports event in Asia at that time, to be set as the official events and second, the OCA authorised Ali sports as the technical supplier for this competition, bypass the IeSF. Chinese team easily won three gold, two silver and one bronze due to the absence of the Korean athletes (Titan, 2018b). Another breaking news in the Chinese esports industry that year was the 'League of Legends' S7 Global finals held at the National Stadium 'Bird's Nest' on 4 November 2017, which attracted more than 40,000 players to watch the game at the stadium (Titan, 2018b). With a peak of more than 100 million Chinese viewers watching live online (China lost to South Korea in the final), making it a landmark of China esports history.

After the 2017 'AIMAG', Kenneth Fok, son of a Hong Kong member of IOC and OCA Vice President Timothy Fok, was elected as the new President of the Asian Esports Federation (AESF) (Titan, 2018b). As the official organising entity for the management and promotion of esports in Asia recognized by the OCA, AESF dominated the 2018 Asian Games in Jakarta where esports became a performance event for the first time and the shortlisted games set 'League of Legends', 'Arena of Valour-NS', 'Clash Royale', 'PES2018', 'StarCraft2' and 'Hearthstone'. The Chinese team eventually won two gold and one silver in all six events and South Korea won one gold and one silver (Titan, 2018b), especially the crucial final of 'League of Legends' between China and South Korea, and the Chinese team successfully took the crown. In 2018 S8 finals from China's Invictus Gaming (IG) team 3:0 victory over Europe's FNATIC (FNC) team, it is the first time to win the tournament's global finals championship.

At the Southeast Asian Games in December 2019, esports are set in the Medal table as an official sport (Hong, 2021). 'DOTA2', 'StarCraft', 'Hearthstone', 'Mobile Legends', 'Arena of Valor', 'And Tekken7' six events were set, and two mobile games 'Mobile Legends' and 'Arena of Valor' developers were from China. On 16 December 2019, Global Esports Federation (GEF) supported by Tencent was formally established. On 23 June 2020, the OCA and the GEF announced a strategic partnership between the two sides. In December 2020, the OCA General Assembly approved the selection of esports as an official sport in the 2022 Hangzhou Asian Games (Hong, 2021). This marked the starting point of the esports as an official event in the mega international sporting event. AESF continues to be appointed as the technical representative for this competition, organising and managing the test events for each esports event at the Games. China finally won four esports gold medals out of seven matches at the Hangzhou Asian Games, and Korea won two esports gold medals (Titan, 2023a).

THE ANALYSIS OF STAKEHOLDERS AND THEIR INTERACTION IN INVOLVING ESPORTS AT THE ASIAN GAMES

Elias (1969) argues that the social process is a shifting power (dis)equilibrium relationship between people who depend on each other in an ever-expanding and complex network in various different ways, such as association or confrontation. The general form and process of such a situation vividly described by Elias through the progressively complex 'game model', which starts from a simple confrontation between two players and gradually adds new players, which is divided into many specific situations such as weak-weak union and weak-strong combination (Li, 2006). Once the game model is large enough to be quite ambiguous, phenomena as split, reorganization, layering and so on will appear and new network structures will be formed. Analysing the process of esports' inclusion the Asian Games, we found that the time during the early days of the AIMAG to the later days of the Asian Games, technical officials of esports events has gradually transferred from KeSPA and IeSF, which the international esports organization that the Korean dominated to Ali sports and AESF with China supported, formed a series complex network interactions, power restructuration and balance of interests around the Hangzhou Asian Games' esports events, on the levels of the OCA and Hangzhou organising committee, game developers and publishers.

During the 2022 Hangzhou Asian Games, a total of seven medal event in esports were held, including Arena of Valor – Asian Games version, DOTA 2, Dream Three Kingdoms 2, FIFA Online4, League of Legends, Game for Peace-Asian Game, Street Fighter 5, along with 2 demonstration events focused in robotics and VR. It should be pointed out that Hearthstone was removed from the list of events as mentioned later (see Table 8.1).

From the perspective of esports promotion, the set of sufficiently influential and representative events is the legal basis for the existence of esports organizations. AESF President Kenneth Fok has briefly introduced for the entry of esports of the Asian Games, who saying that on the one hand, it is necessary to take full care of the members and try to choose events that popular in the vast majority of countries and regions throughout Asia. In addition, Multiplayer Online Battle Arena (MOBA), virtual sports, cards and other familiar esports events are to be covered as much as possible. Furthermore, computers and mobile phones should also be taken into account (Titan, 2018a).

From the perspective of the impact on game manufacturers, the final chosen esports game titles which are directly related to Tencent occupied four, two of which were Tencent original game titles. Tencent is a Chinese multinational technology and entertainment conglomerate. It is also the world's largest company in the video game industry based on its investments. The NetEase and the Perfect World, as the two largest game companies in China below the Tencent, separately have one China-agency operating event that be chosen. NetEase is a Chinese Internet technology company providing online services, another one of

Table 8.1. Esports Titles of the 2022 Hangzhou Asian Ga.

Title	Type	Platform	Developer/ Nationality	Operator
AOV – Asian Game version	MOBA	Mobile	Tencent/CHN	Tencent
DOTA 2	MOBA	PC	Valve/USA	Perfect World
Dream Three Kingdoms 2	RTS	PC	Electronic Soul/CHN	Electronic Soul
FIFA Online 4	SPG	PC	EA/USA	Tencent
HearthStone	CAG	PC	Blizzard/USA	NetEase
League of Legends	MOBA	PC	Riot/USA	Tencent
Game for Peace-Asian Game version	Battel Royale	Mobile	Tencent/CHN	Tencent
Street Fighter 5	FTG	PC	CAPCOM/JPN	

MOBA (Multiplayer Online Battle Arena), RTS (Real-Time Strategy Game), BR (Battle Royale).

the largest Internet and video game companies in the world, and also partnered with Blizzard to operate Chinese versions of their games (Titan, 2023b). Perfect World is a 3D adventure and fantasy MMORPG with traditional Chinese settings. Perfect World is Valve's Chinese partner as the publisher of Dota 2 and Counter-Strike: Global Offencive in China.

Compared to the 2018 Asian Games in Jakarta, Tencent's MOBA games 'League of Legends' and 'Arena of Valor' continue to be retained; although the agency's card game 'Clash Royale' was discarded, the original BR mobile game 'Game for Peace' and the agency's 'FIFA Online4' were added. The result is reasonable, and the inclusion of the two 'Mobile Game' somehow allows Tencent to occupy the commanding height of mobile gaming in Asia is more important to Tencent. With 'StarCraft2' and 'PES' absent from the list the list, 'Hearthstone' on the initial list but removed from Hangzhou Asian Games after collapse of US publisher Blizzard's licencing deal with NetEase in March 2023, if NetEase is loser, then the MOBA personal computer game (PC Game). The inclusion of 'DOTA2' makes Perfect World an undoubtedly winner, considering the status of 'DOTA2' in the global esports market. This is somehow a correction of the imbalance in the decision of esports events to the Asian Games in Jakarta. In the SPG market, EA 'FIFA' series is more excellent than KONAMI 'PES' series in terms of sales performance and cooperation ecology (ECA, 2021), 'FIFA' instead of 'PES' is quite reasonable, while 'Street Fighter5' as the 'only' Japanese game inclusion is a necessary balance of interests to unite the power of Asian esports. In 2019 it was determined that FIFA 19 was outselling PES 2019 at a high rate, at a 22–1 ratio (see Noel, 2019).

After all, esports has also been officially designated as one of the 41 medal sports for the Asian Games 2026 to be held in Nagoya, Japan (AESF, 2023). As the failure of the traditional esports games like 'Counter-Strike', 'StarCraft2', 'Warcraft3' and 'Overwatch', the 'Dream Three Ancient Kingdoms' in Hangzhou Electric Soul is a big surprise, which should be a reward as the 'Host Benefits' (Hong, 2022). This is important to note because both the game's influence and the corporate scale is dwarf to that of other games. Except consideration of market factors, another tacit understanding is the gold medal as host advantage, the three esports events in Jakarta Asian Games were not replaced, happened to be won the gold medals of Chinese team and Chinese Hong Kong players. Considering that the IOC also has rule to the host privilege of additional events on the Olympic Games, this compromise is acceptable, except that the organisers need to decide the 'limitation' for the esports games and events long-term development.

By comparing the Hangzhou Asian Games with the World Electronic Sports Games (WESG), a third-party esports event originally organised by Ali Sports, it is clear that behind the esports events set of Macau AIM to Hangzhou Asian Games, and it is a competition not only between from the China and South Korea but also Alibaba and Tencent. In March 2016, Ali sports launched WESG in an attempt to access the esports industry through third-party events and create a new global top third-party esports tournament in the post-WCG era (Hong, 2022). In July 2016, IeSF announced its exclusive global strategic partnership to

Ali Sports, supporting Ali Sports to develop WESG (Hong, 2022). The first WESG set events including 'DOTA2', 'Counter-Strike', 'StarCraft2' and 'Hearthstone', two of them are from Valve and two from Blizzard, respectively agented by Perfect World and NetEase in China, and none of them is from Tencent.

The third WESG added the simulation esports game called 'PES' and the MOBA game 'Vainglory' from NetEase. In 2019–2020 esports competition season, the fourth WESG back to four events, including 'Counter-Strike', 'StarCraft2', 'DOTA2' and 'PES', the most popular esports game 'League of Legends', 'Arena of Valour' owned by Tencent were still absent. WESG influence in the domestic marketing response is small (Hong, 2022). The decline of WESG, and Tencent's move to the centre of the world esports is a consequence of the strategic battle between Alibaba and Tencent, which also proves the critical influence of Video Game Intellectual Property on esports.

The stakeholders involved in the Hangzhou Asian games is also complex, as displayed in the conceptual diagram presented in Fig. 8.1. There are indications that IeSF, the traditional international esports organisation established in South Korea, and GEF, the emerging international esports organisation supported by Tencent, will become the two giants of the world geopolitical landscape international esports organizations for the inclusion of esports in the Olympic Games. Until October 2020, IeSF has 88 national and regional members on five continents. Partners include American game company VALVE (with its popular esports games DOTA2, Half-Life, Counter-Striker, etc.) and the famous

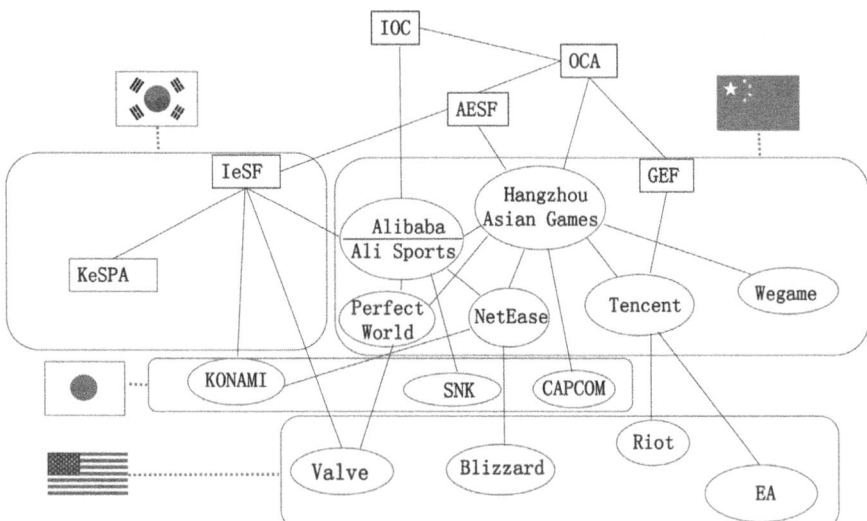

Fig. 8.1. Network Interaction of Stakeholders Involving the Esports Setting of Hangzhou Asian Games.

Japanese game company KONAMI. According to the Korean, as intended, IeSF is going to take the role of the global esports management in the future (Hong, 2021).

Unlike the IeSF membership expansion strategy, the GEF has taken the upper route, including hiring Paul J. Foster, the former head of protocal,event and hospitality at the IOC, as Chief Operate Officer, inviting Hideki Okamura, president of Japanese video game giant Sega Group and Japan eSports Union, to be a member of the GEF Executive Committee, and cooperating with the international Federrations such as ITA, ICF, WKF, UIPMB, ISA, WTF, and ITF, as well as the OCA and the Commonwealth Games Federation (GEF, 2020; Hong, 2021). Following the establishment of the GEF, IeSF sought to establish a partnership with AESF, which committed to considering IeSF as the only global governing entity for esports. So, these two federations are competing for global governance leadership (IeSF, 2020). The latest trend is GEF and IESF are likely to explore collaboration with potential merger in the future after GEF Vice President Prince Faisal been elected as the permanent president of IESF in 2023 (Ivan, 2023).

INFLUENCING FACTORS OF ESPORTS AT THE ASIAN GAMES

ANT is an attempt to understand society as the result of 'the networking of connections between human actors, technologies, and objects,' and 'an actor is any element that bends the surrounding space, makes other elements dependent on it, and translates the volition of others into its language.' In other words, the actor can be not only human but also non-human (Callon, 1986). In this way, the technological object is the formative result of many related and heterogeneous elements, in the sense that it is technical, political and economic. A central concept of ANT is 'translation', 'an explanation given by fact constructors on interests of themselves and those they absorb.' Simplification is the result of translation – the interpretation of a complex world in a translational way. A simplified entity usually exists in a context of Juxtaposition with the others to which it is linked.

Based on this, esports, as an innovative social practice driven by digital technology, is also a 'simplification'. As a translator, the AESF or Tencent 'juxtaposed' esports into the Hangzhou Asian Games, the global esports economic geography, local cultural economy/politics and Olympic values all have the influence on it.

Industrial Factors

According to Newzoo (2021), the global esports games market is foreseen to grow from $175.8 billion in 2021 to over $200 billion by 2023. Among the global esports games market share in 2021, the PC game market declined by 2.8% to $35.9 billion and the console market declines by 8.9% to $49.2 billion.

By contrast, the mobile game market generates a market proportion of $90.7 billion in 2021; it is a rise of 4.4% up against last year (Newzoo, 2021). The Asia-Pacific region has the largest number of players in the world, accounting for 55% of the total number of players worldwide. In addition to China, the number of players in India and South Korea is also rising rapidly. The number of European and American players is only 14% (Europe) and 7% (North America) of the world. But on the other hand, players in Europe and America contribute over 40% of the global game market revenue (Newzoo, 2021).

The world's major game developers are mainly based in the US and Japan, such as Microsoft, Activision Blizzard, Valve, EA, Take-Two in the United States, Sony, Nintendo, KONAMI, CAPCOM, SNK and so on in Japan. Because of China's huge gaming population, Tencent and NetEase have developed a large number of original games while acting as agenting for US and Japanese games and now became the top international game companies in terms on game business revenue, especially mobile games have even become an important Chinese brand going abroad. These are reflected in the previous analysis.

Cultural Factors

Among the esports events selected for the Hangzhou Asian Games, there are three original Chinese games events (Hong, 2022). In Tencent's MOBA game Honour of Kings, the character design is primarily based on Chinese historical or mythological figures, but it also includes characters from Japanese history (such as Musashi Miyamoto) and Western mythological figures (such as King Arthur). In League of Legends (LOL), there is a character inspired by Sun Wukong (also known as Monkey King).

The only esports game title within a core of Chinese culture is 'Dream Three Ancient Kingdoms' but with relatively limited influence (Hong, 2022). This RTS online gaming is based on the Three Kingdoms culture and the main features of DOTA, the roleplay game (RPG) map of Warcraft and mixed RTS elements into RPG online games; it was officially operated in 2015. Such the game with publicity and popularity was not qualify but to be finally chose, the core reason is the Electronic Soul is a Hangzhou local company, and the Three Kingdom theme is also an important factor in promoting Chinese traditional culture at the Asian Games. In recent years, Hangzhou has accelerated the layout of esports and is fast moving towards the 'esports city'. In June 2017, Xiacheng District built China (Hangzhou) esports digital entertainment town; Hangzhou Asian Games esports venue is located in the district (Hangzhou, 2020).

In October 2019, the Bilibili Gaming esports (BLG) Zhejiang headquarters opened in Yuhang District, and the home of the 'Hangzhou Lightning team' (Overwatch League) was settled in Yuahang District (Hangzhou, 2020). The truth is that the Electronic Soul has also begun to explore the overseas market. In 2020, Electronic Soul invested in the establishment of subsidiaries in Japan and Singapore, focussing on the East and Southeast Asian markets where users are similar and there is a certain awareness of the Three Kingdoms story. 'We hope to let players in Asia and even the whole world see the charm of our Chinese cities through esports,' Zhang Yijia, general manager of Tencent Hoot suite's TIMI gaming centre and general director of Honour of Kings, said that the AOV (Asian Games version) will incorporate designing elements of Hangzhou's famous attractions, landmarks and city culture (Zhang, 2022). Fu Hua, Vice Minister of the Publicity Department of the Communist Party of China believes that Chinese gaming titles are going to play a key role in communicating Chinese culture around the world (Hong, 2022).

Olympic Values

At the press conference announcing the event setting, the Hangzhou Asian Organising Committee clearly mentioned that the esports event setting of the Hangzhou Asian Games has been discussed by many parties by the AESF, the OCA and the State General Administration of Sports, taking into account the factors such as the fairness of the competition rules, the value orientation of content, international influence, propaganda and so on (Qian, 2021). The Constitution of the OCA clearly stated that the OCA is responsible for the promotion and development of the Olympic Movement and its noble ideals among the people of Asia, without infringing on Olympic values (Article III of The OCA Constitution and Rules, 'General Target'). Tomas Bach, president of the IOC, said in an interview with the Associated Press in 2018: 'we can't allow some games that advocate violence and discrimination into the Olympic Games, that is the so-called "Killing" games. From our point of view, they are contradictory to Olympic values and therefore they are unacceptable' (AP, 2018). But Bach doesn't have that preconception on all game genres, as he has previously said: 'If players are competing in a virtual world for soccer or other sports, we are interested in that.' Therefore, if the IOC admits esports, simulation sports games will be the first choice. In other words, games such as FPS and MOBA are difficult to become Olympic sports because they contain mildly violent or fantastically violent content. According to this standard, 'Game for Peace', as a shooting game, is the furthest kind from the current IOC standard among the popular esports games. To adapt to Olympic values, 'Game for Peace (Asian Games Edition)' has made significant adjustments. Unlike the traditional battle royale gameplay, the competition is no longer the form of mutual shooting between humans, but a combination of real sports elements, such as cross-country, shooting and racing online. The game is divided into several sections, each section needs to complete the shooting task, then the team needs to drive the vehicle to complete the track event, and the final ranking is decided according to the order of the team reaching the finish line. It can be said that 'Game for Peace' is the closest to the real sports and sports state in the Asian Games version among the eight esports games except 'FIFA'.

IMPLICATIONS AND FUTURE OUTLOOK OF ESPORTS AT EVENTS

Esports and traditional sports have areas of overlap. Generally speaking, scholars agree that both traditional sports and esport are self-motivated activities engaged in primarily for the purpose of having fun with commonly accepted rules to guide the process that feature competition as the central part of the play. The debate on labelling esport as a kind of sport has mainly centred on what characteristics define sport. Some of the debates regarding esports as a sport stem from imprecision even in established academic definitions of 'sport' (such as Guttmann (1978), who proposed that sports must involve at least a modicum of physicality, but does not clarify the relative threshold of this physicality). Some treat physical excellence as the defining characteristic of sport, while others see teamwork and tactics as the central sport value.

Scholars also note that some traditional sports focus more on gross motor skills, while other activities widely regarded as sports concentrate on fine motor skills including precision, accuracy or reflex speed. Based on this reasoning, scholars have made the case that esports should not be treated separately from many fine-motor-skill-oriented sports such as auto racing or chess (Hou et al., 2020). Esports is a discipline of so-called 'mind game' on the Hangzhou Asian Games. The mind game also include chess, Go and bridge, which are recognized by the IOC and the GAISF (General Association of International Sports Federations) but have not yet been included in the Olympics. However, as early as 2006, chess became a medal event for the 2006 Asian Games in Doha.

Some scholars also believe that esports have not yet been institutionalised, specifically that the history of esports as a sport is not long enough to incorporate institutionalised, organizational operations as well as the stability of the rules has not been tested (Abanazir, 2019). In a way, the practice of esports at the Hangzhou Asian Games is of historic importance in the process of institutionalising esports. In the process of esports becoming an official event in mega international sporting games, can the emerging supranational esports organization overcome the limitations of traditional third-party esports events and reach an agreement with competing esports game publishers owning the esports game titles intellectual property? The coexistence of the Hangzhou Asian Games esports events 'League and Legends' and 'DOTA2' shows a possibility.

Some observers worry that the national heroes honour to the winners in traditional sports events such as the Asian Games is not attractive enough against the huge bonuses to professional athletes of tournaments or commercial events organised by operators, which may greatly reduce the enjoyment of esports competition on traditional mega sporting games (LÜ, 2021). There may still be a long way to go to break the situation where game operators dominate the esports ecology. The ANT points out that 'heterogeneous combinations created by actor words are not guaranteed to be real because actors are totally capable of constructing different, disconnected worlds' (Callon, 1986).

As practiced in 'Dream Three Ancient Kingdoms2' and 'Game for Peace Asian Games Version', it does not matter whether it is called RTS or MOBA,

FPS and simulating sports can also be integrated and the boundaries between game genres are permeable. Kenneth Fok, the chairman of the AESF, advocated a broader concept of esports, 'esports not only include the esports competitions as we see, but also drones, artificial intelligence, robot competitions, etc., it is a broader concept' (2020). 'Mech Master' as a performance event on Hangzhou Asian Games showcases another possibility of esports. Some institutions predict that esports will completely surpass finger controllers and buttons in the next five years. Game control will involve limbs, facial expressions and even brain neural activity. In the next 5–20 years, online and offline sports could be synchronized to adapt to the player's location and capabilities, and the combination of haptic feedback interface virtual and reality augmentation technology makes the perfect mixture of remote and live games (Yang, 2016).

Based on ANT, esports as an innovative social practice driven by digital technology is also a 'simplification' – connect a variety kind of games from real-time Strategy (RTS), first-person shooting (FPS), Battel Royale, MOBA, fighting game, card and simulation sports game – as to the IOC created a separate conception of 'Virtual Sports' to show the difference (Parry, 2021). In March 2021, the IOC plenary Session adopted the 'Olympic 2020 + 5 Agenda', which specifies that the future development of the digital strategy will focus on 'virtual sports'. Virtual sports require real physical exercise, such as cycling and taekwondo, similar to exergaming. To implement the 'Olympic 2020 + 5 Agenda' and encourage the virtual sports development, the IOC held the first 'Olympic Virtual Sports Series (OVS)' before the start of the Tokyo 2020 Olympic Games, with the participation of games such as 'e-baseball2020', the cycling fitness game 'Zwift', the Virtual Regetta, an open virtual rowing 'Virtual Regetta', and 'GT Racing'. Due to the coronavirus, all competitions took place online, with approximately 250,000 participants from over 100 countries around the world, attracting a total of 750,000 viewers on the official Olympic website (IOC, 2021a, 2021b). In comparison, in the 2021 'League of Legends' S11 Global Finals EDG vs DK, Esports Charts only counted the peak number of oversee viewers streaming platforms reached 4.01 million without domestic live (EC, 2021).

Commenting on the esports strategy of the IOC, Trent Murray, a veteran esports observer, said

> If the IOC wants to strengthen its relationship with the gaming community, do it the right way. Empower esports communities, support underdeveloped scenes, and create something that speaks to our culture. Otherwise, don't expect an audience who grew up on Fortnite, to be particularly interested in virtual rowing. Trent (2021)

In this sense, the more aggressive esports strategy of the Asian Games may have referential meaning for the Olympics. On the Olympic Esports Week created by the IOC in Singapore 2023, Fortnite becomes an official esports discipline. Unlike the original edition Fortnite Battle Royale game mode (in which 100 players battle it out on an island until only one is left), it features a special International Shooting Sport Federation Island created in Fortnite, which be designed to reflect sport shooting competition. It is difficult to deny that it was inspired by the Hangzhou Asian Games esports event 'Game for Peace (Asian Games Edition)'.

The Asian Games, as a traditional mega sporting event, is facing a development dilemma similar to the Olympic Games: it is increasingly losing the attention of young people, and it is urgent to consolidate the market and economic foundation through reform. On 17 April 2014, Nguyen Tan Dung, then Prime Minister of the Vietnam Government, announced that Hanoi would give up the right to host the 2018 Asian Games (Hanoi, 2024). Later, Jakarta, Indonesia, accepted the host. By 2022, only Hangzhou participated in the bid for the Asian Games (Zhang, 2022). It can be said that the Asian Games has become a money-losing business. It is against this background that esports firstly became a performing event at the 2018 Asian Games. According to the '2018 Jakarta Top 10 Hot Sports of the Asian Games' released by Gu Yu and Zhiwei, the online popularity of esports in China is still far beyond the traditional sports like basketball, volleyball, and swimming, in the absence of CCTV coverage (Hong, 2021). The inclusion of esports in the Asian Games signifies the recognition of esports as a competitive sport on par with traditional sports. The inclusion of esports in the Asian Games and its potential impact on the Olympic Games demonstrate the evolving nature of sports and the need to adapt to the interests and preferences of new generations.

Although the term 'sport' is used in many places in the Olympic Charter, it has not clearly defined. In 2002, when auditing the application for bridge and chess to set as an Olympic sports, the IOC Olympic Programme Commission considered that the IOC should clarify the difference between 'mind sport' and Olympic sports and made it clear that bridge and chess should not be allowed to enter the Olympic sports. At the 114th Plenary Session in IOC Mexico City, it was also agreed that the competitions relying on mechanical assistance and 'mind sports' were 'not qualified to be included in the Olympic Games'. This is also a rigid clause in the existing rules that prohibits esports from becoming an Olympic sport entirely because the esports based on hand-brain coordination and computer display results are just mechanical and intelligent events (Carcuro & Colomboa, 2004).

Since the 2017 Olympic Summit, the IOC has been actively maintaining close attention and continuous interaction with esports. In 2017, the sixth Olympic Summit hold a belief that esports could be seen as an official sport (Yi, 2022); the following is the main reason: The players involved prepare and train with an intensity which may be comparable to athletes in traditional sports. Therefore, the Summit recognized that Competitive 'esports' could be considered a sporting activity. The seventh Olympic Summit held in 2018 discussed the issue of 'whether esports should be included in the Olympics' and concluded that it was 'too early' (Yi, 2022). However, the IOC also said that it would try to keep in touch and cooperate with the esports industry. On the eighth Olympic Summit held in 2019, issues related to esports were discussed again (Yi, 2022). The summit received a report from David Lappartient, the head of the Esports Liaison Group, on the proposal to promote the Olympic Movement and Olympic values in esports. In the 'Declaration of the Eighth Olympic Summit' issued subsequently, it was suggested that the two-speed cooperation mode should be adopted for esports and games: first, consider how to manage their electronic and virtual sports and explore opportunities for cooperation with game publishers and second, consider building a dialogue platform between sports stakeholders and esports communities.

The ninth IOC Olympic Summit held in 2020 heard the report of David Lappartient on the latest development of virtual sports and gaming (Yi, 2022). Lappartient emphasised that virtual sports have both physical forms (such as cycling) and non-physical forms (such as football), and games include competitive games (such as League of Heroes) and leisure games (such as Super Mario). The Summit believes that the IFs must accept both the physical and non-physical virtual forms of their respective sports, putting the emphasis on regulating fair competition, respecting the virtual sports values and reaching out to and expanding new audiences. The Summit agrees to maintain contact with game players as a way to promote sports activities and sports values to the younger generation. To conclude, the IOC is now more accepting and encouraging individual sports federations to develop virtual forms of existing sports events, including physical and non-physical ones.

One of the most substantial initiatives of the IOC is to hold the Olympic Virtual Series. Some international sports organisations also intend to set up their Olympic virtual series in the future. FIFA has successfully held the first FIFA esports World Cup (EA's 'FIFA 19') in April 2019, and FIBA also held the first esports Open in June 2020. IOC President Bach believes that the Olympic virtual series can bring a new digital experience, enhance the relationship with fans and spectators in the virtual sports field, encourage more and more young people to participate in sports and promote Olympic values (IOC, 2021a, 2021b, pp. 21–22). The IOC had held the first Olympic esports Week in Singapore from June 22 to 25, 2023. Bach said: 'The first Olympic esports Week shows our ambition to support the development of virtual sports in the Olympic movement, it is a milestone' (see again IOC, 2021a, 2021b, pp. 21–22). Of course, a more imaginary propose in the future to IOC may make esports games be a parallel game as the Paralympics, which scheduled between the Olympic game and the Paralympics.

According to the existing strategies of the IOC on esports, although the virtual series of the Olympic Games is not an official Olympic event, it is not excluded that virtual sports appeared as a discipline or event in the future Olympic Games (Yi, 2022). According to the basic requiring on the Olympic events accords to the 'Olympic Charter', 'Sport' refer to those sports managed by the International Federations recognized by IOC (Yi, 2022). 'Discipline' refers to a branch of the Olympic sports consist of one or more events. 'Event' refers to a competition with final result and medal awarded that has included in the sport or discipline.

It is important to note that there are many factors affect the evaluation of Olympic events. Events setting is a complex decision-making process with multiple stakeholders' combat. The IOC cannot unilaterally decide on the inclusion of 'esports', there were a lot successful cases of other stakeholders lobbying, such as BMX in Beijing 2008, golf, rugby sevens in Rio 2016, etc. From the current situation analysis, there are three reasons why the virtual sports game barely has the chance to become an official Olympic event: First, the existing Olympic sport evaluation standards are disadvantage to esports. The biggest weakness of esports lies in the two first-level indicators of 'athletes' health and international organization operation status'; second, the interest structure of esports ecology is unstable or even unbalanced, which is difficult for the IOC to control at present.

CONCLUSIONS

The author believes that virtual and simulated sports games may be set in the 2028 or 2032 Olympic Games as one event or several disciplines or sports. There are three reasons why: At first, the Olympic virtual series games since 2021, which was owned by IOC, have accumulated experience, from which the interest balance model and the market-acceptive commercial value are accepted by the IOC; Second, in addition to the current virtual series events, there are a lot more powerful international sports organisations may also hold the virtual series events in recent years, which may form more virtual sports with physical strength (which have enough physical ability) that can be recognized by the IOC and the international sports organisations; Third, Los Angeles or Brisbane, the host of the 2028 and 2032 Olympic Games, may take the initiative of developing local and even domestic esports industry, it may put pressure on the IOC and relevant international sports organisations to accept virtual sports as disciplines or events attached to traditional Olympic sports. In September 2023, IOC has announced the creation of a new official commission focused on esports – Esports Commission. This could pave the way for potential inclusion of esports in future Olympic Games.

However, for the Los Angeles or Brisbane Olympics in 2028 and 2032, respectively, there may also be several variables to accept esports as an Olympic event. First, according to the current rules of the Olympic sport setting, it will be decided by the IOC plenary session at least three years which means in 2025 or 2029 in advance. At that time, there will be a new IOC President, and there will be a large number of 'new officials' among its members. It is hard to say that the concepts like 'sports organization mission' and 'physical strength emphasised' would remain as stable as they are now is the most decisive factor and a key factor affecting the President, the Executive Committee and the plenary session's decision. Second, after 6 or 7 years of development of the Olympic Games and esports, the status of both sides may also undergo some subtle changes. It is unpredictable to know if the international esports organisations development got rid of unstable and unbalanced situation nowadays, and if existing organisations would be integrated or reorganised, if it is possible to had an international esports organization with clear conception, stable interest structure, strong organizational capacity and extremely strong mobile ability in the world? And so on.

Or maybe IOC would be in decline at that time, and esports with its organizations would be popular, which will also make it possible for the former to invite the latter to join. Third, the tendency of division of esports development might also appear. The current mainstream esports game and other functional game development might achieve a bigger development in the meta-universe environment. Virtual sports in traditional Olympic event might also integrated latest technology and emerged a more prosperity trend welcomed by special groups. At that time, esports and the Olympic Games may develop in separate, which will deprive the motivation and desire of the traditional esports to be an official Olympic sport.

FIVE KEY READINGS

Taylor, T. L. (2014). *Raising the stakes: Esports and the Professionalization of computer gaming.* **MIT Press.**

This book explores the emerging scene of professional computer gaming and the accompanying efforts to make a sport out of this form of play. In the course of her explorations, Taylor travels to tournaments, including the WCG Grand Finals (which considers itself the computer gaming equivalent of the Olympics) and interviews participants from players to broadcasters. She examines pro-gaming, with its highly paid players, play-by-play broadcasts, and mass audience; discusses whether or not esports should even be considered sports; traces the player's path from amateur to professional (and how a hobby becomes work) and describes the importance of leagues, teams, owners, organisers, referees, sponsors and fans in shaping the structure and culture of pro-gaming. Taylor connects professional computer gaming to broader issues: our notions of play, work and sport; the nature of spectatorship; the influence of money on sports. And she examines the ongoing struggle over the gendered construction of play through the lens of male-dominated pro-gaming. Ultimately, the evolution of professional computer gaming illuminates the contemporary struggle to convert playful passions into serious play.

Ryan, R. (2019). *Understanding esports: An introduction to the global phenomenon.* **Lexington Books.**

This book provides a broad view of the history, experience, and impact of professional Esports as it has shifted the cultural and athletic landscape during its rise.

Dal Yong Jin. (2021). *Global esports: Transformation of cultural perceptions of competitive gaming.* **Bloomsbury Publishing.**

Global esports explores the recent surge of esports in the global scene and comprehensively discusses people's understanding of this spectacle. By historicising and institutionalising esports, the contributors analyse the rapid growth of esports and its implications in culture and digital economy. Dal Yong Jin curates a discussion as to why esports has become a global phenomenon. From games such as Spacewar to Starcraft to Overwatch, a key theme, distinguishing this collection from others, is a potential shift of esports from online to mobile gaming. The book addresses why many global game players and fans play and enjoy online and mobile games in professional game competitions, and therefore, they investigate the manner in which the transfer to, from and between online and mobile gaming culture is occurring in a specific subset of global youth. The remaining focus identifies the major platforms used to enjoy esports, including broadcasting and smartphones. By analysing these unexamined or less-discussed agendas, this book sheds light on the current debates on the growth of global esports culture.

Summerley, R. (2019). The development of sports: A comparative analysis of the early institutionalization of traditional sports and esports. *Games and Culture, 15*(1), 51–72. **https://doi.org/10.1177/1555412019833809**

This article takes the definition of a sport as 'an institutionalised game' under which both 'traditional sports' and 'esports' fall. It takes a comparative analytical approach that examines the historical documentation and cultural output of these two major categories of sports and their early institutionalisation. Given the increasing interest in, engagement with and spectator numbers of esports, it is worth considering the key similarities and differences between various institutions. This article examines traditional sports institutions from the mid-19th to late 19th century alongside Esports institutions that emerged from the mid-1990s to the present day. First, the processes of institutionalisation are analysed with these examples in mind and, second, are compared to draw out the significant differences and similarities between the factors affecting early institutionalisation.

Miah, A. (2021). The esports question for the Olympic movement. *Journal of Olympic Studies, 2*(2), 14–26.

This article examines the historical development of the relationship between esports and the Olympic Movement, harnessing the metaphor of the 'family' as an explanation for why the relationship is complex, multifaceted, unresolved and intimately tied to a variety of processes that continue to limit further integration.

REFERENCES

Abanazir, C. (2019). Institutionalisation in esports. *Sport, Ethics and Philosophy, 13*(2), 117–131.

AESF. (2023). Esports continues to stage as an official medal sport at the 20th Asian Games Aichi-Nagoya 2026. https://www.aesf.com/news-media/esports-continues-to-stage-as-an-official-medal-sport-at-the-20th-asian-games-aichi-nagoya-2026

Associated Press. (2018). Esports has no Olympic future with violence. *Thomas Bach Says*. https://olympics.nbcsports.com/2018/09/01/esports-olympics-violence/

Callon, M. (1986). The sociology of an actor-network: The case of the electric vehicle mapping the dynamics of science and technology. *Sociology of Science in the Real World*, (1), 19–34.

Carcuro, F., & Colomboa, J. (2004). The future of the Olympic programme: Adding value to the Olympic Games through change in its sports composition. *Centre International d'Etude du Sport International Master (MA) in Management, Law and Humanities of Sport*.

Cui, L., Kim, E. J., & Kim, J. Y. (2023). How Chinese media addresses esports issues: A text mining comparative analysis of online news and viewers' comments on the Hangzhou Asian Games. *Electronics, 12*(24), 4961.

Elias, N. (1969). *The civilizing process: Sociogenetic and psychogenetic investigations*. University of Florida Press.

Elias, N., & Dunning, E. (1986). *Quest for excitement: Sport and leisure in the civilising process*. Blackwell.

Esports Charts (2021). *LoL Worlds 2021 – Viewership and detailed stats.* https://escharts.com/tournaments/lol/worlds-2021. Accessed on 6 November 2021.

European Club Association. (2021). Esports: Curse or blessing for football clubs? https://www.ecaeurope.com

GEF. (2020). Global Esports Federation confirms key leadership roles in line with plans to convene the world's esports ecosystem. https://globalsports.org/news/

Guo, Z. (2016). Sport sociological imagination: Perspective and expanding of historical sociology. *Journal of Shenyang Sport University*, (05), 19–23.

Guttmann, A. (1978). *From ritual to record: The nature of modern sports.* Columbia University Press.

Hangzhou Investment Promotion Bureau. (2020). Jia Su Xiang "Dian Jing Zhi Dou" Mai Jin! Hang Zhou Miao Zhun Dian Jing Chan Ye Xin Lan Hai. http://tzcj.hangzhou.gov.cn/art/2020/12/11/art_1621408_58891016.html/

HANOI. (2014, April 18). Vietnam pulls out of hosting Asian Games. *China Daily* (p. 001).

Hong, J. (2021). A political economic study on the inclusion of E-sports as official Olympic events: Disputes, interests and influences. *Future Communication,* (03), 70–77+125. https://doi.org/10.13628/j.cnki.zjcmxb.2021.03.009

Hong, J. (2022). Network interaction and interest balance in institutionalization: Research and judgment of E-sports events in Hangzhou Asian Games. *Journal of Chengdu Sport University*, (03), 18–23.

Hou, J., Yang, X., & Panek, E. (2020). How about playing games as a career? The evolution of esports in the eyes of mainstream media and public relations. *International Journal of Sport Communication*, *13*(1), 1–21.

IeSF. (2020). *Esports world body and Asian Esports Federation unite.* https://ie-sf.org/news/4094

IOC. (2021a). *Olympic agenda 2020 + 5:15 recommendations.*

IOC. (2021b). Inaugural Olympic virtual series successfully concludes with nearly 250,000 participants from over 100 countries around the world. https://www.infobae.com/aroundtherings/press-releases/2021/07/19/inaugural-olympic-virtual-series-successfully-concludes-with-nearly-250000-participants-from-over-100-countries-around-the-world/

Ivan, Š. (2023). *Esports federations GEF and IESF announce strategic partnership.* https://esportsinsider.com/2023/12/gef-iesf-strategic-partnership

Latour, B. (1987). *Science in action: How to follow scientists and engineers through society.* Harvard University Press.

Li, K. (2006). *Xi Fang She Hui Xue Li Lun.* Peking University Press.

Lu, X. (2010). Construction on visual fields of sports sociology research. *China Sport Science*, (11), 9–16. https://doi.org/10.16469/j.css.2010.11.002

Lü, Z. (2021). *Esports' Olympic inclusion: Obstacles and challenges.* Report of the 2021 international conference of sport history and culture.

Newzoo. (2021). Global games market report 2021. https://newzoo.com/insights/trend-reports/newzoo-global-games-market-report-2021-free-version/. Accessed on 1 July 2021.

Noel, A. (2019, September 18). FIFA 19 Outsells PES 2019 at 22 to 1 Ratio. *Sports King.* https://www.sports-king.com/fifa-19-vs-pes-2019-sales-2665/

Parry, J. (2021). *Esports will not be at the Olympics.* https://olympicstudies.org/esports-will-not-be-at-the-olympics/

Qian, C. F. (2021, November 5). *Hang Zhou Ya Yun Hui 8ge Dian Zi Jing Ji Xiao Xiang Zheng Shi Bu.* https://www.chinanews.com.cn/ty/2021/11-05/9603038.shtml

Ryan, R. (2019). *Understanding esports: An introduction to the global phenomenon.* Lexington Books.

Sun, L. (2010). *Jie Gou-Zhi Du Fen Xi, Hai Shi Guo Cheng Shi Jian Fen Xi?* Social Sciences Academic Press.

Taylor, T. L. (2014). *Raising the stakes: Esports and the professionalization of computer gaming.* MIT Press.

Tian, E. (2020). A prospect for the geographical research of sport in the age of big data. *Sport in Society*, *23*(1), 159–169.

Tian, E., & Wise, N. (2020). An Atlantic divide? Mapping the knowledge domain of European and North American-based sociology of sport, 2008–2018. *International Review for the Sociology of Sport*, *55*(8), 1029–1055.

Titan. (2018a). Du Jia Zhuan Fang Huo Qi Gang: 6 Xiang Mu Ru Ya Yun Hui, Jiang Ban Dian Jing Ya Zhou Bei. *Ti Tan Sports*, 001. April 13.
Titan. (2018b). Ya Zhou Dian Jing Di Li Er: Shu Yu Han Guo Dian Jing De Shi Dai Zheng Zai Jie Shu Ti Tan. *Ti Tan Sports*, 001. October 8.
Titan. (2023a). Guan Yu Ya Yun Hui Dian Jing De Shi Ge Gu Shi. *Ti Tan Sports*, 001. October 9.
Titan. (2023b). Hearthstone Bei Yi Chu Hang Zhou Ya Yun, Ying Xiang Jiu Jing You Duo Da? *Ti Tan Sports*, 001. March 16.
Trent, M. (2021). *Opinion: Why the Olympics should create a separate 'esports games'*. https://www.sportsbusinessjournal.com/en/Esports/Sections/People-and-Pop-Culture/2021/02/Opinion-Olympics-esports
Wise, N. (2015). Geographical approaches and the sociology of sport. In R. Giulianotti (Ed.), *Routledge handbook of the sociology of sport* (pp. 142–152). Routledge.
Wise, N., & Kohe, G. Z. (2020). Sports geography: New approaches, perspectives and directions. *Sport in Society*, *23*(1), 1–10.
Wise, N., & Maguire, K., (Eds.). (2022), *A research agenda for event impacts*. Edward Elgar.
Yang, Z. (2016). Wei Lai Ti Yu Chuan Bo De Fa Zhan Qu Shi Tan Xi. *Journal of Physical Education*, *32*(6), 49–52.
Yi, J. (2022). Analysis on the possibility of including E-sports into Olympic Games from the choice criteria and procedure, concept and trend of sports and events for Olympic Programme. *Journal of Chengdu Sport University*, *3*, 10–18.
Zhang, S. (2022). Integration strategies of building the city image of Hangzhou Asian Games. *International Journal of Frontiers in Sociology*, *4*(2), 26–31.

CHAPTER 9

RUNNING CULTURE IN CHINA: CONCEPTUALISING NOTIONS OF POWER AND SELF

Zhanbing Ren

Shenzhen University, China

ABSTRACT

In the past 10 years, the scale of running events in China has increased dramatically, and the forms of running events have also become rich and diverse. Running is not only a social phenomenon but also a historical and cultural phenomenon as an organic part of human culture with its own sociological values in China. This chapter offers insight into the development of Chinese running culture and how this has emerged from ancient and modern Chinese running cultures based on Foucault's disciplinary power theory, biopower and the technologies of the self. This chapter argues that running culture in China constructs the subjectivity of the Chinese runners under the joint action of the technologies of power and the technologies of the self. The findings acknowledge how Chinese Runners present and express themselves by showing a 'sense of presence'. Runners illustrate the implicit or explicit meaning and value of a particular way of life through running. Runners regard running as the technology of the self for self-expression and self-creation so that individuals can control their bodies and soul, thoughts, behaviours and ways of existence. Emerging technologies of power provide possibilities for the production of running culture in China, and the current policy under the technologies of power meets the needs of runners. In Chinese running culture, power was not oppressive but productive.

Keywords: Running culture; the technologies of power; the technologies of the self; disciplinary power; biopower

INTRODUCTION

After humans learn to walk, they run (Gotaas, 2012). Long-distance running is also unique in terms of physical and psychological requirements for participants (Buman et al., 2008). This kind of competitive running has been a subculture since the 20th century and has become a non-mainstream part of people's lives. Part of a localised cultural phenomenon, running has transformed from a once-pursued physical activity to a lucrative sports industry (Small, 2010). People run to maintain a healthy life because there are many uncertain factors in the daily life of this risk society, and these uncertain factors may affect physical health (Beck et al., 1992). Running as an accessible and pleasurable leisure activity can play a potential health role. Scholars across the social sciences have found running enhances one's physical and mental health and promotes interpersonal relationships (Kostrubala, 1976; Loughran et al., 2013; Oswald et al., 2020).

In the past 20 years, the scale of running events in China has increased dramatically, and the forms of running events have also become rich and diverse. Running is not only a social phenomenon but also a historical and cultural phenomenon as an organic part of human culture with its sociological values in China. This chapter offers insight into the development of Chinese running culture and how this has emerged from ancient and modern Chinese running cultures based on Foucault's disciplinary power theory, biopower and the technologies of the self. This chapter discusses running culture in China for the first time under Foucault's theoretical framework and argues that running culture in China constructs the subjectivity of the Chinese runners under the joint action of the technologies of power and the technologies of the self. In Foucault's research, technologies of power are regarded as the opposite of the technologies of the self. The technologies of power aim to discipline individuals, while the technologies of the self-attempt to enable individuals to 'self-constitute', not just 'be constituted'.

This chapter embraces the work of Foucault to interpret the development of running culture in China and explains the phenomenon of running culture in China through Foucault's theory. Through this paper, the findings acknowledge how Chinese Runners present and express themselves by showing a 'sense of presence'. Runners illustrate the implicit or explicit meaning and value of a particular way of life through running. Runners regard running as the technology of the self for self-expression and self-creation so that individuals can control their bodies and souls, thoughts, behaviours and ways of existence. Through their strength or the help of others, they achieve self-transformation to obtain a particular state of happiness, purity, wisdom, perfection, or immortality. On the other hand, the 'presence' mode of runners was also constructed from the perspective of the technologies of power, which determines the individual behaviour of runners and makes them subject to a specific purpose or domination, that is, objectifying the subject. The emerging technologies of power, for example, biopower, continue to provide possibilities for the production of running culture in China. China's running market has become the living environment driving China's running culture, which was an inseparable part of China's running culture. China's running policy under the technologies of power meets the needs of runners. In Chinese running culture, power was not oppressive but productive.

This chapter argues that Chinese running culture shapes the subjectivity of runners through the historical development of running practices in China and individual self-construction. On the one hand, the historical development of running practices in China has gradually formed discourses, knowledge and power related to running. These factors influence the subjectivity of individuals and shape their behaviours and cognition. As subjects of power relations and knowledge, the subjectivity of runners is not only a result of power control but also a result of the power–knowledge relationship. Through long-term and repetitive running practices rooted in the knowledge domain of running, Chinese runners gradually form their subjectivity. On the other hand, the subjectivity of Chinese runners is also shaped by individual self-construction. Chinese runners develop specific identities and values throughout the prolonged history of running practices. They perceive running as a technology for shaping their identities and ways of existence. Through bodily practices, they express their presence and engage in self-expression. By exerting effort and undergoing self-transformation, they further strengthen their subjectivity. Chinese runners utilise their physical fitness and abilities to create experiences and realities that diverge from everyday life while running. This embodied reality serves as the foundation of their subjectivity. Through these genuine practices, runners express and showcase themselves while running, ultimately shaping their subjectivity through their running practices.

CONCEPTUAL CONSIDERATIONS FOR RUNNING RESEARCH

Considering different conceptual considerations related to running, Chinese Confucianism concerns inner virtue and morality and ignores competition (Confucius, 2014). Meanwhile, Chinese Taoism advocated quiet and inaction, returning to simplicity and conforming to nature, instructing believers to live in harmony with the universe (Tzu, 2006). As a form of leisure and for being competitive, running has been a popular activity in Western developed countries for a long time. It appeared in the first ancient Olympic Games (Golden, 1998) and the first modern Olympic Games. Today, this kind of competitive running is more popular than ever among the Chinese middle class (Sui & Yang, 2022). Running has become a hot fashion sport (Ronkainen et al., 2018) and a widespread sociological phenomenon (Xie et al., 2020). In recent years, more and more researchers have applied Western perspectives, with many considering Foucault's theoretical writings to sports sociology research (Andrews, 1993; Birrell & Cole, 1994; Denison, 2019; Markula, 2004; Mohamad & Chung, 2018; Rail & Harvey, 1995; Smith Maguire, 2002; Thorpe, 2008; Wachs & Chase, 2013) and confirmed through a recent systematic review study (Tian & Wise, 2020).

One study using Foucault's theory as applied to running suggested that the body-philosophic meaning of the cultural phenomenon of running might produce indulgent manipulative power over people (Yuan & Hou, 2019). Another study found that permission to engage in conversation during a run was only granted to experienced runners who have acquired the 'correct' running term (Lev & Zach, 2020). From a coaching standpoint, researchers have illustrated the effectiveness of daily instructional practices and the importance of coaching that balances maintaining endurance and disciplinary techniques (Denison, 2007, 2010; Denison et al., 2017; Denison & Mills, 2014). To develop effective coaching, coaches must understand how power operates in and around their coaching environment (Mills & Denison, 2018). Thus, running, as the technology of the self, realizes the impact on the runner's body, psychological thoughts and behaviour to change the runner to achieve a specific state of happiness (Wang, 2019).

Foucault differentiated between four main types of technologies: production (i.e. producing, transforming and manipulating something), sign systems (i.e. using meanings or symbols), power (i.e. determining conduct) and self (i.e. transforming oneself to attain a desired state) (Foucault, 1988). Foucault is arguably regarded for this notion *technologies of power*, which appears in most of the scholars' writings. In the '*History of Sexuality*', Foucault turned to the issue of the cognitive subject, focussing on the agency of the body whereby a new concept was coined: *the technologies of the self*. The emergence of the concept of the technologies of the self is described as a sublimation of Foucault's thought. Scholars today explore Foucault's technologies of the self-concept in critical social research, involving almost every conceivable aspect of bodily existence. In this chapter, Foucault's theory is utilised as a handy tool for studying the social phenomenon of running culture in China.

This study attempts to understand the phenomenon of running fever in China that has been sanctified by the consumer society based on Foucault's theory. Foucault's ideological pedigree has experienced the ideological evolution from power technology to the technologies of the self. This process can just be used to understand one of China-running culture's most popular consumer society phenomena. With the mastery of the body, we may become a recipient of abuse under the supervision of power, or we can rediscover the hope of self-production from the gap between us and our body.

HISTORY OF RUNNING IN CHINA

Running Culture in Ancient China

Running culture in China can be traced back to before the fifth century to the myth and legend of Kuafu chasing the sun. This myth and legend tell the process of the leader of the Kuafu tribe in the Yellow Emperor period looking for water sources, building water conservancy and leading the tribe to migrate and work during the drought period in ancient times (Birrell, 2000). Running became a popular form of movement because, at that time, the Chinese lived primitive lifestyles, feared the natural world and resigned themselves to fate. The cultural symbolism of Kuafu chasing the sun is a fantasy of ancient Chinese ancestors to conquer nature, reflecting the strong desire of ancient Chinese ancestors to understand and overcome nature (Li, 2010). The running culture in ancient China illustrates the spirit of human resistance to natural oppression. It inspires the confidence of ancient Chinese ancestors through a myth and points out how ancient Chinese ancestors adapted to the natural environment.

The ancient Chinese running culture has a particular relationship with the early post system (Hao, 2011; Li, 2010; Qiu & Liu, 1999; Su & Chen, 2010). The post system began in the Yin and Shang dynasties (1300 BC–1046 BC). It was mainly used for the transmission of government orders and military information. One of the most primitive and primary express delivery methods in ancient times was *step delivery*, that is delivery by manual walking. The oracle bone has a *post-delivery* record (Confucius, 2014). Posts allowed people who were good at running fast to deliver official letters or information during the Spring and Autumn and Warring States Periods (770 BC–221 BC) (Mencius, 2005). In 221 BC, after the Qin dynasty unified the six kingdoms, it began to build post roads. There was a specific relationship between the short-distance delivery in this period and the step delivery and running of ordinary mail. Mail carriers should walk about 5 kilometers to deliver the post on the same day (Loewe & Shaughnessy, 1999).The Han dynasty inherited the Qin system, and a post station was set up every 15 kilometers for staying. During the Wei and Jin dynasties (AD 220–AD 420), the management system of the Han dynasty was inherited. At that time, some people were good at running fast in the *Budi* network post stations, called *Jijiaozi*, and those who sent government documents were good long-distance runners (Qiu & Liu, 1999).

In the Jin dynasty (AD 1115–AD 1234), there appeared a post-transfer form for transmitting official documents called *Jijiaodai*, a long-distance weight-bearing relay race, with a station every 5–7.5 kilometers. They are robust, carrying paperwork, self-defence weapons, rain gear and hanging bells on their waists. These are all good runners from the military and can be said to be professional long-distance runners in the military (Li, 2010). Express delivery at post stations in the Song Dynasty (AD 960–AD 1279) also adopted the long-distance running relay method to deliver documents. This relay method avoids the physical fatigue caused by the long-distance delivery of the same person and ensures the speed and efficiency of official document delivery (Kuo, 2011). Yuan, Ming and Qing dynasties all continued the post system. With the establishment of the new post, the old post system was gradually abolished in the late Qing dynasty (Qiu & Liu, 1999). This post system has laid a particular foundation for running culture in China.

The needs of ancient Chinese warfare prompted the infantry to have good running ability. During the Xia and Shang dynasties, due to the requirements of war, the trained soldiers must be able to achieve extraordinary strength and the running ability to chase four-horse chariots (Sima, 2011). In the Zhou dynasty of China (1046 BC–256 BC), 'infantry running with chariots' appeared. The bronze inscription '*Ling Ding*' in the Western Zhou dynasty recorded an incident of infantry running with chariots. (Feng, 2013; Loewe & Shaughnessy, 1999). The chariots of the Western Zhou dynasty were called *Si*, which consisted of four horses and one chariot. On the battlefield, in addition to having this kind of chariot charge in front and clear obstacles, 72 infantrymen were required to follow behind to expand the battle results. The cooperation between chariots and infantry on this battlefield requires infantry to have the ability to run long distances (Aimei et al., 2015; Feng, 2013; History, 2019). From the Warring States Period to the Han dynasty (202 BC–AD 220), as chariot battles were transformed into large-scale corps battles, soldiers' walking and running became the troops' main training methods. In the Han Dynasty of China, people who followed the carriages professionally appeared called *five hundred*. Their duties were to clear the way in front of the carriages of senior officials, and the basic skills needed were to keep up with the running speed of the carriages (He, 1956; Loewe & Shaughnessy, 1999). In AD 1287, Kublai Khan, the emperor of the Yuan dynasty of China, formed a guard army named *Guiyouchi* and set up many post stations to transmit military information, responsible for *Yuan Dadu* (located in today's Beijing, China) and *Yuanshangdu*. (located in Xilin Gol League, Inner Mongolia, China). The Praetorian Guards were observed and trained by participating in an annual long-distance race. There are two routes in this running competition. One is the East Route, starting from *Hexiwu* (located in today's Tianjin, China) and ending in *Huangcheng Danei* (located in today's Beijing), with a total distance of about 67.6 kilometers (Hao, 2011).

Running Culture in Modern China

From the end of the 19th Century to the beginning of the 20th Century, Western sports culture profoundly influenced the development pattern of Chinese sports. Modern Chinese sports mainly came from Western sports (Hong & Zhouxiang, 2015; Morris, 2004). More social elites pay attention to the development of running, and more people have started to participate in running. As early as 1904, Shanghai held the first 'Shanghai Wanguo Cross-Country Race', the earliest outdoor cross-country running event in Shanghai. China's first marathon was held in Nanjing in November 1910. In 1929, the Shanghai Sports Association also had the first city marathon in Shanghai, with a total course of 17 miles (about 27 kilometers) (Shunlin, 1930). At that time, foreign nationals mainly participated. After that, the event was held every spring and lasted until the 1930s at the end (Kang, 1926). During this time, marathon training methods also began to spread among people (Qi, 1933).

Sports events at this stage played a role that was more than that of a sporting event but one of shaping Chinese independent nationhood and national identity (Li & Hong, 2015). The significance of mass sport was demonstrated in the landmark slogan by Chairman Mao Zedong in 1952: 'Develop physical culture and sports and strengthen the people's physiques *(fazhan tiyu yundong zengqiang renmin tizhi)*' (Zheng et al., 2018). Since then, the fundamental purpose of running has been to improve the national quality and strengthen the national physique.

The Chinese economy has developed significantly since Deng Xiaoping started the reform and opening-up policy in 1978. In 1981, the first Beijing International Marathon was successfully held in Beijing, marking the first time that marathon running events have been held continuously in China after the reform and opening up. Running has become a vital sport to improve Chinese people's health (Luping, 2021). In the early stage of China's reform and opening up, the reform of the rural economic system was the main driving force in promoting urbanisation (Tan et al., 2016). Urbanisation played an essential role in promoting marathon fever in China. From 1981 to 1984, the Beijing Marathon became the leader of Chinese marathon events. At this time, the organisation mode of the Beijing Marathon belonged to professional events held in urban streets, and the number of participants was relatively small. For example, only 195 players from 19 countries signed up for the second Beijing Marathon, of which 181 participated, only 143 players and 38 foreign players (Luping, 2021).

Since 1985, under the initiative of the President of the International Olympic Committee (IOC) Samaranch, the organizational model of the Beijing Marathon has undergone unexpected reform. Participation was open to the public, and more than 10,000 players participated in the fifth Beijing Marathon. The marathon has become a mass event held in the city. Then, in May 1987, the Chinese Athletics Association and the Dalian Municipal People's Government co-hosted the first Dalian International Marathon, one of the long-distance races initiated and sponsored by President Samaranch (Luping, 2021). Subsequently, in October 1987, Hangzhou hosted the China–Japan West Lake Osmanthus Marathon, making Hangzhou the third city in Chinese history to host a marathon. The achievements of Chinese elite sports have gradually promoted the development of Chinese mass sports (Shen, 2020).

With the support of the IOC, marathon running events have progressively become running events with a more significant proportion of amateur runners. The IOC has also successively supported Chengdu, Dalian, Luoyang, Kunming and Guangzhou in marathon events, with tens of thousands participating. The IOC has been essential in promoting marathon running events in China. Marathon events originated from Western sports and have gradually been recognized by Chinese players. However, at this stage, running-related events were still dominated by the state-mandatory planned economy, and the market economic mechanism was almost blank. The state mainly funded, planned and operated the official national marathon events. Although corporate sponsorship is allowed, The market is limited (McMillan & Naughton, 1992; Shen, 2020; Zheng et al., 2018). At the same time, residents' awareness of sports consumption has not yet been formed, and the quota for domestic runners to participate in the marathon has been allocated according to the planned economy model. Because there were no registration places, the social youths who loved to run's enthusiasm for participating was relatively low, and the degree of marketisation of the marathon was deficient at this stage. The main participants in the marathon are mainly professional elite athletes. The marathon running event aims to create excellent athletic performance, stimulating the Chinese people's national pride, self-confidence and patriotic enthusiasm at home and abroad and improving international influence (Ma & Kurscheidt, 2019; Zheng et al., 2018).

Under the planned economic system, the state has greater power and strict management, which limits the initiative of economic development and the vitality of sports events. In 1992, the Chinese government established the reform goal of the socialist market economy with Chinese characteristics (Sigley, 2006), which has become a booster for the further development of marathon running events. In 1992, the Chinese government proposed 'forming a new pattern of combining state and social-run sports, with social-run sports as the mainstay' (Zheng et al., 2018). Subsequently, China International Sports Tourism Corporation became an advertising and investment company for the Beijing Marathon, raising much more social funds and promoting the marathon development. The marketisation significantly improved the overall service quality of the Beijing Marathon (Luping, 2021). China's urbanisation has also fully developed from the coast to the inland, promoting the rapid development of cities. The city's unique gathering space has also laid a specific material foundation for Chinese running culture (Henderson et al., 2009). And then, in 1996, Shanghai successfully held the first International Marathon. In 1998, qualifications for the Beijing Marathon were open to the whole society, announcing the birth of a marathon consumer market centred on public experience.

After entering the 20th Century, the number of marathon running events in China increased (see Zuo et al., 2019). In March 2003, Xiamen City held the first International Marathon; in May 2006, Yangzhou City had the first Jianzhen International Marathon; in May 2007, the first Zhengzhou-Kaifeng Marathon was born; in September 2010, Taiyuan held the first marathon (Zuo et al., 2019). However, the primary funding source for Chinese marathons at this stage was national finance, and the main body of supply and operation of sports events was still government sports departments. The marketisation of marathon events has just begun to advance gradually (Wei et al., 2010). In 2010, the State Council of China proposed 'striving *to develop the market for sports competitions and performances*' and '*actively guide and standardise the market-oriented operation of various sports competitions and performances.*' The capital introduction has been emphasised in the marathon market (Liu et al., 2017). As of 2011, the number of marathon events registered with the Chinese Athletic Association has increased to 22.

Meanwhile, the Chinese economy has performed admirably for about three decades since the Chinese reform and opening-up policy, with even double-digit growth rates. Marathon events have formed an operation mode of '*government leadership, enterprise participation, and market operation.*' (Zheng et al., 2018). The Chinese middle class was encouraged to take responsibility for their identity construction and well-being (Tsang, 2014; Zhang, 2017) and began to pursue the spiritual culture while pursuing material culture. Participating in marathons has become a serious leisure activity in China (Qiu et al., 2020). In 2014, the State Council of China issued 'Several Opinions on Accelerating the Development of the Sports Industry and Promoting Sports Consumption', which elevated national fitness to a national strategy and cancelled the approval of commercial and mass sports events. This policy broke the social force organisation and institutional barriers to hosting sports events. The local governments have much more enthusiasm to support the event development. At the same time, the government has gradually withdrawn from the micro-level of event operation, focussing on macro-guidance, support and supervision (Zheng et al., 2018). According to official data from the Chinese Athletic Association, the number of running-related events increased from 219 in 2015 to 1,828 in 2019 (including road running with more than 800 participants and cross-country and hiking activities with more than 300 participants). Participants increased from 1.5 million in 2015 to 7.12 million in 2019 (Wei et al., 2020).

RUNNING CULTURE IN CHINA AND THE TECHNOLOGY OF DISCIPLINARY POWER

Foucault pointed out that disciplinary power is about creating efficient systems that lend to economic control (Foucault & Ewald, 2003). Disciplinary power manifests itself as the technique of disciplining the body. The body becomes the field of the technologies of power, playing a role in social structures such as prisoners, schools, hospitals and factories. Running in ancient China was just a tool, which, in a sense, symbolises the control of disciplinary power over the body, which was docile by effective discipline. At the same time, the individual effectively forces himself to operate within these spaces. The soldier of that era bore specific running capacity attributes that signed their unique status as violent tools of the state. The soldier displayed the sign of their running capacity and the capacity of the state whose banner he fought be inner. Foucault points out that mastering and preparing oneself is a form of preparedness (Foucault, 2012b). For Foucault, 'external' factors – important 'external' technologies, 'external' shapes, etc. – are all crucial in shaping the subject as an 'inner' dimension.

Running in ancient China was also a form of obedience, not a movement in a spontaneous state, but a passive acceptance under a specific power. The military was uniquely dependent on disciplinary power over the body. Disciplinary power plays an essential role in the birth of the disciplinary process. Disciplinary power inevitably standardises life and body through various disciplinary techniques. For example, infantry needs to have an excellent running performance to meet the needs of marching such as events. Therefore, the running event, *Guiyouchi,* was born in China's Yuan dynasty. This running event was just a training technique required by the military. Disciplinary power has a normalising and oppressive effect on the disciplinary techniques of the body. In this way, the body was manipulated, shaped and disciplined. From then on, the body becomes obedient, cooperative and docile. Foucault (2012b) explains

> 'what was then being formed' 'was a policy of coercions that act upon the body, a calculated manipulation of its elements, its gestures, its behaviour. The human body was entering a machinery of power that explores it, breaks it down and rearranges it. A "political anatomy", which was also a "mechanics of power", was being born; it defined how one may have a holdover others' bodies, not only so that they may do what one wishes, but so that they may

operate as one wishes, with the techniques, the speed and the efficiency that one determines. Thus discipline produces subjected and practised bodies, "docile" bodies'. (p. 138)

From this perspective, the runner's body became a machine. Disciplinary power was in the techno-political sphere, consisting of rules and methods of controlling or correcting the workings of the human body, empirical and computational, concerning armies, schools and hospitals. Although these two spheres were pretty different, the central idea was the same: 'docile'. That was to say, no matter what method the ruling class adopted, their purpose was only one: to make the ancient runners' bodies docile through discipline on the bodies of the ruled class. While being docile, the runner's body became the production of disciplinary power in ancient China. The dominant effect of power produced a submissive subject, which was undoubtedly passive, such as the running body of the ancient Chinese soldier and postman. As Foucault (2012b) stated, these bodies can be made docile by being '*subjected, used, transformed and improved*' (p. 136).

RUNNING CULTURE IN MODERN CHINA AND THE TECHNOLOGIES OF BIOPOWER

Foucault proposed that in the 19th Century, a new technology of power emerged: 'biopower'. Biopower, as a particular technique, appeared slightly later than discipline power. This concept was featured only in the last chapter of a book published in 1976 (see Foucault, 2019a). Foucault pointed out that biopower was a positive take and influence on one's life, and repeating attempts allows one to master a technique (Foucault, 2019a). *The* new biopower operates instead through dispersed networks named the dispositif, which refers to the various institutional, physical and administrative mechanisms and knowledge structures Foucault & Ewald, 2003). Foucault has started recognising a macro-power pointed at the species and populaces through administrative instruments, different from disciplinary micro-power, which lends to a sense of control (Foucault, 1982). Government intrigue moved from security over territory to security over people to population governance. Governance was to be affected not by dictator management but by direct and indirect means of influence, as necessary governance (Foucault, 2007). According to Foucault, this change in governance methods constitutes what is deemed power in the present time with a target population and with a major base following (Foucault, 2007). Foucault also indicated a growing governmental interest in public health, which can be interpreted as an important discourse for promoting running activities and competitions in China.

Biopower was not the discipline of individuals by the will of the state but the means and guaranteed to maintain and guide the operation, development and construction of society. China established various modern sports systems, including the non-governmental National Olympic Committee and the sports administration system, from the end of the 19th century to the beginning of the

20th century. Meanwhile, the provincial, municipal, regional and national levels have formed three-level competitive sports systems (Li & Hong, 2015). The construction of public sports venues has begun and showcases China's rising influence as a host nation for major events (see Wise, 2020). This means that modern Chinese sports have moved from expatriates and schools in the concession to society. For example, A simple runway appeared in the newly built Shanghai Public Stadium (covering 28 acres, about 1.87 hectares) on 30 March 1917. Through running, the social function of strengthening the race and the country has gradually changed to fitness, entertainment, and competition (Morris, 2004).

Running culture in China was more influenced by the Soviet Ready for Labour and Defence fitness promotion system after the founding the People's Republic of China in 1949. The sports policy concentrated all resources on a small number of elite athletes to achieve excellent international results. The primary purpose of running was to train people to be healthy, courageous and optimistic defenders of the motherland and socialist workers (Wei et al., 2010). In 1978, China implemented a profound internal reform and opening-up policy to modernise and strive to integrate into the world economy. In 1979, China renewed its membership in the IOC an essential role in stimulating national enthusiasm, motivating people to modernise and enhancing China's new image on the international stage (Wei et al., 2010). The Chinese government also started concentrating nationwide effort and resources on marathon running event development. In 1992, the Chinese government established the reform direction of the socialist market economic system. In June 1995, promulgating the *Outline of the National Fitness Program*me laid the foundation for China to carry out mass sports activities more widely and improve people's physical fitness (Tan, 2015). In 2001, China joined the WTO, and Beijing's successful bid to host the 2008 Olympic Games, especially the State Council of China, cancelled the approval system for commercial and mass sports in 2014, significantly promoting the running fever in China.

From Foucault's perspective, biopower achieves regulatory control of the population as life and life processes are regulated through specific and nuanced interventions in modern China. The running culture in contemporary China was also one of the results of Foucault's so-called biopower plant being concerted and practiced in various institutional structures. The most specific goal of biopower was population control, and the practice of power was to save lives instead of banishing them. Improving health was precisely the core goal of biopower, which played an essential role in promoting the development of running culture in China. These results aligned with the Chinese '*Outline for Building a Leading Sports Nation*' and the '*Outline of the Nationwide Body-building Plan*'. These were also the inherent requirements of biopower at work. From this point of view, biopower was rather like pastoral power, which '*is fundamentally a beneficial power*' (Foucault, 2007), and its shape was of '*someone who keeps watch*' (Foucault, 2007).

RUNNING CULTURE IN MODERN CHINA AND THE TECHNOLOGY OF SELF

Foucault (1986) speaks to the notion of technologies of the self whereby individuals focus on helping others move towards happiness and positive vibes through healthy activities and to lead healthier lifestyles. From a Foucaulian standpoint, running can thus be seen as a form of individual behavioural sovereignty (see Foucault, 2007). Foucault (2007) also notes we must pay attention to two different power systems impacting controlled behaviours. Of course, control can also be exercised, as effectively but less blatantly, through self-regulation: the disciplined self was achieved through internalized norms of behaviour. The technologies of the self as a subject speak in connection to technologies of power, the technologies of the self-developed within the handle of subjectification and the shaping of oneself as a subject inside power relations (Thorpe, 2008). Foucault notes that we can impact this self-creation or self-fashioning through ethical practice, meaning practice is necessary to develop professional skills and techniques (Foucault, 1997). Under the concept of the technology of the self, the subject shapes its free practice for its purpose, which does not involve surrender to external power. Foucault regards this kind of subject as free (Foucault, 2012a).

According to Foucault (2019b), self-techniques, as does running culture, come in different forms. Neoliberalism's development is rooted in the political function of market freedom, as it allows consumers to exercise free will (Hayek, 1976). The Chinese government has increasingly adopted a form of neoliberal governance that encourages citizens to take personal responsibility for their health, success and happiness (Tsang, 2014; Zhang, 2017). However, China's modernisation has led to social differentiation (Lu, 2012; Tian & Wise, 2022), and consumer capitalism fosters the individualistic self (Guitart, 2011). There is a strong tendency to move towards utilitarian individualism in social relations in China. In the ever-changing modern society, the social challenge of status makes separating individuals and society more and more apparent. Family and social groups, which used to give people a sense of security, are no longer as crucial as before (Beck et al., 1992). Neoliberalism views health as a personal responsibility (LeBesco, 2011). Therefore, the growing Chinese middle-class individuals need to identify themselves and find a sense of security. They pay much more attention to self-enrichment, career success and leisure time. They recognized the symbolic value of leisure (Tsang, 2014). In this case, running becomes an important safety strategy for individuals (Crawford, 2006). Running as a recreational activity has become an integral part of an active and healthy lifestyle among the middle class (Abbas, 2004). It can help increase participation levels in exercise and physical activity (Shipway & Holloway, 2010).

People regard running as a healthy lifestyle, and their motivations are mainly to lose weight, maintain good health and improve their quality of life (Shipway & Holloway, 2016). In addition, running is inherently geographical, with spaces, places, movements and bodies central to the practice (Cook & Larsen, 2022). As a convenient and accessible exercise, running is an element of the conscious good life in space and time (Bale, 2004). Runners turn the place and route of running into a place for social interaction in daily life. Running members of the group have positive social interactions and support during and outside the running (Xie et al., 2020). Running creates positive relationships between the runner's self and others, mediating the relationship between self and society, mind and body, and idea and object (Allen-Collinson & Hockey, 2015). Many people suffer from depression and other mental illnesses; for them, running has become an effective treatment (Greist et al., 1979). Regular runners have plastic changes in brain structure and function (Cao et al., 2021), and anxiety and fatigue begin to decrease gradually (Sparling et al., 1993); some people use running as a treatment for alcohol or other addictions. A practical pathway to addictive behaviours and physical achievement through running can enhance a runner's self-esteem (Shipway & Holloway, 2016).

CONCLUSIONS

Running enables individuals to explore the emotional potential of the body. This effective atmosphere might condition and discipline runners' affective capacities for health (Cai et al., 2021), and subcultural groups of runners can provide individuals with health-related professional knowledge. Behavior norms in daily life can also provide social support, and the runners have a sense of identity with running, an important consideration in research concerning sport and place of where activities happen (Wise, 2015). All these technologies affect and regulate runners' lifestyles (Haslam et al., 2009). Currently, physical activity, including running, has emerged as a practical technology of the self (Crawford, 1980), through which *'the subject constitutes itself in an active fashion'* (Foucault, 2019b).

In Foucault's research, he regards the technology of power as the opposite of the technology of the self. But today, the meaning of Foucault's panopticon has a new interpretation in modern Chinese running culture. The meaning of Foucault's panopticon has a new interpretation in modern Chinese running culture. There seems to be a new panopticon around the runner, material, spiritual and institutional factors forming an invisible wall. For example, these factors include running-related values, ethics, psychological quality, self-image, wearable devices, digital technology, natural environment and climate (Ren, 2016; Ren et al., 2020; Zuo et al., 2019). Surveillance of runners can potentially divert runners' attention away from the actual scene, weakening the runner's true feelings, experience or participation in the background (Goffman, 2021), which is often true of runners. When they run, they may lose the devotion and concentration of actual participation because of the existence of this panopticon. It creates a particular meaning without proving that the body is present. Running is a kind of self-identification practice, but similarly, this self-identification process is mainly based on physical activities. The running body is also disciplined by external forces from time to time, which is related to the staged requirements of the entire social environment and the feedback of others. In forming the running culture in China and constructing individuals as runners, the invented, perfected and ever-evolving procedures and knowledge of power relations as 'technology' played the most fundamental roles.

ACKNOWLEDGEMENTS

This chapter was supported by the National Social Science Fund of China [grant number 18BTY033]

FIVE KEY READINGS

Foucault, M. (2012). *Discipline and punish: The birth of the prison.* **Vintage Books.**
Foucault analysed the social and theoretical mechanisms behind the changes in Western penal systems during the modern age based on historical documents from France. Foucault argues that prison did not become the main form of punishment just because of the humanitarian concerns of reformists. He traces the cultural shifts that led to the predominance of prison via the body and power. According to Foucault, prison is used by the 'disciplines' – new technological powers that can also be found in places such as schools, hospitals and military barracks.

Foucault, M. (2007). *Security, territory, population: Lectures at the Collège de France, 1977–78.* **Springer.**
This book derives from Foucault's lectures at the College de France between January and April 1978, which can be seen as a radical turning point in his thought. Focussing on 'bio-power', he studies the foundations of this new technology of power over population and explores the technologies of security and the history of 'governmentality'.

Foucault, M. (1988). Technologies of the self. In: L. H. Martin, H. Gutman, & P. H. Hutton (Eds.), *Technologies of the self: A seminar with Michel Foucault* **(pp. 16–49).**
Foucault defines 'technologies of the self' as 'reflected and voluntary practices by which men not only fix rules of conduct for themselves but seek to transform themselves, to change themselves in their particular being and to make their life an oeuvre'. In other words, technologies of the self are what Michel Foucault refers to as the processes and procedures by which people define themselves. He holds that people are constantly involved in processes that define and develop certain ethical self-understandings. In this sense, these processes are political because they reveal the interplay between the micro-relations between individuals and the macro-structures or forces of power, which is necessary to comprehend subjectivity or the self.

Bale, J. (2004). *Running cultures: Racing in time and space.* **Routledge.**
John Bale brings the sport into the realm of the humanities by drawing on sources including literature, poetry, film, art and sculpture, as well as statistics and training manuals to highlight the tensions, ambiguities and hidden complexities beneath the commonplace notion of running. The text explores local,

personal, communal and global aspects of running and its practitioners. It examines the streets, tracks and stadiums where athletes run, the races in which they compete, and the running relationships that exist between the athlete and the coach, between runners and between the athlete and spectator. It discusses the importance of speed and records, how running has been used to symbolise resistance and transgression and how it can be associated with a healthy lifestyle.

Wei, F., Hong, F., & Zhouxiang, L. (2010). Chinese state sports policy: Pre- and post-Beijing 2008. *The International Journal of the History of Sport, 27*(14–15), 2380–2402. http://doi.org/10.1080/09523367.2010.504583

Wei, F provides an overview of Chinese sports policy and practice, the origin, challenge and continuity from the 1920s to the 2000s, particularly emphasising the post-Beijing Olympics. It states that political, economic and educational requirements have always shaped the development of Chinese sports policy.

REFERENCES

Abbas, A. (2004). The embodiment of class, gender and age through leisure: A realist analysis of long distance running. *Leisure Studies, 23*(2), 159–175. http://doi.org/10.1080/0261436042000226354

Aimei, H., Xueqin, L., & Zhikun, G. (2015). *The history of Western Zhou dynasty*. Shanghai People's Publishing House.

Allen-Collinson, J., & Hockey, J. (2015). From a certain point of view: Sensory phenomenological envisionings of running space and place. *Journal of Contemporary Ethnography, 44*(1), 63–83. http://doi.org/10.1177/0891241613505866

Andrews, D. L. (1993). Desperately seeking Michel: Foucault's genealogy, the body, and critical sport sociology. *Sociology of Sport Journal, 10*(2), 148–167. http://doi.org/10.1123/ssj.10.2.148

Bale, J. (2004). *Running cultures: Racing in time and space*. Routledge.

Beck, U., Lash, S., & Wynne, B. (1992). *Risk society: Towards a new modernity* (Vol. 17). SAGE Publications.

Birrell, A. (2000). *The classic of mountains and seas*. Penguin Classics.

Birrell, S., & Cole, C. L. (1994). *Women, sport, and culture*. Human Kinetics.

Buman, M. P., Omli, J. W., Giacobbi, P. R., & Brewer, B. W. (2008). Experiences and coping responses of "Hitting the Wall" for recreational marathon runners. *Journal of Applied Sport Psychology, 20*(3), 282–300. http://doi.org/10.1080/10413200802078267

Cai, X., Woods, O., & Gao, Q. (2021). Running bodies and the affective spaces of health in and beyond marathon running in China. *Health & Place, 70*, 102612. http://doi.org/10.1016/j.healthplace.2021.102612

Cao, L., Zhang, Y., Huang, R., Li, L., Xia, F., Zou, L., Yu, Q., Lin, J., Herold, F., Perrey, S., Mueller, P., Dordevic, M., Loprinzi, P. D., Wang, Y., Ma, Y., Zeng, H., Qu, S., Wu, J., & Ren, Z. (2021). Structural and functional brain signatures of endurance runners. *Brain Structure and Function, 226*(1), 93–103. http://doi.org/10.1007/s00429-020-02170-y

Confucius. (2014). In D., Reader (Ed.), Book of rites. Dragon Reader.

Cook, S., & Larsen, J. (2022). Geographies of running cultures and practices. *Geography Compass, 16*(10). http://doi.org/10.1111/gec3.12660

Crawford, R. (1980). Healthism and the medicalization of everyday life. *International Journal of Health Services, 10*(3), 365–388.

Crawford, R. (2006). Health as a meaningful social practice. *Health, 10*(4), 401–420.

Denison, J. (2007). Social theory for coaches: A Foucauldian reading of one athlete's poor performance. *International Journal of Sports Science & Coaching, 2*(4), 369–383.

Denison, J. (2010). Planning, practice and performance: The discursive formation of coaches' knowledge. *Sport, Education and Society*, *15*(4), 461–478.
Denison, J. (2019). What it really means to 'think outside the box': Why Foucault matters for coach development. *International Sport Coaching Journal*, *6*(3), 354–358. http://doi.org/10.1123/iscj.2018-0068
Denison, J., & Mills, J. P. (2014). Planning for distance running: Coaching with Foucault. *Sports Coaching Review*, *3*(1), 1–16. http://doi.org/10.1080/21640629.2014.953005
Denison, J., Mills, J. P., & Konoval, T. (2017). Sports' disciplinary legacy and the challenge of 'coaching differently. *Sport, Education and Society*, *22*(6), 772–783.
Feng, L. (2013). *Early China: A social and cultural history*. Cambridge University Press.
Foucault, M. (1982). The subject and power. *Critical Inquiry*, *8*(4), 777–795.
Foucault, M. (1986). *The care of the self: The history of sexuality* (Vol. 3). Trans. Robert Hurley. Penguin.
Foucault, M. (1988). Technologies of the self. In *Technologies of the self: A seminar with Michel Foucault* (pp. 16–49). The University of Massachusetts Press.
Foucault, M. (1997). Self writing. *Ethics: Subjectivity and Truth*, *1*, 207–223.
Foucault, M. (2007). *Security, territory, population: Lectures at the Collège de France, 1977–78*. Springer.
Foucault, M. (2012a). *The history of sexuality, vol. 2: The use of pleasure*. Vintage.
Foucault, M. (2012b). *Discipline and punish: The birth of the prison*. Vintage.
Foucault, M. (2019a). *The history of sexuality: 1: The will to knowledge*. Penguin UK.
Foucault, M. (2019b). *Ethics: Subjectivity and truth: Essential works of Michel Foucault 1954–1984*. Penguin UK.
Foucault, M., & Ewald, F. (2003). *"Society Must Be Defended": Lectures at the Collège de France, 1975–1976* (Vol. 1). Macmillan.
Goffman, E. (2021). *The presentation of self in everyday life*. Anchor.
Golden, M. (1998). *Sport and society in ancient Greece*. Cambridge University Press.
Gotaas, T. (2012). *Running: A global history*. Reaktion.
Greist, J. H., Klein, M. H., Eischens, R. R., Faris, J., Gurman, A. S., & Morgan, W. P. (1979). Running as treatment for depression. *Comprehensive Psychiatry*, *20*(1), 41–54. https://doi.org/10.1016/0010-440X(79)90058-0
Guitart, M. E. (2011). The consumer capitalist society and its effects on identity: A macro cultural approach. *Revista Psicologia Política*, *11*(21), 159–170.
Hao, Y. (2011). Study on Mongolian Guiyouchi movement. *Sports Culture Guide*, (05), 93–95.
Haslam, S. A., Jetten, J., Postmes, T., & Haslam, C. (2009). Social identity, health and well-being: An emerging agenda for applied psychology. *Applied Psychology*, *58*(1), 1–23. http://doi.org/10.1111/j.1464-0597.2008.00379.x
Hayek, F. A. (1976). *The road to serfdom*. Routledge.
He, C. (1956). *On the development of the form of land occupation in the han dynasty*. Shanghai People's Publishing House.
Henderson, J. V., Quigley, J., & Lim, E. (2009). *Urbanization in China: Policy issues and options*. Brown University. Unpublished manuscript.
History, C. (2019). *Ancient China: A captivating guide to the ancient history of China and the Chinese civilization starting from the Shang dynasty to the fall of the Han dynasty (ancient Asia)*. Independently published.
Hong, F., & Zhouxiang, L. (2015). *The politicisation of sport in modern China: Communists and champions*. Routledge.
Kang, B. (1926). School news: Cross-country race news: Chronicle of cross-country races. *Nanyang Weekly (Shanghai 1919)*, *7*(10), 58–59.
Kostrubala, T. (1976). *The joy of running*. Lippincott.
Kuo, S. (2011). In W. Hong & Z. Zheng (Eds.), *Brush Talks from Dream Brook*. Paths International Ltd.
Mencius. (2005). In D. C., Lau (Ed.), *Mencius*. Penguin Classics.
LeBesco, K. (2011). Neoliberalism, public health, and the moral perils of fatness. *Critical Public Health*, *21*(2), 153–164.

Lev, A., & Zach, S. (2020). Running between the raindrops: Running marathons and the potential to put marriage in jeopardy. *International Review for the Sociology of Sport, 55*(5), 509–525. http://doi.org/10.1177/1012690218813803
Li, X. (2010). Postrider in silk road and sports. *Sports Culture Guide*, (12), 117–119. http://doi.org/10.3969/j.issn.1671-1572.2010.12.034
Li, L., & Hong, F. (2015). The national games and national identity in the Republic of China, 1910–1948. *International Journal of the History of Sport, 32*(3), 440–454. http://doi.org/10.1080/09523367.2015.1004888
Liu, D., Zhang, J. J., & Desbordes, M. (2017). Sport business in China: Current state and prospect. *International Journal of Sports Marketing & Sponsorship, 18*(1), 2–10. http://doi.org/10.1108/IJSMS-12-2016-0086
Loewe, M., & Shaughnessy, E. L. (1999). *The Cambridge history of ancient China: From the origins of civilization to 221 BC*. Cambridge University Press.
Loughran, M. J., Hamilton, D., & McGinley, M. (2013). Motivations and perceived benefits of marathoning: An exploratory study. *Athletic Insight: Online Journal of Sport Psychology, 5*, 113–127.
Lu, X. (2012). *Social structure of contemporary China* (Vol. 31). World Scientific.
Luping, Z. (2021). *Big era of Chinese marathon*. Electronic Industry Press.
Ma, Y., & Kurscheidt, M. (2019). The national games of China as a governance instrument in Chinese elite sport: An institutional and agency analysis. *International Journal of Sport Policy and Politics, 11*(4), 679–699.
Markula, P. (2004). "Tuning into one's self:" Foucault's technologies of the self and mindful fitness. *Sociology of Sport Journal, 21*(3), 302–321. http://doi.org/10.1123/ssj.21.3.302
McMillan, J., & Naughton, B. (1992). How to reform a planned economy: Lessons from China. *Oxford Review of Economic Policy, 8*(1), 130–143.
Mills, J. P., & Denison, J. (2018). How power moves: A Foucauldian analysis of (in)effective coaching. *International Review for the Sociology of Sport, 53*(3), 296–312. http://doi.org/10.1177/1012690216654719
Mohamad, S. O., & Chung, H. J. (2018). Foucault's history of the present: The birth of the games concept approach in Singapore's physical education curriculum. *International Journal of the History of Sport, 35*(12–13), 1325–1334. http://doi.org/10.1080/09523367.2019.1593151
Morris, A. D. (2004). *Marrow of the nation: A history of sport and physical culture in Republican China* (Vol. 10). University of California Press.
Oswald, F., Campbell, J., Williamson, C., Richards, J., & Kelly, P. (2020). A scoping review of the relationship between running and mental health. *International Journal of Environmental Research and Public Health, 17*(21). http://doi.org/10.3390/ijerph17218059
Qi, Z. (1933). Marathon running practice method (with Olympic marathon rules). *Li Xing (Nanchang), 2*(5), 78–88.
Qiu, R., & Liu, G. (1999). *Historical materials of Chinese courier*. Beihang University Press.
Qiu, Y., Tian, H., Lin, Y., & Zhou, W. (2020). Serious leisure qualities and participation behaviors of Chinese marathon runners. *International Review for the Sociology of Sport, 55*(5), 526–543. http://doi.org/10.1177/1012690218822303
Rail, G., & Harvey, J. (1995). Body at work: Michel Foucault and the sociology of sport. *Sociology of Sport Journal, 12*(2), 164–179. http://doi.org/10.1123/ssj.12.2.164
Ren, Z. (2016). Problems of marathon competition culture in China. *Journal of Sports Adult Education, 32*(5).
Ren, Z., Zuo, Y., Ma, Y., Zhang, M., Smith, L., Yang, L., Loprinzi, P. D., Yu, Q., & Zou, L. (2020). The natural environmental factors influencing the spatial distribution of marathon event: A case study from China. *International Journal of Environmental Research and Public Health, 17*(7), 2238.
Ronkainen, N. J., Shuman, A., Ding, T., You, S., & Xu, L. (2018). 'Running fever': Understanding runner identities in Shanghai through turning point narratives. *Leisure Studies, 37*(2), 211–222. http://doi.org/10.1080/02614367.2017.1324513

Shen, L. (2020). Olympic strategy, nationalism and legitimacy: The role of ideology in the development of Chinese elite sports policy in the first reform decade, 1978–1988. *International Journal of the History of Sport, 37*(Suppl. 1), 26–40.

Shipway, R., & Holloway, I. (2010). Running free: Embracing a healthy lifestyle through distance running. *Perspectives in Public Health, 130*(6), 270–276.

Shipway, R., & Holloway, I. (2016). Health and the running body: Notes from an ethnography. *International Review for the Sociology of Sport, 51*(1), 78–96. http://doi.org/10.1177/1012690213509807

Shunlin, Z. (1930). Photography of the 2nd Shanghai 17-Mile Marathon. *Shanghai Pictorial,* (581), 2.

Sigley, G. (2006). Chinese governmentalities: Government, governance and the socialist market economy. *Economy and Society, 35*(4), 487–508. http://doi.org/10.1080/03085140600960773

Sima, Q. (2011). In B. Watson (Ed.), *Records of the grand historian.* Columbia University Press.

Small, H. (2010). The loneliness of the long-distance runner in Browning, Sillitoe, and Murakami. *Essays in Criticism, 60*(2), 129–147. http://doi.org/10.1093/escrit/cgp023

Smith Maguire, J. (2002). Michel Foucault: Sport, power, technologies and governmentality. *Theory, Sport & Society*, 293–314.

Sparling, P. B., Nieman, D. C., & O'Connor, P. J. (1993). Selected scientific aspects of marathon racing. *Sports Medicine, 15*(2), 116–132. http://doi.org/10.2165/00007256-199315020-00005

Su, Q., & Chen, Z. (2010). Review and reflection of the research on history of posts in China. *Journal of Beijing University of Posts and Telecommunications, 12*(05), 58–66.

Sui, W., & Yang, J. (2022). Running middle-class–marathon craze in transforming period of China. *Sport in Society*, 1–12. http://doi.org/10.1080/17430437.2022.2054337

Tan, Y., Xu, H., & Zhang, X. (2016). Sustainable urbanization in China: A comprehensive literature review. *Cities, 55*, 82–93.

Tan, T. (2015). The transformation of China's national fitness policy: From a major sports country to a world sports power. *International Journal of the History of Sport, 32*(8), 1071–1084. http://doi.org/10.1080/09523367.2015.1036240

Thorpe, H. (2008). Foucault, technologies of self, and the media: Discourses of femininity in snowboarding culture. *Journal of Sport & Social Issues, 32*(2), 199–229. http://doi.org/10.1177/0193723508315206

Tian, E., & Wise, N. (2020). An Atlantic divide? Mapping the knowledge domain of European and North American-based sociology of sport, 2008–2018. *International Review for the Sociology of Sport, 55*(8), 1029–1055.

Tian, E., & Wise, N. (2022). Dancing in public squares – Toward a socially synchronous sense of place. *Leisure Sciences.* https://doi.org/10.1080/01490400.2022.2099490

Tsang, E. (2014). *The new middle class in China: Consumption, politics and the market economy.* Springer.

Tzu, L. (2006). *Tao Te Ching: A new English version.* Harper Perennial Modern Classics; Reprint edition.

Wachs, F. L., & Chase, L. F. (2013). Explaining the failure of an obesity intervention: Combining Bourdieu's symbolic violence and the Foucault's microphysics of power to reconsider state interventions. *Sociology of Sport Journal, 30*(2), 111–131. http://doi.org/10.1123/ssj.30.2.111

Wang, J. (2019). Body management and rationalization in running fitness: A qualitative study based on marathon runners. *China Sport Science, 39*(12), 34–42.

Wei, F., Hong, F., & Zhouxiang, L. (2010). Chinese state sports policy: Pre- and post-Beijing 2008. *International Journal of the History of Sport, 27*(14–15), 2380–2402. http://doi.org/10.1080/09523367.2010.504583

Wei, H., Wu, J., & Zhang, Y. (2020). 2019 China marathon big data: The number of world athletics-certified events ranks first in the world.http://sports.people.com.cn/n1/2020/0501/c401891-31695749.html. Accessed on 1 May 2020.

Wise, N. (2015). Geographical approaches and the sociology of sport. In R. Giulianotti (Ed.), *Routledge handbook of the sociology of sport* (pp. 142–152). Routledge.

Wise, N. (2020). Eventful futures and triple bottom line impacts: BRICS, image regeneration and competitiveness. *Journal of Place Management and Development, 13*(1), 89–100.

Xie, H., Chen, Y., & Yin, R. (2020). Running together is better than running alone: A qualitative study of a self-organised distance running group in China. *Leisure Studies*, *39*(2), 195–208. http://doi.org/10.1080/02614367.2019.1698647

Yuan, B., & Hou, T. (2019). Habits, discipline and struggle: The mirror metaphor of the marathon fever. *Journal of Sports Science*, *40*(04), 62–67.

Zhang, L. (2017). The rise of therapeutic governing in postsocialist China. *Medical Anthropology*, *36*(1), 6–18. http://doi.org/10.1080/01459740.2015.1117079

Zheng, J., Chen, S., Tan, T., & Lau, P. W. C. (2018). Sport policy in China (Mainland). *International Journal of Sport Policy and Politics*, *10*(3), 469–491. http://doi.org/10.1080/19406940.2017.1413585

Zuo, Y., Zou, L., Zhang, M., Smith, L., Yang, L., Loprinzi, P. D., & Ren, Z. (2019). The temporal and spatial evolution of marathons in China from 2010 to 2018. *International Journal of Environmental Research and Public Health*, *16*(24), 5046.

CHAPTER 10

CHALLENGES IN REFORMS OF CHINESE ELITE SPORTS: TOWARDS A NEW DEVELOPMENT MODE

Dehao Ma and Liu Ji

East China Normal University, China

ABSTRACT

Along with the national government's expectation transformation, administrative system reform, economic transition, social demand structure's upgrading and population change, these negative effects are turning increasingly obvious and thus become huge powers that push the reform of traditional elite sports development mode forward. Against this background, in order to make this reform better adapted to China's reality and future development, the chapter suggests that Chinese traditional elite sports development mode should shift its driving forces of development from single to multiple, change its administrative system from government-oriented to society-oriented, develop its training concepts from instrumentalism to humanism, improve its construction of development from unbalanced to balanced and alter its effectiveness of development from extensive to intensive so as to achieve sustainable development.

Keywords: China; elite sports; development mode; reform; sustainable development; transformation

INTRODUCTION

Being influenced by the transformation of economic and political systems, China's social and population structures have changed deeply, which gives more opportunities as well as challenges to elite sports development (Hu & Henry, 2017). Those variations put more pressure on Chinese traditional elite sports development modes and calls for new innovations. This is important as sport in China looks to progress following the Beijing Olympic Games. So, the General Administration of Sport of China (GASC) issued *The Twelfth Five-Year Plan of Chinese Sports Development* in 2011 (see Zheng et al., 2018). Events are an important reflection of society (Wise & Harris, 2019), and in China, sports development plans are aimed at success in international competitions.

An important topical area of research in sociology of sport work is mega-events and Olympics and sports development and performance is important to this (Tian & Wise, 2020). This five-year plan focused on development between 2011 and 2015 and beyond to reform traditional elite sports development mode to adapt to the new social condition better. The State Council of China (SCC) issued the *Outline for Building a Strong sports Country* in 2019 (Su et al., 2023). This also pointed out that it was necessary to improve the development model of elite sports that combined national system with market mechanism. The purpose of this was to adhere to the principle of opening up to run sports for the purpose of forming an elite sports management system that combined both state and society. Against this background, we addressed Chinese traditional elite sports development mode's challenges coming from China's whole transformations and proposed several suggestions for this reform.

CHALLENGES OF CHINESE ELITE SPORTS DEVELOPMENT MODE

Challenges From the National Government's Expectation Transformation

The first trait of Chinese traditional elite sports development mode is its driving force of development, which mainly comes from government's political expectations. Caldwell (1982) has argued that the growth of nationalism, the conduct of war and the flourishing development of international sport must all happen simultaneously. The phenomenon of taking international competitive sports as an opportunity to demonstrate the virtues of a country's political system is common to both western and eastern nations. In fact, it is prevalent to view sport as a sign of quality of life in countries where the regime has a kind of inferiority complex in some direction. These words well explain the reason why China has put so much money and so many resources into the development of elite sports.

China had created a splendid civilization which lasted for thousands of years and was halted by the western colonialists from 1840 to 1945 (Xu, 2019, p. 19). Before the first opium war, Chinese always viewed themselves as descendants of the dragon. But during the first and second opium wars, they were treated as 'the sick man of Asia'. That was a big disgrace they had never experienced before. Consequently, after the People's Republic of China was founded in 1949, the Chinese were very eager to restore their country's great-power status in a short time, which was also an important reason for the movement of Great Leap Forward (*Dayuejin*). This strong desire has made the government always put main resources into projects that have dominant diplomatic values, such as nuclear weapons, satellites, intercontinental missiles and, also, the so-called *Juguo Moshi*.

Compared with other projects, the investment of elite sports is fewer, but no less significant. Just as Lorenz (1987) notes, sport was a special ritualised form of battle developed by human culture. The Chinese, too, often view the wining of Olympic medals as a sign that the state is strong, and see hosting the Olympic Games as a symbol of China's rejuvenation. According to statistics, 95% of the citizens in Beijing supported hosting the Olympics, and 94% of them wanted to serve as volunteers. The Beijing Olympic Games Bid Committee received numerous support letters and donations from both home and abroad (Fan & Lu, 2012, p. 150). Driven by this nationalism, the government invested lots of resources into the development of elite sports, which also achieved its expected goals.

However, Caldwell (1982) believes to driving for international sport success is a testament to the insecurity of a country's identity, as events create social and economic impacts (Wise & Maguire, 2022). This points to a country's growing maturity (or declining insecurity) may well rest upon drawing identity from a variety of sources in addition to sport, such as the arts, political diplomacy or the manifestation of virtues in the world. After 30 years of rapid development, China's GDP has become the second, foreign currency reserves the first in the world, which makes its power status admitted by most other counties and its national self-confidence greatly improved too (Chhabra et al., 2021). This also means that the government's political expectations of elite sports become lower, especially after the Beijing Olympic Games. Besides, the understanding of elite sports in China also becomes more rational. For example, Chinese athletes won a total of 199 gold medals in the 16th Asian Games in 2010, which took up 41.7% of the games' whole medals (Associated Press, 2020). However, these medals did not cause national rejoice but, rather, gave birth to Chinese 'gold medal fatigue'. Yang Ming, a reporter of Xinhua News Agency, wrote an article named 'The Fact Behind Gold medals' that sparked off Chinese public's reflections on the traditional elite sports development mode and discussions on the topic which is more important between elite sports and mass sports.

The strategy that China has insisted on gives priority to the elite sports' development for a long time, which causes the mass sports' development to relatively lag behind. Let us take the distribution of funds as an example. Mass sports accounted for 22.45% of whole sports funds from the government in 2008, and the others were mostly used for elite sports. This figure, however, dropped to only 7.15% in 2016. Due to the lack of fund, the public sports venues are also in short supply. According to the *Statistical Survey of National Stadium in 2021*, China's per-capita sports venues were only 2.41 square metres in 2021, which were lower than the world average level (GASC, 2022a). Strapped by these restrictions, the proportion of Chinese population who participate in regular exercise is low. According to the *Survey Bulletin of National Fitness Activities in 2020*, the proportion of residents aged 7 and above who regularly participated in physical activity was only 37.2% (GASC, 2022b). This is an important reason for the decline of Chinese physical fitness. *The Fifth Monitoring Bulletin on National*

Physical Fitness showed the adult overweight rate and obesity rate were 35.0% and 14.6% respectively in 2020, an increase of 2.3 and 4.1 percentage points over 2014; the declining trend of maximum muscle strength in adults was also evident (GASC, 2022c). According to *The Eighth National Survey on Student Physical Fitness and Health*, compared with 2014, the morphological development indicators such as height, weight and chest circumference continued to improve and physical fitness such as flexibility, strength, speed and endurance changed for better in 2019. However, there were also problems such as the detection rate of poor eyesight among students, the increase in the rate of overweight and obesity and the decline in grip strength level (Ministry of Education of China, 2021).

However, a big crisis caused by changes of China's population structure hides in such national physical fitness. According to the Department of Economic and Social Affairs of United Nations (2012), China's working-age population (from ages 15 to 64) will gradually decrease through this century, while the ageing population (65+) will increase until around the year 2060. Such a decrease in the working-age population and a rise in the ageing population 65 and over means that total population dependency ratios will rise. This means that the whole country's dependency burden has been increasing from 2010 (Department of Economic and Social Affairs of United Nations, 2012). According to statistics, from 2010 to 2021, Chinese residents' per capita disposable income increased 2.8 times. But during the same period, Chinese residents' per capita health care costs increased 3.4 times. So, the growth of health spending was faster than that of the income. The change of population structure also results in a rising trend of labour costs. For example, from 2010 to 2021, Chinese urban residents' average annual wages (equivalent to labour costs) increased 2.3 times (National Bureau of Statistics of China, 2023).

Based on these changes of China's population structure and labour costs, Cai Fang, a famous demographer, made the followed prediction:

> China's first demographic dividend will be over around 2030. According to the demographic economic theories, there will be another demographic dividend when the first finishes, which can be called the second demographic dividend. Assimilating foreign countries' experiences, saving rate and labour supply are the key factors to realize the second demographic dividend. Referring to the saving rate, it mainly depends on a series of system arrangements such as education system, employment system and social security system. As for the labour supply, only through making full use of labour and improving human capitals can the labour productivity get increased under the condition that the absolute number of labours is shrinking. However, the ascent of both human capital and labour productivity is inseparable from people's health. Therefore, constructing Chinese public health service system is a main developing strategy in the next twenty years for the government. (Cai, 2010, p. 8)

The service system of public health should include medical security and mass sports as well because the medical security is, to some extent, a kind of wasting spending when people lose their labour capacity, but the mass sports is a kind of protecting measure to keep it. Doing sports regularly in the youth can not only keep people's current labour productivities but also lay well foundations for working efficiencies when they get old. Therefore, compared with medical security, mass sports is a kind of public health service with production capacity (Yang, 2011, p. 14). In addition, mass sports can also promote the development of relevant industries, which will alleviate the government's pressure from public health costs. Based on this, many developed countries are paying more and more attention to the positive roles of mass sports to promote national health, and their public health security system is now transforming from the traditional mode that takes medical security alone as the core to the new mode which takes both medical security and mass sports. Under such a background, the government of China also needs to pay more attention to mass sports to promote the nation's public health.

In fact, before Beijing won the right to host the 2008 Olympic Games, Chinese government had realised the importance of mass sports and decided to adjust the traditional strategy that gave priorities to the elite sports' development. For instance, in 1996, former president Jiang Zemin pointed out that the central task of sports was to promote the health of the Chinese (Wu et al., 1999, p. 237). In the same year, *The Ninth Five-Year Plan of National Economy and Social Develop* issued by the SCC in 1996 made this adjustment clear and put Chinese sports' tasks of 'implementing national fitness programme to improve national health' in front of 'carrying out Olympic strategy to promote athletic level', which meant that in the aspect of sports, the mass sports would be in the first position to develop. But this adjustment was delayed by the holding of the Beijing Olympic Games. However, after the Beijing Olympic Games, former president Hu Jintao emphasised this turning again:

> We must take promoting public health and improving the quality of Chinese people's life as our fundamental goals, attach great importance to the functions of sports in promoting people's all-round development, economic growth and social harmony, and realize the coordinated development between elite sports and mass sports.

According to this call, the SCC set the August 8th as the National Sports Day and then promulgated *The Regulations on National Fitness* issued by the SCC in 2009 to protect people's rights to participate in sports. In 2012, the SCC issued *The Twelfth Five-Year Plan of National Basic Public Service System*, took the mass sports as a national basic public service and confirmed government's responsibilities for mass sports (Zheng et al., 2018). Since the 18th National Congress of the Communist Party of China, the country's overall sports development strategy has gradually changed from giving priority to the development of elite sports to the integrated development of elite sports and mass sports and given more support to the development of mass sports (Zheng, 2018).

For example, the SCC issued the *Several Opinions on Accelerating the Development of Sports Industry and Promoting Sports Consumption* in 2014 (Zheng, 2018), proposed to attach more importance to national fitness and support sports industry as a green industry. The '*Healthy China 2030' Planning Outline* promulgated by the SCC in 2016 implemented a series of measures to improve public service system for national fitness and widely launch national fitness campaign. The *Outline for Building a Strong sports Country* proposed to coordinate construction of venues and facilities for national fitness, optimise network organisations for national fitness and promote intelligent development of national fitness. *The Fourteenth Five-Year Plan of Chinese Sports Development* issued by the GASC in 2021 once again emphasised that 'giving priority to meeting the health needs of people and promoting the all-round development of people as the aim of sports work, strengthening the function of sports public services, and fully implementing the strategy of national fitness' (Li et al., 2023). The *Opinions on Building a Higher Level Public Service System for National Fitness* issued by the SCC in 2022 formulated a future goal that

> by 2035, a national fitness public service system in line with modern socialist countries will be fully established, the proportion of people who regularly participate in physical exercise has reached more than 45%, and physical fitness and leisure sports activities have become a common part of life, and people's physical qualities and health levels rank in the forefront of the world. (Li et al., 2023)

These measures were all signs that the government would attribute more resources to mass sports, which means the dividend policies that traditional elite sports development mode depends on are disappearing along with the government's expectation transformation.

Challenges From the National Administrative System Reform

The second trait of Chinese traditional elite sports development mode is its centralised administrative system. The biggest advantage of this system is that it is able to gather resources in a short time, especially at the time of economic hardship, and the rapid development of China's elite sports has proved its high-efficiency. However, along with the growth of economic reform and the upgrading of social demands, some drawbacks of this administrative system arise quickly.

The first drawback is that the government has all power of managing and operating elite sports, which seriously restricted the development of professional sports that should have followed market regulations and laws. In 1994, the State Physical Education and Sports Commission (SPESC) decided to take football as the pilot to launch professional league to adapt to socialist market economy (Riordan & Jones, 1999). In the initial stage, there were 12 clubs participating in the Chinese Series A Professional Football League (CSAPFL), all recombined by previous local provincial or municipal football teams. The players came from provincial or municipal sports schools, and the teams' stadiums also belonged to the local government. Though football clubs got the local enterprises' capital injection with government's help, most of enterprises were state-owned, whose purposes were not to make profits but to butter up government officials to get more benefits from other fields. For example, in 1999, there were 22 football clubs whose main shareholders were state-owned or collective enterprises, which occupied 84.6% of all football clubs (Cheng, 2005, p. 24). In fact, even if they wanted to manage football clubs in accordance with modern enterprises' mode, they still faced lots of restrictions coming from the confusion of property rights, as according to the original agreement, the property of clubs and players both belonged to local governments and enterprises.

In addition, the property right of CSAPFL also belonged to the Chinese Football Association (CFA), which was an official association affiliated to the SPESC, rather than an independence social association. According to the principle that investors are owners, most profits of CSAPFL should be assigned to clubs, but in fact, only a handful of them was given to the CFA. For example, the CFA had got $12 million from the International Management Group's sponsorship fees from 1999 to 2003, but only divided $3 million to football clubs playing in the CSAPFL (Cheng, 2005, p. 25). Moreover, the CFA also imposed its affiliated company China's Football Industry Development Corp to exclusively take charge of the CSAPFL's naming and television rights as well as other relevant league products, which further reduced the clubs' profit margins and made them fall into fiscal troubles. For example, in 2000, only 35% of football clubs playing in the CSAPFL can make profits or keep financial balance, and the others were all in deficit (Jin, 2004, p. 27). The bad financial situations cause frequent change of club's investors, which leads to obvious fluctuation of clubs' competition performance and makes it hard to cultivate fixed faithful fans. An example is that in clubs that have played in CSAPFL or the Chinese Football Association Super League (CFASL) from 1994 to now, all football club names in China have been changed. Moreover, the implicit distribution of properties and the unbalanced division of profits often cause the conflicts between football clubs and the CFA. In a word, although the CSAPFL had a primal form of western professional league, it still took many characteristics of planned economy.

The second drawback of the centralised elite sports administrative system is that it can easily produce rent-seeking and corrupt behaviours in the government as there is a lack of effective supervision mechanism. Let's also take the CFA as an example. As discussed above, the CFA is affiliated to the GASC, and its main leaders are also appointed by the GASC. Even the members of the supervising committee whose responsibilities are monitoring the operation of CFA are also designated by the GASC. In fact, this system design is the 'government supervises government', which makes it quite easy for some officials to obtain illegal income through manipulating matches. For instance, in 2009, judiciary authorities of China carried out the investigation related to manipulating matches and found that there were more 20 clubs, five referees, 40 football players and seven CFA officials participating in manipulating football matches from 1999 to 2009 (Watts, 2009). These fraudulent behaviours seriously affected the league's credibility and image, which made its television ratings decline rapidly. The low television ratings caused CFASL's failure to find main sponsor in 2005. In 2007, China's most influential sports television also stopped the live broadcast of CFASL. These behaviours also exist in basketball and volleyball leagues. In short, being influenced by the centralised administrative system, Chinese professional sports lost its vitality, audience and China's rapidly growing market.

Actually, the centralised elite sports administrative system is facing a gradually imminent crisis of the acceleration of China's government administrative system reform. Before 1978, China's development mode manifested high planning in economic and the government had absolute power in controlling society, which was also the base of the centralised elite sports administrative system. Since China's reform and opening up, this mode has begun to dissolve, which mainly displays in three aspects:

> The first aspect is that the government takes a market orientation in economic fields and gives enterprises more resources; the second is that the government transfers more power to the society and more space to social organizations; the third is that the government reinforces the restriction of its power and conducts a series of administrative system reform. (Lu, 2010, pp. 329–243)

China has restructured its government agencies eight times since the 1980s to optimise its administrative structure and downsize its civil service and improve its operational efficiency (Pan, 2019). It is predicted that the next round of reforms may be in the near future.

As we've discussed above, the SCC planned to cancel the SPESC and to transfer its power to the All-China Sports Federation (ACSF) in 1998, but this was delayed by the hosting of the Beijing Olympic Games. However, the trend that the SCC wants to reform traditional elite sports administrative system doesn't change. For instance, the *Several Opinions on Accelerating the Development of Sports Industry and Promoting Sports Consumption* put forward such measures as 'separating government administration from commune management and speeding up the decoupling of sports industry associations from administrative organs' thus providing an institutional guarantee for sports social organisations and market organisations to participate in the development of competitive sports (Zheng, 2018). The *General Plan for Reform and Development of Chinese Football* issued by SCC in 2015 put forward measures such as 'decoupling the CFA from the GASC' and 'establishing a professional league council with independent association legal personality', which provided direction for the professionalisation and socialisation of other sports (Li et al., 2023). Then, later in 2019, 10 national ministries and commissions jointly issued the *Implementation Opinions on Comprehensively Promoting the Reform of Decoupling Industry Associations and Chambers of Commerce from Administrative Organs*; in order to further transform government functions and innovate management methods, 67 sports social organisations such as the Chinese Basketball Association, Chinese Gymnastics Association and Chinese Athletics Association, affiliated with the General Administration of Sports, were included in the list of proposed decoupling and required to complete the decoupling within a time limit (Li et al., 2023). This has played an important role in promoting materialisation process of sports social organisations and building an elite sports governance system with participation of multiple entities.

Challenges From the National Economic Transition

The third trait of Chinese traditional elite sports development mode is its training concepts always take the result of competition as the core aim and pay less attention to athletes' education. In order to develop Chinese elite sports, the government built a complete system to foster elite athletes from training to competing. Fan Hong has explained this system clearly:

> When boys and girls between the age of six and nine are identified with some talent in a particular sport, they will be selected to the local sports schools, which are all around the country. They are trained three hours a day, and four or five times a week. After a period of hard training, the promising ones will be promoted to semiprofessional training. And they are trained four to five hours a day, and five or six days a week. Then, the ones with potentials are selected to the provincial sports schools or training centres, and train four to six hours a day, and five or six days a week. Their aims are to reach to the second stage and become professional athletes in provincial teams, and eventually reach to the third stage, becoming members of national squads and Olympic teams. (Fan et al., 2005, pp. 516–517)

In the times of planned economy, most athletes could get jobs from the government or obtain opportunities to enter schools after they retire from sports teams, which also got the SCC's legal support. The Organization Department of Central Committee of China (ODCCC) issued the *Notice of Selecting and Training Athletes Together* in 1952 to affirm athletes' contribution to the country and promise to give them appropriate placement. In 1963, the SPESC published the *Draft Notice of Sports Team's Regular Work* and underlined that the retired athletes could enjoy the same treatment as national public servants (Wu et al., 1999). According to Wu et al. (1999), these favourable terms attracted many parents to put their children into sports schools. According to statistics, in 1958, there were about 770,000 young athletes training and studying in 16,000 sports schools in China.

But after 1978, the year when China started its reform and opening up, the placement policies of retired athletes have been fundamental changed step by step. For instance, in 1980, the SPESC published the *Notice of Recruiting and Allocating Elite Athletes* and pointed that the government would arrange works for retired athletes according to their athletic performance (Wu et al., 1999). This principle broke the original average placement criteria and put competition into retired athletes' placement. And then, the SPESC promulgated the *Measures for Implementation of Retired Athletes Fee* in 1986 and proposed that the government encouraged retired athletes to find works by themselves and promised to give them some money based on their training ages and athletic performance, which also indicated that the government would not arrange works for athletes as noted by Wu et al. (1999). With the implementing of these measures, problems that athletes were lacking in education and social occupational skills caused by long-term training in a closed environment began to highlight out. Along with national marketisation reform, the original planning-employment mode was broken, which made it more difficult to place retired athletes. Influenced by these factors, more and more retired athletes became unemployed crowds. In 1981, there were 2,432 retired athletes waiting for jobs. This number was up to 5,212 in 1989, which took up 26.49% of the total number of retired athletes (Tian et al., 1993).

In 1992, the SCC quickened China's reform and opening-up process, which also promoted the reform of elite sports development mode. In 1993, the SPESC issued the *Advice on Deepening Reform of China's Sports System* and proposed to promote sports' socialisation, enrich athletes' training system and transform retired athletes' placement policies (Wu et al., 1999). In this context, the government was more inclined to provide certain monetary compensations to retired athletes rather than to arrange works for them. Furthermore, technological advancements prompted job skills to become so specialised that the retired athletes could hardly find jobs by themselves, for they spent too much times on training and competing instead of learning career skills and knowledge, which also promoted the media and people to start begin to pay attention to living conditions of retired athletes and to doubt whether the athletes' training mode was reasonable. But these doubts were swamped by the joy that Beijing won the right to host Olympic Games in 2001. In order to get more medals, the GASC expanded the scale of national sports teams and increased the number of students in sports schools. According to statistics, there were 1,316 full-time Olympic athletes in China's national teams in 2002, and this figure was soon up to 3,222 in 2004 (Fan et al., 2005, p. 523).

Depending on these human and financial resources invested, China got 51 gold medals in the Beijing Olympic Games (Zhu, 2010). But what lies behind the glory is trouble in looking for jobs. It was reported that there were 4,343 retired athletes waiting for jobs in 2009, and the number would increase to 6,536 in 2010, which meant that the government would face more pressure in next eight years (Zhu, 2010). On account of this, the GASC restarted the reform of athletes training mode which was shelved by the holding of the Beijing Olympic Games. In 2010, the SCC issued the *Guidance for Promoting Culture Education and Security Works of Athletes* and proposed that the government should diversify athletes' training mode, reform athletes' curriculum and establish monitoring mechanism to ensure the athletes' education quality.

In short, affected by Chinese traditional training system, the number of retired athletes who could not find work will increase with the reforming of China's market economy system. This is also an important external motivation that pushes the reform of Chinese current athletes' training mode forward.

Challenges From the Upgrading of National Social Demand Structure

The fourth trait of Chinese traditional elite sports development mode is that there exists serious imbalance in its construction of development. Although the SCC had already recognised the importance of Olympic Games in 1952, mainland China still did not participate in Olympic Games from 1953 to 1984 (Chan, 1985). So, it was in 1979 when China renewed its membership of the International Olympic Committee (IOC) and other international sports organisations that the SCC really paid more resources to Olympic sports.

In order to maximise effects of resources, the SPESC identified 16 key sports events of the summer Olympic Games, which were athletics, swimming, diving, gymnastics, weightlifting, shooting, archery, fencing, judo, wrestling, rowing, sailing, basketball, volleyball, table tennis and badminton, and three of winter Olympic Games, including speed skating, sprint way speed skating and figure skating, as national key events in 1984. In 1995, the SPESC published the

Program of Striving for Olympic Glory from 1994–2000 and proposed to increase the number of athletes for Olympic sports events up to 17,000 and to expand the number of athletes for the key Olympic sports events to over 13,600 (Li et al., 2023). Moreover, it proposed that the number of Olympic sports events' full-time coaches should be increased up to 4,900, and that the number of the key Olympic sports events' full-time coaches should exceed 4,100.

In 2001, Beijing won the bid for the Olympic games. The GASC drew up the *Program of Striving for Olympic Glory from 2001 to 2010* in 2002 (Li et al., 2023). In this file, the GASC further divided China's Olympic sports events into four categories, which were the traditional strong events such as table tennis, badminton and diving, the capable events such as gymnastics, weightlifting, shooting and judo, the potential events such as athletics, swimming and water sports, and the weak events such as boxing, horsemanship, men's soccer, men's volleyball and baseball. Different sports events got different resources according to this classification. Relied on the *Juguo Moshi* and unbalanced developing strategy, China became a powerful sports nation rapidly and finally achieved its great aim in the Beijing Olympic Games.

But this unbalanced developing strategy attached too much importance to certain sports events and seriously limited the others. China has found the most success in diving, weightlifting, gymnastics, table tennis, shooting, badminton and judo. These sports make-up about 81% of China's total gold medals from the 23rd to the 30th Olympiads (from 1984 to 2012) (see Zheng & Chen, 2016). The reason why China could get rapid development in these events is that they have a lower degree of public participation in the world, diving, weight lifting, gymnastics, shooting and judo in particular. The demands for venues and equipment of these sports events are too high for ordinary people to participate in. In these sports events, the advantages of *Juguo Moshi* could show up obviously, as the government provides free venues, equipment and coaches for athletes and gives them professional training in their youth, which is hard to imagine in many other countries.

However, the *Juguo Moshi* could not work well in some sports events with a higher degree of public participation in the world. For example, China is far behind the US, Russia and Britain in athletics, swimming and cycling. There were 302 gold medals in total in Beijing Olympic Games, and athletics, swimming and cycling took up 99, showcasing their presence in international sporting competition (Rick & Li, 2023). China only got one gold medal in these three sports events, while the US got 20, Russia got seven and the UK got 11. In fact, the unbalanced construction of sports events also drives China to another crisis. Some China's key sports events, like the table tennis and badminton, have such a low degree of public participation in the world that they may be removed from Olympic Games. This crisis requests China to develop new key Olympic events.

Chinese often feel ashamed of their lower athletic level in men's football, basketball and volleyball. According to new ranking, Chinese men's football team took the 97th place in the world, men's basketball team was in the 27th place in the world and men's volleyball team came the 26th place in the world. The advantages of *Juguo Moshi* could not work well on these popular events with huge market value either. Conversely, the unbalanced sports developing strategy even restricted the development of these events because the resources were mainly invested to diving, weightlifting, shooting, gymnastics, etc. This is also an important reason why Chinese professional sports couldn't get well operation. Worse yet, the resources of these sports events' reserved athletes are decreasing rapidly. For example, the number of Chinese football reserved athletes reduced by 65% from 1995 to 2009 (Mu, 2011); basketball reserved athletes dropped by 42% from 1980 to 2006 and volleyball reserved athletes decreased by 33% from 1980 to 2006 (Yang, 2010).

However, with the fast development of Chinese economy, its gross domestic product (GDP) increased 310.9 times and its per capita GDP increased 210.3 times from 1978 to 2021. The Engel coefficient of Chinese residents also reduced from 63.9% in 1978 to 29.8% in 2021 (National Bureau of Statistics of China, 2023). This has changed Chinese social demand structure profoundly, which reveals the upgrading from private products to public ones and from pursuit of material comforts to that of spiritual comforts. These changes make people's sports demands no longer simply focus on the national pride coming from gold medals but also on the enjoyment of high-level professional games. However, against the huge market demands, Chinese professional sports cannot develop well due to the influence of the unbalanced developing strategy and the centralised administrative system, which also influences the development of the nation's whole sports industry. Compared with foreign developed countries, the added value of China's sports industry accounted for 1.14% of GDP in 2019, which is not only less than the proportion of developed countries such as the US, the UK and France but also less than Brazil, which is also a developing country (see Ma, 2021). But comparing the rise of China and Brazil here showcases their presence in the international sporting landscape (see Wise, 2020). In addition, the structure of China's sports industry is not reasonable. In the total output structure of China's sports industry in 2019, the manufacturing of sporting goods and related products accounted for 46.2%, while the sports service industry accounted for 50.6%, which is quite different from the structure of sports industry in developed countries, for example, the sports service industry in the United States respectively account for 82.23% of the total output value of sports industry (Ma, 2021).

However, along with the arrival of multimedia times, lots of foreign professional league encroach on China, attracting lots of Chinese sports audience and resulting in the low television ratings and tournament's attendance of the domestic matches. These influences make China's sports clubs operate difficultly and athlete's competitive enthusiasm decline, which in turn affect the tournament's attendance. This has formed a vicious cycle. Therefore, if Chinese elite sports want to achieve sustainable development, it is necessary to adjust the unbalanced developing strategy and spend more resources to the sports events that have high degrees of public participation and market value such as football, basketball and tennis.

Challenges From National Population Change

The fifth trait of Chinese traditional elite sports developing mode is that its effectiveness of development manifests high input and low output, especially in human resources. As we know, cultivating an advantageous sports event not only needs lots of money but also requires many athletes to endure a long time of hard training. So, the selection of excellent athletes is very strict, demanding the youth to have both great athletic talent and good psychological quality. China's well-organised and tightly structured three-level selection system (based on total, child and old-age populations), which is also an important support system to promote elite sports development. According to statistics, there were about 400,000 young boys and girls trained at more than 3,000 sports schools throughout China in 2004, but only five percent of them could go into national teams, and the others would leave sports schools with no formal primary or secondary education (Dai, 2004). Therefore, it can conclude that this extensive selection system highly depends on population. In this sense, we can say that the rapid developments Chinese elite sports obtained in past three decades were partly for the rich reserved population.

China's population growth rate was more than 1% from 1950 to 1995, which caused its total population to increase rapidly from 540 million to 1.008 billion (Department of Economic and Social Affairs of United Nations, 2012). More importantly, the proportion of the population aged 15–24, the main sources of sports athletes' reserve, remained more than 15% from 1950 to 2010 (Department of Economic and Social Affairs of United Nations, 2012). This 'demographic dividend' gave Chinese traditional elite sports development mode support.

However, in order to control population growth, China started its one-child policy in 1973, which has become a basic national policy from 1982. The main content of this policy is encouraging citizens to get married and bear only one child at a late age, which changed China's population construction immensely. China's population growth rate has presented a rapid downward trend since 1973, and it already dropped to 0.51% in 2010 according to the Department of Economic and Social Affairs of United Nations (2012). According to the United Nations' prediction, China's population would enter negative growth stage, and its total population would decline from 1.3 billion in 2010 to 800 million based on its constant-fertility variant in 2100. And its population aged 15–24 will also decrease from 200 million in 2010 to 70 million in 2100 (United Nations, 2012). This trend puts forward more challenges for China's experiential and extensive traditional athletes' selection mode.

Moreover, with the economy growing, China's employment opportunities increase rapidly. But the proportion of population aged 15–64 who are the main labour population is decreasing gradually. In this background, people have more career options, which will decrease people's motivations of engaging in elite sports. In addition, with the increase of education fund, the youth have more opportunities to accept higher education, which will also reduce the youth's motivations of engaging in elite sports. Furthermore, with the coming of the 'few-generating' society, parents prefer their children to engage in steady jobs rather than become professional athletes with certain risks. According to statistics, the number of China's athletes who were over the second athletic grades has reduced from 63,095 in 1995 to 20,092 in 2019, and the number of amateur sports schools has reduced from 3,236 in 1993 to 1,603 in 2019 (Ma, 2022). In a word, the selection of reserved athletes is facing more and more challenges from population, society and economy, which is also an important external power pushing the reform of Chinese elite traditional sports development mode forward.

THE REFORMS OF CHINESE ELITE SPORTS DEVELOPMENT MODE

Shifting Its Driving Forces of Development From Single to Multiple

As we have stated, the driving forces of Chinese traditional elite sports development mode mainly come from government's political expectations, but these traditional driving forces are weakening along with the changes of government's expectation. In this context, finding new driving forces and dividend policies becomes more important and urgent. From the experiences of developed countries, there are mainly three sources of driving forces of elite sports development, the market, society and government, and they present a diversified trend. However, the sources of Chinese elite sports development are simplex, and mainly depend on the government. Therefore, if Chinese elite sports want to keep growing in the future, it is necessary to dig the sources come from the market and society.

In fact, as we've discussed above, China's current economic strength and consumption level can basically meet the needs of elite sports development. It is just because of the closed and planned elite sports development mode that the sources from the market and society could not be used properly. Therefore, if Chinese elite sports want to shift the driving forces from single to multiple, the traditional development mode must be reformed to provide institutional foundations for professional sports to make good use of China's enormous market. At the same time, the power of developing elite sports should be gradually transferred to sports associations to fully employ China's abundant social resources. In addition, it is important to actively play a role in national identity and political propaganda to get support from the government. Of course, it should be emphasised that the driving forces from the society are thought to be dominant in the future and those from the market and government follow.

Shifting Its Administrative System From Government-Oriented to Society-Oriented

The Chinese traditional elite sports administrative system is government-oriented, which on one hand promotes its athletic level rapidly, but on the other hand limits the development of its professional sports. As China's reform and opening-up process goes on, this administrative system is facing more and more pressure from national political reforms, especially after the Beijing Olympic Games. The government's political demands for elite sports present a downward trend. Moreover, with the acceleration of globalisation and the coming of multimedia era, sports industries urgently need to get out of the closed administrative system to embrace the market. In short, these changes prompt the government to shift elite sports administrative system from government-oriented to society-oriented.

There are two possibilities for Chinese elite sports administrative system reform. The first is a radical reform which means that the SCC will cancel the GASC and transform the power of administrating elite sports to the ACSF directly. And the other is a gradual reform that means the SCC will steadily give the power of administrating elite sports to the ACSF stage by stage. According to the current situation, the gradual reform is more likely to come true, because the radical reform can easily make Chinese Olympic gold medals decrease rapidly, which will be hard for the government to accept. If the government suddenly transfers the power of administrating elite sports to sports associations, it could easily cause chaotic management that will influence athletes' athletic performance, as the sports associations are seriously restricted by the traditional administrative system. Therefore, the gradual reform will be more suitable.

We can estimate the implementation progress of this gradual reform according to the general period (5 years) of China's administrative system reform. From 2023 to 2033, in order to pave the way for the targeted society-oriented administrative system, the government will delegate more power (such as personnel and financial power) to sports management centres to make them independent legal official organisations. During this period, the CCC may merge the GASC to the Ministry of Culture of China or the Ministry of Education of China and give certain power to the ACSF at the same time to implement the mode that the government and the ACSF co-manage elite sports for some time. From 2034 to 2044, the government will give the power of regulating elite sports to ACSF. At the same time, the sports management centres will also gradually transfer the power of administering and operating sport events to each national sports association according to the sports events' public participation, market value and developing characteristics. So, the national sports associations will gradually replace sports management centres and become independent legal social organisations in administering and operating sport events. At last, Chinese elite sports administrative system will truly become society-oriented (see Fig. 10.1).

Shifting Its Training Concepts From Instrumentalism to Humanism

As we have described, the Chinese government views elite sports as an instrument for political propaganda, which makes the training system often pay more attention to athletes' competitive abilities, but less to their education. This causes athletes' lack of job skills, which brings more trouble to them in finding jobs after they retire along with China's economic reform. Moreover, as Chinese legal construction advances, the citizens' consciousness of human rights has been greatly promoted, which gives more challenges to the traditional athletes training concept. In this context, the humanism that takes the athletes' lifelong

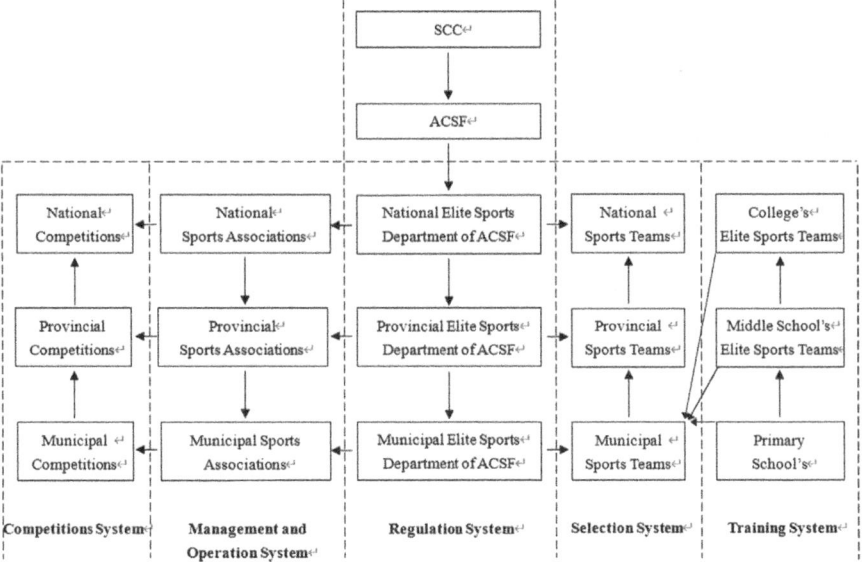

Fig. 10.1. The Main Constructor of China's Future Elite Sports Development Mode.

development as the basic principle and views elite sport as a measure to cultivate well-rounded people surely will become Chinese future training concept.

We have stated that China's sports schools are attached to sports administrative departments, not to education departments. These schools have their own independent curriculums, class arrangements and evaluation standards, which makes it hard for the education department's resources to flow in. In fact, the sports departments also take a negative attitude in supervising athletes' education, because they, like coaches and sports school's officials, also view getting gold medals as the first target. This enclosed training system seriously affected the quality of athletes' education. Therefore, the key measure to shift Chinese training concepts from instrumentalism to humanism is to promote the transformation of sports school.

Considering the progress of elite sports administrative system reform, we suggest that the transformation of sports schools take the following steps. The first step is from 2023 to 2033. In this step, the strategy that education departments and sports departments co-manage sports schools will be more practicable because the GASC may be merged into China's Ministry of Culture or Ministry of Education, but it still has some power of administrating elite sports. As for the division of function, the education department is mainly responsible for the athletes' education, such as curriculums, class arrangements and teachers' assessments, while the sports department is mainly responsible for athletes' training and competition. Besides, the two departments should hold joint meetings termly to communicate and coordinate with each other in athletes' education and training. The second step is from 2034 to 2044. During this step, sports schools will be gradually transformed into ordinary schools that are in the charge of education departments because sports departments' functions will be further weakened, and their main functions will be just regulating the developing direction of elite sports, not directly administrating in its management and operation. And sports associations can establish cooperative relationship with education departments to give athletes guidance in training and competition.

Shifting Its Construction of Development From Unbalanced to Balanced

In order to maximise the effects of resources, China chose an unbalanced developing strategy, which on one hand rapidly promotes its athletic levels in the sports events whose public participation rate is low in the world, while on the other hand limits the development of sports events with a high public participation rate. Moreover, as the national social demand structure upgrades, this unbalanced developing strategy becomes increasingly unable to satisfy China's need for a high-level professional league. Besides, with the era of multimedia coming, lots of foreign sports league matches encroach on China, attracting lots of Chinese sports audience and resulting in the low television ratings of the domestic league matches. These pressures are the external powers to push the adjustment of China's unbalanced elite sports developing strategy forward. In fact, the unbalanced developing strategy is also the reason for Chinese elite sports' internal demand for new growth points of achieving medal in the future, for China has already stretched to its limits in some key summer Olympic sports events. In the Beijing Olympic Games for example, Chinese athletes won all the gold medals in table tennis, eight of the nine in diving, nine of the 14 in gymnastics, three of the five in badminton and eight of 15 in weightlifting. And the number of the gold medals that China gained in these five sports events accounts for 60.78% of its total number. Besides, some of Chinese key sports events (such as table tennis and badminton) may be removed from Olympic Games. What's worse, this unbalanced strategy also limits the development of Chinese traditional sports, and makes Chinese elite sports lost their diversity, nationality, characteristics and attraction. So, if Chinese elite sports want to achieve sustainable development, it is necessary to adjust the unbalanced developing strategy and attribute more resources on the sports events that have high degrees of public participation (such as athletics, swimming, and cycling), those with market values (such as football, basketball and tennis) and the traditional sports events (such as wushu, dragon boat and diabolo).

At the operational level, Chinese sports departments should implement three measures. The first is changing the traditional strategy that organises national games' sports events according to Olympic Games and properly adding some non-Olympic items. The second is changing the traditional approach that allocates resources to sports events according to their potentials for wining Olympic medals and properly spending more resources on the sports events with high degrees of public participation. The third is protecting traditional sport and regularly organising traditional sports section.

Shifting Its Effectiveness of Development From Extensive to Intensive

Chinese traditional elite sports development mode manifests high input and low output, especially in human resources. However, with the enriching of education resources and the expanding of job choices, the teenagers' intention to engage in elite sports begins to decline. Coupled with the change of population structure, Chinese elite sports face the big crisis that the number of reserved athletes is dropping fast. The disappearance of demographic dividend requires Chinese elite sports to shift the effectiveness of development from extensive to intensive.

At the operational level, Chinese sports departments should implement the following measures. The first is increasing the investment in scientific research to raise the success rates of athletes' selection. The second is selecting athletes according to different regions' population developing trend. For example, China's eastern regions' trend of population ageing is more serious than that of the west. The proportion of young population in the east is less, but the job opportunities and education resources are more, which makes the intention of teenagers there to engage in elite sports weaker. So, the coaches can consider tilting to western region when they select athletes. The third is enhancing the scientific level of athletes' training to increase the training yield. The fourth is increasing the support for professional sports to attract more people to pay attention or participate in elite sports. The fifth is improving the athlete's disability security system to reduce the teenagers' anxiety of engaging in elite sports.

CONCLUSION

Joseph Stiglitz, the recipient of Nobel Prize, said that Chinese reform was standing in the middle of the river and looking for the position of the other shore (Qin, 2010). This is also suitable for describing the state of Chinese elite sports development mode reform. From the main evolution process of traditional elite sports development mode, we can see that this mode promotes Chinese athletic level rapidly on the one hand but also caused lots of negative effects on the other hand. Along with the national government's expectation transformation, administrative system reform, economic transition, social demand structure's upgrading and population change, these negative effects are increasingly highlighted and become huge powers that push Chinese traditional elite sports development mode reform forward. In this context, how to design and implement this reform has become an urgent, complex and important topic, as it is not simply tinkering on the traditional development mode but a profound change which will deeply affect the future development of Chinese elite sports. In this paper, we just offered some macroscopic suggestions. Further research is still needed to develop these suggestions into operational measures.

ACKNOWLEDGEMENTS

The chapter is funded by the Major Project of Chinese National Social Science Fund (project number: 20&ZD335).

FIVE KEY READINGS

Cai, F. (2010). Demographic transition, demographic dividend, and Lewis turning point in China. *Economic Research Journal, 34*(4), 4–13.

Based on the empirical evidence of population dynamics, this paper proves the judgement of diminishing demographic dividend and incoming Lewis turning point in China. It also argues that the further economic growth and thus faster entrance of high-income cavalcade is the key and only avenue to close the 'ageing before affluence' gap. Accordingly, this paper concludes with proposing measures of exploiting potentials of first demographic dividend, creating conditions for second demographic dividend and tapping new sources of economic growth.

Hong, F., & Zhouxiang, L. (2012). Beijing's two bids for the Olympics: The political games. *The International Journal of the History of Sport, 29*(1), 145–156.

Fan Hong, Ping Wu and Huan Xiong point out that China's confidence in launching bids twice in eight years would not have happened without its strong economic development and its increasingly important role on the international political stage. Through the two bids, China learnt about international political games and connected itself to the world, in particular the Western world. The success of the bid in 2001 was seen by most of the Chinese people as a landmark in Chinese history. They celebrated not only Beijing's Olympics victory, but more importantly, the rise of China in the 21st century.

Elliott, R., & Harris, J. (Eds.). (2015). *Football and migration: Perspectives, places, players.* Routledge.

Football serves as a compelling microcosm of globalisation and migration, explored in the first book dedicated to dissecting its intricate migratory processes. Drawing from sociology, history, geography and anthropology, it analyses migration patterns in established and emerging football contexts. Case studies delve into elite men's football leagues in Europe, South America, North America and Asia, while also spotlighting underrepresented groups like female players, youth and amateurs. The book underscores football's unique global influence, making it essential reading for scholars interested in sports, sociology, geography, migration, globalisation and post-colonial studies.

Xiong, X., & Zheng, G. (2007). The formation, evolution and reconstruction of competitive sport development in China. *China Sport Science, 27*(10), 3–17.

Xiong Xiaozheng and Zheng Guohua consider that Chinese elite sport development model is based on the constant effort to resolve problems encountered in practice as an answer to actual needs. It is not the transcendental model of experience as a whole, actually the formation and evolution of

China's social development is a continuous exploring process for the compatible routine for social needs. However historical experience tells that sports would acquire its development on the condition of the coherence of sports development model and social development model.

Yue, Y. (2010). From Big Sports Country to Sports Power: The Demand of China Economic and Social Development on Sports Business in Future Ten Years. *China Sport Science, 30*(3), 3–10.

Yang Yue argues that sports business is an important part in modern economic and social development blue-print in each country. The trend of Chinese sports business depends on economic and social development including the economic and social system of our sports business based on the developing strategy followed in each historical phase, future population trend, the future economic development and social undertaking development.

REFERENCES

Associated Press. (2020). China dominates Asian games. https://www.nytimes.com/2010/11/29/sports/global/29iht-GAMES.html

Cai, F. (2010). Demographic transition, demographic dividend, and Lewis turning point in China. *Economic Research Journal, 34*(4), 4–13.

Caldwell, G. (1982). International sport and national identity. *International Social Science Journal, 15*(2), 173–184.

Chan, G. (1985). The "Two-Chinas" problem and the Olympic formula. *Pacific Affairs, 58*(3), 473–490.

Cheng, Y. (2005). Management of China's professional football club. *Journal of Chengdu Sport University, 31*(2), 24–27.

Chhabra, T., Doshi, R., Hass, R., & Kimball, E. (Eds.). (2021). *Global China: Assessing China's growing role in the world*. Brookings Institution Press.

Dai, Q. (2004, September 7). Chinese sports need a new era. *Chinese News Weekly*.

Department of Economic and Social Affairs of United Nations. (2012). *Population division*. http://esa.un.org/wpp/country-profiles/country profiles_1.htm. Accessed on 24 October 2012.

Fan, H., & Lu, Z. (2012). Beijing's two bids for the Olympics: The political games. *International Journal of the History of Sport, 29*(1), 145–156.

Fan, H., Ping, W., & Huan, X. (2005). Beijing ambitions: An analysis of the Chinese elite sports system and its Olympic strategy for the 2008 Olympic Games. *International Journal of the History of Sport, 22*(4), 510–529.

GASC. (2022a). Survey Bulletin of national fitness activities in 2020. https://www.sport.gov.cn/n315/n329/c24335053/content.html. Accessed on 7 June 2022.

GASC. (2022b). *Statistical survey of national stadium in 2021*. https://www.sport.gov.cn/n315/n329/c24251191/content.html. Accessed on 29 April 2022.

GASC. (2022c). The fifth monitoring bulletin on national physical fitness. https://www.sport.gov.cn/n315/n329/c24335066/content.html. Accessed on 7 June 2022.

Hu, X., & Henry, I. (2017). Reform and maintenance of Juguo Tizhi: Governmental management discourse of Chinese elite sport. *European Sport Management Quarterly, 17*(4), 531–553.

Li, J., Wan, B., Yao, Y., Bu, Te, Li, P., & Zhang, Y. (2023). Chinese path to sports modernization: Fitness-for-all (Chinese) and a development model for developing countries. *Sustainability, 15*(5), 4203.

Lorenz, K. (1987). *Human aggression: Theories, research, and implications for social policy*. The Writers Publishing House.

Jin, Q. (2004). Investigation and analysis on current situation of our professional soccer club operation. *China Sport Science and Technology, 40*(1), 26–31.

Ma, D. (2021). Contradictions between supply and demand in China's sports industry and countermeasures. *Sports Culture Guide*, (3), 67–73.
Ma, D. (2022). The overseas experience and enlightenment of elite sports reserve talents' training: Taking UK, USA and Russia as examples. *China Sport Science and Technology*, *58*(9), 46–51.
Ministry of Education of China. (2021). Release report of the eighth national survey on student physical fitness and health. *Chinese Journal of School Health*, *42*(9), 1281–1282.
Mu, L. (2011). Chinese football reserved athletes reduced rapidly. http://sports.xinmin.cn/2011/01/17/8915404.html. Accessed on 17 January 2011.
National Bureau of Statistics of China. (2023). *China statistical yearbook (1978–2021)*. https://data.stats.gov.cn/easyquery.htm?cn=C01. Accessed on 9 January 2023.
Pan, X. (2019). The retrospect and summary of seventy-years Chinese governmental reforms. *Chinese Public Administration*, (10), 25–32.
Qin, L. (2010, June 1). The reform needs top-level design. *Economic Weekly*.
Rick, O., & Li, L. (2023). *Global sports and contemporary China: Sport policy, international relations and new class Identities in the People's Republic*. Palgrave Macmillan.
Riordan, J., & Jones, R. (Eds.). (1999). *Sport and physical education in China*. ISCPES.
Su, L., Agudamu, L. Y., & Zhang, Y. (2023). China's new urban clusters strategy for coordinated economic growth: Evidence from the sports industry. *PLoS One*, *18*(10), e0292457.
Tian, M., Li, D., & Zhang, R. (1993). Arrangement of retired elite players in China and measures to improve it. *Journal of Beijing Sports University*, *16*(1), 2–8.
Tian, E., & Wise, N. (2020). An Atlantic divide? Mapping the knowledge domain of European and North American based sociology of sport, 2008–2018. *International Review for the Sociology of Sport*, *55*(8), 1029–1055.
Watts, J. (2009). China shows red card to football match-fixing with over 20 arrests. *The Guardian*. https://www.theguardian.com/world/2009/dec/31/china-football-match-fixing
Wise, N. (2020). Eventful futures and triple bottom line impacts: BRICS, image regeneration and competitiveness. *Journal of Place Management and Development*, *13*(1), 89–100.
Wise, N., & Harris, J. (Eds.). (2019). *Event, places and societies*. Routledge.
Wise, N., & Maguire, K. (Eds.). (2022). *A research agenda for event impacts*. Edward Elgar.
Wu, S., Xiong, X., & Hua, T. (1999). *Sports history of the People's Republic of China*. Zhongguo Shuju Publishing House.
Xiong, X., & Zheng, G. (2007). The formation, evolution and reconstruction of competitive sport development in China. *China Sport Science*, *27*(10), 3–17.
Xu, G. (2019). *Olympic dream: China and sports, 1895–2008*. Guangdong People's Publishing House.
Yang, Y. (2010). From big sports country to sports power: The demand of China economic and social development on sports business in future ten years. *China Sport Science*, *30*(3), 3–10.
Yang, Y. (2011). Research on China sports development strategy during the shutdown of demographic dividend window. *China Sport Science*, *31*(1), 10–18.
Zheng, J. (2018). *Elite sport development in China – Structure and strategy*. Routledge.
Zheng, J., & Chen, S. (2016). Exploring China's success at the Olympic Games: A competitive advantage approach. *European Sport Management Quarterly*, *16*(2), 148–171.
Zheng, J., Chen, S., Tan, T.-C., & Lau, P. W. C. (2018). Sport policy in China (Mainland). *International Journal of Sport Policy and Politics*, *10*(3), 469–491.
Zhu, Y. (2010, January 20). There are nearly half of Chinese athletes with no jobs. *Nanjing Daily*.

CHAPTER 11

FROM 'IMPORTED' TO 'LOCAL': FRAMING FOUNDATIONS ON THE SOCIOLOGY OF SPORT IN CHINA

Qiang Gao and Le Zhou

East China Normal University, China

ABSTRACT

This chapter explores the development of sport sociology in China from its transition from an 'imported' Western concept to a 'localised' Chinese discipline. Specifically, this chapter considers the role of the body in this process. This chapter offers some descriptive insight into the development of sport sociology in China, focussing on how it has transitioned from an 'imported' Western concept to a 'localised' discipline with its own unique characteristics. It also seeks to address some differences and similarities between Eastern and Western ideologies regarding the concept of the 'body' and how these differences influence the study of sport sociology in China. The chapter uses a historical and philosophical approach to analyse the development of sport sociology in China. It examines the concept of the body in both Western and Chinese contexts and how these concepts have influenced the development of sport sociology in China. The value of this work is it provides a unique perspective on the development of sport sociology in China, highlighting the role of the body and the process of localization. It contributes to the understanding of the interaction between Western and Eastern ideologies in the field of sport sociology.

Keywords: Sport sociology; localization; body theory; Eastern and Western ideologies; philosophy of sport

INTRODUCTION

The study of the 'body', as a theoretical research topic in modern and contemporary times has indeed made significant progress in various academic disciplines such as sociology, anthropology and philosophy (Merleau-Ponty, 2010; Nietzsche, 2008; Tian & Wise, 2020). These disciplines have seen vertical development in their theoretical approaches to understanding the concept of the 'body'. Moreover, the study of the 'body' has not only seen development at the theoretical level but has also led to fruitful academic contention among different regional philosophical schools (Turner, 2012). This academic contention has contributed to the conceptualisation of various ideas related to the body, and these concepts have gradually gained resonance and reference in multi-disciplinary fields. New concepts, including the reconstruction of research paradigms, and the evolution of thinking across different disciplines direct how we think about the body in sociology of sport research (Shilling, 2012). Then it is gradually formed the concept construction, the reconstruction of research paradigm and thinking, and it finally affected the underlying thinking mode of the general public (Sartre, 1960). The development of body studies goes beyond just progress in theory; it represents a process of academic debate and integration of ideas. It reflects a focused debate between 'traditional-contemporary & Chinese-Western' perspectives, as observed by the Chinese philosopher Yang Guorong (2019).

Body theory delves into the realm of sport research from philosophical concepts to practical aspect of the human body. Abstract concepts related to the body involves concrete physical behaviours of humans in sport activities. This process is deeply consistent with the theory of 'Cultural-Psychological formation' proposed by the Chinese philosopher Li Zehou (1979) and the theory of 'Civilising Process' proposed by the German sociologist Norbert Elias (2000). Both two philosophers paid close attention to sociological theory and imported them to the study of 'body'.

The formation of sport sociology in China is 'imported'. As the theory of sport sociology gradually enters China, it inevitably incorporates concepts and theories from Western sociology and sport sociology (Lu, 1996), as well as a focus on events to develop the nation's international image and competitiveness (Wise, 2020). This process leads to an understanding of the localization of sport, which are generally accepted as a form of physical or leisure activity (Tian & Wise, 2022), and offers geographical dimensions that complement sociological considerations (Wise, 2015). In other words, Chinese sport sociology scholars analyse local sport activities and phenomena from the perspective of the local Chinese, using Western concepts and theories as tools.

After continuous thinking of several generations of sports theory researchers, the concept, theory and research paradigm of the body have a universal academic proposition of 'worldwide' and 'wholeness'. This is full of human thinking. From the ancient to present, progressing continually and historically to more contemporary changes in thought and use of theory. The development of sport sociology is a process of the introduction of Western academic system to Chinese one, revealing the distinction between the East and the West. In summary, with the penetration of the study of the body, it is clearer how the thought of sport sociology changes from 'imported' identity to 'local' one. Through the inheritance and dialogue of sport sociology ideas between the East and the West, a more inclusive research orientation can be established for sport sociology in China.

CHINESE BODY AND WESTERN BODY: THE STRUCTURE OF DISSONANCE BETWEEN 'SOCIAL EXISTENCE' AND 'IDEOLOGICAL PRESENTATION'

Human being has a flesh, but from the flesh to the body is a historical process of the interaction of the between holistic culture and individual psychology (Li, 1979). From the perspective of debate of 'traditional-contemporary & Chinese-Western', although Eastern and Western cultures are distinct, the transition from 'flesh' to 'body' follows a converging path. This convergence is particularly evident in the context of world modern history (Li, 1979).

In traditional Chinese culture, the development from 'fresh' to 'body' is fundamentally a process of integrating meanings rather than transcending or breaking apart (Yang & Zhang, 2017). From the perspective of Chinese expression, Chinese philosophy places a greater emphasis on the concept of 'ti' (体), which signifies three connotations. First, it is 'tiyan' (体验), which accompanies personal experiences. Second, it is 'embodiment' (体现), which refers to the state personally experienced by an individual. Third, it is 'human action', which denotes allowing something happening. Therefore, the ancient Chinese understanding of the body is largely interpreted as a paradigm for recognising the self and the universe (Yang & Zhang, 2017).

In Western society, the understanding of the body has undergone significant fluctuations. There is a noticeable dissonance between 'social existence' and 'ideological presentation'. This can be observed in ancient Greek times, where the body and Mind were often seen as coexisting in harmony (Robert, 2023). However, with the establishment of Christianity's dominant position in society, a contradictory relationship between the body and Mind emerged, marked by conflicts. Nevertheless, with the shift in contemporary beliefs and the advancements in neuroscience, the connection between the body and Mind has been re-established through new modes (Robert, 2023)

SPORT SOCIOLOGY IN CHINA

Sport sociology was introduced to China and has undergone a process of localization, largely influenced by the dissonance between 'social existence' and 'ideological representation' (Feng, 2014). The process from 'importation' to 'localization' can be summarised as follows: it begins with the demand formed by China's contemporary perception of the body as a social existence framework, followed by selective absorption of the ideas and theories of Western sport sociology. The localization process of sport sociology, however, unfolds based on the integration of Chinese social body and individual body. This process can be divided into three stages: the emergence (before and to the early 1980s), the development (mid-1980s to mid-1990s) and the reflection (and mid-1990s to present).

Research on sport in China is looked at in several phases. There are earlier considerations during times of dynasties, the establishment of New China, and developments after the 1980s. Constrained by cultural ideological beliefs deeply rooted in China since ancient times of Qin dynasty, such as 'Those who govern others with their intellectual mind and those who are governed with their physical labour' and 'Those who excels in mental study can follow the official career', traditional notions widely accepted in modern Chinese society continue to prioritise mental development over physical enhancement. Therefore, when the Physical Education systems of Germany, Japan and the Soviet Union, as well as various forms of modern Western sport, gradually introduced into Chinese society in the last century, most people only considered Sport and Physical Education as 'the education for Body' with less emphasis on its connection to 'Mind'. This led to the initial introduction of sport sociology, primarily focused on improving the education for the individual body in schools and for the public. It enriched sociological theories and methodologies with 'the education for Body' as the core, gradually establishing disciplines in university education and research after China's Reform and Opening-up period to express its own value attributes and practical applications. In this stage, sport sociology was often supported by the '真义体育观' (the narrow/true definition of 'tiyu' which exclusively covers only Physical Education) and closely associated with the field of education.

The second stage is when we begin to see gradual development in the 1980s to the formal establishment of the discipline in the mid-1990s. Unlike Western sports sociology, which engages in multifaceted thinking in functionalism, semiotics and critical research, it possesses multiple perspectives in empirical analysis, interpretation and clarification of sport social phenomena. Under the continued influence of the traditional 'Cultural-Psychological Framework', China tends to place more emphasis on the cultivation of personal experience and character development of 'Practical Rationality'. It involves integrating abstract and dialectical thinking into the 'mundane and unnoticed yet' aspects of social and cultural life in a profound manner. This indicates that from the initial introduction of sport sociology in China to its attainment of a certain level of local social status, it has already become inseparable from the extensive everyday sport culture of the people. Through its own theoretical innovations and practical applications, sport sociology plays a role in creating a more positive social order. During this stage, sport sociology, supported by an immature theoretical framework, focused more on the practical cultivation of the social body and was closely associated with its parent discipline, sociology.

The thirst stage is where we find the formal establishment of the discipline in the mid-1990s to the present in the 21st century, the research in sport sociology has experienced robust development. Benefiting from the successful transformation of China's socialist market economy with Chinese characteristics and the continuous enhancement of comprehensive national strength, the people's material production, living standards and socio-cultural levels have entered a new historical era. At this stage, in addition to personal physical conditioning and the construction of social rationality, the body also calls for more psychological and emotional space. Therefore, the introduction of sport sociology, after initially focussing on natural education of the body and the cultivation of social order, further shifts its focus to opening up the 'mind' of the people, aiming to establish its roots from the fundamental level. In this context, research studies that focus on the integration of social body and individual body have involved psychological experiments leading to the development of measurement scales and exploration of latent emotional energy. Also important to address is social group identification and belonging, which provide the field of sport sociology with disciplinary expectations and future path choices. This will help address contradictions between unbalanced and inadequate development and the people's ever-growing needs for a better life. At the same time, the unprecedented economic development has also led to a series of 'alienation phenomena' in society, including the field of sport. In this stage, sports sociology tends to focus on the holistic development of individual personalities, always in association with psychology.

FUTURE OUTLOOK

In the Western academic context, sport sociology is a relatively mature discipline within the field of the humanities of sport, while sociology, as its parent discipline, is a subject with a high degree of integration in both Western and Chinese research. Therefore, the development of Chinese sport sociology provides a favourable platform for the continuation and advancement of Western sport sociology (Lu, 2023). However, transforming Western theories and methods into research tools that Chinese scholars can readily use requires the process of 'localization'. The considerations outlined in this chapter remind us of the importance of focussing on the transformation of 'bodily awareness', to a large extent, integrating the differences between Eastern and Western ideologies into the emergence and expansion process of universal human bodily awareness. This process reveals the absorption of Western sport sociology theories into Chinese sport sociology, forming its own characteristics. Of course, the transformation of 'bodily awareness' into theoretical insights can extend to the process of generating theories in various disciplines of Humanities of Sport and delve into the broad interactions between theories and disciplines in the East and the West.

FIVE KEY READINGS

Guorong, Y. (2019). *Philosophicail horizons: Metaphysical investigation in Chinese philosophy.* **Brill.**

It delves deeply into the metaphysical inquiries within Chinese philosophy, enlightening readers with rich information and perspectives, fostering a deeper understanding of the prevalent metaphysical underpinnings in Chinese philosophy. Serving as an illuminating guide, it elucidates the intricacies of metaphysical investigations within the scope of Chinese philosophical thought.

Zehou, L. (2008). *Historical ontology: The five discourses of Ji-Mao.* **Sanlian Bookstore.**

It is a noteworthy work in the field of philosophy. The book delves deeply into the ontological issues of history, showcasing Li Zehou's unique and profound thoughts. Based on the concept of the five discourses of Ji-Mao, he explores the essence of history, its spatiotemporal structure, the forms of civilization throughout history, the macroscopic perspective of history and the practicality of historical issues. Among these, Li Zehou's discussion on the spatiotemporal structure and forms of civilization within history is particularly thought-provoking.

Elias, N. (2000). *The civilizing process: Sociogenetic and psychogenetic investigations.* **Wiley Blackwell Publishing.**

It is a pivotal work in sociology and history. Published in 2000, it deeply explores civilization's evolution, examining societal changes and individual behaviour. Elias intricately dissects how social structures and individual psyches influence each other over time, bridging sociology and psychology.

Arasse, D. (2005). *Histoire du corps* **(Vol. 3). A. Corbin, J. J. Courtine, & G. Vigarello (Eds.). Seuil.**

The series of the books, spanning three volumes, covers the period from the Renaissance to the 20th century. From perspectives such as religion, art, medicine, sexuality, hygiene, violence, sports and performance, it discusses the cultural history of the body, showcasing the comprehensive impact of Western societal changes on human self-awareness regarding the body.

Chen, R. (1999). Analysis of the true essence of sports perspective, the characteristics and discrepancies of the grand sports perspective. *Journal of Xi'an Institute of Physical Education, 16*(4), 1–5.

It mainly introduces the true essence sports perspective and the grand sports perspective that emerged in China in the late 1920s, reflecting the different understandings of the essence, function and objectives of sports today. By revealing the fundamental characteristics of the true essence sports perspective and the grand sports perspective, it is believed that the divergence stems from the differences in their respective domains and value orientations.

REFERENCES

Feng, Y. (2014). *New horizons: The road from China to freedom.* Peking University Press.
Li, Z. H. (1979). *Critique of critique philosophy: A review of Kant.* People's Publishing House.
Lu, Y. Z. (1996). Progress and basic characteristics of Chinese sports sociology. *Sports Science Research, 3,* 1–9.
Lu, Y. Z. (2023). The destiny of Chinese sports and the value of sports sociology. *Journal of Sports Studies, 30*(5), 1–2.
Merleau-Ponty, M. (2010). *Phenomenology of perception.* Routledge.
Nietzsche, F. (2008). *The birth of tragedy.* Oxford University Press.
Robert, A. M. (2023). *History and philosophy of sport and physical education: From ancient civilizations to the modern world.* McGraw-Hill.
Sartre, J. P. (1960). *Critique de la raison dialectique.* Gallimard.
Shilling, C. (2012). *The body and social theory.* Sage.
Tian, E., & Wise, N. (2020). An Atlantic divide? Mapping the knowledge domain of European and North American based sociology of sport, 2008–2018. *International Review for the Sociology of Sport, 55*(8), 1029–1055.
Tian, E., & Wise, N. (2022). Dancing in public squares – Toward a socially synchronous sense of place. *Leisure Sciences.* Latest Articles.
Turner, B. S. (Ed.). (2012). *The Routledge handbook of the body* (pp. 130–144). Routledge.
Wise, N. (2015). Geographical approaches and the sociology of sport. In R. Giulianotti (Ed.), *Routledge handbook of the sociology of sport* (pp. 142–152). Routledge. (pp.
Wise, N. (2020). Eventful futures and triple bottom line impacts: BRICS, image regeneration and competitiveness. *Journal of Place Management and Development, 13*(1), 89–100.
Yang, R. B., & Zhang, Z. L. (2017). *The bodily dimension in the study of Chinese philosophy.* National Taiwan University Press.